Financial Management Information Systems

25 Years of World Bank Experience on
What Works and What Doesn't

THE WORLD BANK
Washington, D.C.

© 2011
The International Bank for Reconstruction and Development / The World Bank
1818 H Street NW
Washington DC 20433
Telephone: 202-473-1000
Internet: www.worldbank.org

World Bank Studies are published to communicate the results of the Bank's work to the development community with the least possible delay. The manuscript of this paper therefore has not been prepared in accordance with the procedures appropriate to formally-edited texts. This volume is a product of the staff of the International Bank for Reconstruction and Development / The World Bank. The findings, interpretations, and conclusions expressed in this volume do not necessarily reflect the views of the Executive Directors of The World Bank or the governments they represent.

The World Bank does not guarantee the accuracy of the data included in this work. The boundaries, colors, denominations, and other information shown on any map in this work do not imply any judgment on the part of The World Bank concerning the legal status of any territory or the endorsement or acceptance of such boundaries.

ISBN: 978-0-8213-8750-4
eISBN: 978-0-8213-8753-5
DOI: 10.1596/878-0-8213-8750-4

Library of Congress Cataloging-in-Publication Data has been requested.

Contents

Tables

Figures

Abbreviations

AAA	Analytic and Advisory Services
AFR	Africa Region
BC	Budget Classification
CFAA	Country Financial Accountability Assessment
CoA	Chart of Accounts
COBIT	Control Objectives for Information and related Technology
COTS	Commercial off-the-shelf Software
EAP	East Asia and Pacific Region
ECA	Europe and Central Asia Region
e-Gov	Electronic Government (e-Government)
FLOSS	Free/Libre Open-Source Software
FMIS	Financial Management Information System
HR	Human Resources
IBRD	International Bank for Reconstruction and Development
ICR	Implementation Completion Report
ICT	Information and Communication Technology
IDA	International Development Association
IDB	Inter-American Development Bank
IEG	Independent Evaluation Group
IPSAS	International Public Sector Accounting Standards
ISR	Implementation Status Report
IT	Information Technology
ITIL	Information Technology Infrastructure Library
LCR	Latin America and Caribbean Region
LDSW	Locally Developed Software
MEF	Macro Economic Forecasting
MoE	Ministry of Economy
MoF	Ministry of Finance
MTBF	Medium Term Budgeting Framework
MTEF	Medium Term Expenditure Framework
MTFF	Medium Term Fiscal Framework
OSS	Open Source Software
PAD	Project Appraisal Document
PBB	Program Based Budgeting
PEFA	Public Expenditure and Financial Accountability
PEM	Public Expenditure Management
PFIC	Public Financial Internal Control
PFM	Public Financial Management
PIB	Performance Informed Budgeting

PIM	Public Investment Management
PREM	Poverty Reduction and Economic Management Network
PSG	PREM Public Sector and Governance Group
SAR	South Asia Region
TS	Treasury System
TSA	Treasury Single Account

Acknowledgments

This paper was prepared by the Public Sector and Governance Group of the World Bank Poverty Reduction and Economic Management Network. The authors would like to acknowledge the World Bank team involved in the preparation of this document. The principle authors—Cem Dener (PRMPS), Joanna Alexandra Watkins (PSP GET), and William Leslie Dorotinsky (ECSP4)—would like to thank Pedro Arizti, Christine de Mariz Rozeira, Ana Bellver Vazquez-Dodero, Alexandre Arrobbio, and Jose Eduardo Gutierrez Ossio (LCSPS) for their suggestions and guidance in developing this study. The authors would also like to thank Ali Hashim, Salvatore Schiavo-Campo, Richard Allen, and Gert Van Der Linde for their invaluable peer review comments on this study. Finally, we would like to thank Jim Brumby, Nick Manning, and Parminder Brar for their substantive contributions. The map was reproduced by the World Bank Map Design Unit.

Preface

Financial Management Information Systems: 25 Years of World Bank Experience on What Works and What Doesn't was prepared as an updated and expanded version of the FMIS review report, originally drafted in 2003, to highlight the achievements and challenges observed during the design and implementation of World Bank–funded FMIS projects since 1984.[1]

Target Audience

The World Bank teams, government officials, and other specialists involved in FMIS projects.

Objective

In conjunction with the development of a new World Bank FMIS database, this study seeks to identify trends in the design and implementation of FMIS solutions in World Bank–funded projects since 1984 and share observed/reported achievements, challenges, and lessons learned with interested parties.

Activities

Sep 2009	Initiation of activities for review of the FMIS projects. Development of a web site to collect and share relevant documents.
Oct 2009	Scanning the operations portal and business warehouse to identify all relevant Treasury/FMIS projects (lending with substantial information and communication technologies (ICT) components). Defining the outline of new FMIS Report.
Nov 2009	Data collection for the FMIS Database (scanning more than 300 Implementation Completion Reports (ICRs), Project Appraisal Documents (PADs), and Implementation Status Reports (ISRs)).
Dec 2009	The first version of FMIS Database ready. Meetings with task teams to verify data.
Jan 2010	Initial findings & FMIS Database shared with task teams/managers for comments.
Jul 2010	FMIS Report and Database shared for final comments.
Oct 2010	FMIS Data Mapper was developed with 94 FMIS projects on Google Maps.
Nov 2010	Review Meeting; Comments on FMIS Report received and incorporated.
Dec 2010	Final FMIS Report delivered as a World Bank Study (WBS).

Key Resources[2]

- The World Bank FMIS Database (1984–2010)—updated in August 2010. Currently available to World Bank users only. An external version is expected to be available in 2011.

- William L. Dorotinsky, Junghun Cho, "World Bank's Experience with Financial Management Information (FMIS) Projects," Draft Report, 2003.
- William L. Dorotinsky, "Implementing Financial Management Information System Projects: The World Bank Experience-Preliminary Results," Reinventing Government with ICT, Presentation, World Bank, November 19, 2003.
- Cem Dener, "Implementation Methodology of the Integrated Public Financial Management Systems in Europe and Central Asia," Presentation, World Bank, May 2007.

Notes

1. This report was commissioned under the auspices of the Public Sector Performance (PSP) Global Expert Team (GET), given the importance of Information Technology in improving the efficiency of public sector processes.
2. Hyperlinks to related web sources will be available in the electronic copy of the study, which can be downloaded from the World Bank web site.

Executive Summary

Financial Management Information Systems

25 Years of World Bank Experience on What Works and What Doesn't

Since 1984, the World Bank has financed 87 Financial Management Information System (FMIS) projects in 51 countries, totaling over US $2.2 billion, of which US $938 million was for FMIS-related ICT solutions.[1] This study presents the World Bank's experience with these investment operations, including substantial ICT components, in order to share the achievements and challenges observed, and provide guidance for improving the performance of future projects. Building on the existing FMIS literature and new data available, this study is structured according to four overarching questions:[2]

- What historical patterns emerge from World Bank–financed Treasury/FMIS projects? This includes an analysis of project scope, cost, duration, design, objectives, and ICT solutions, among other aspects.
- How have such projects performed according to various criteria?
- What are the key factors that contribute to the success and failure of projects?
- What have we learned that could be useful for future projects?

The findings of this study are primarily based on the 2010 FMIS Database, which includes 55 closed and 32 active Treasury/FMIS (T/F) projects implemented between 1984 and 2010 (7 pipeline projects are also analyzed in some sections).[3] The data were gathered primarily from internal World Bank documents and sources: individual project Implementation Completion Reports (ICRs), Project Appraisal Documents (PADs), and the Independent Evaluation Group (IEG) reports, and were complemented by interviews with project leaders and public sector/informatics specialists. The Database contains a rich set of operational data and performance ratings for the benefit of those involved in the implementation of such projects, as well as client countries.

The Latin America and Caribbean region of the World Bank stands out with the largest number of completed (25) and active (4) projects. The Africa region follows with 13 completed and 12 active projects. The majority of these completed projects are comprehensive FMIS solutions (32) or an expansion of such systems (13). The approach followed by World Bank teams in the preparation of completed and active projects is also analyzed by determining the degree of attention to key preparation activities. These aspects were selected in line with the FMIS Design and Implementation Methodology presented in this study to ensure consistency in comparison.

In addition to the dataset, a number of case studies are provided to highlight the design complexities and the important nuances regarding the success and failure of projects. Country cases, rather than individual projects, were selected to illustrate the integrated and sequential nature of multiple projects with large investments in ICT over many years. Cases from Mongolia, Turkey, Albania, Guatemala, and Pakistan are included.

FMIS project performance is analyzed from various angles. The performance ratings in the ICRs indicate that the majority of 55 completed projects were "satisfactory" along most dimensions of performance (67% of outcome, 87% of sustainability, 56% of development impact, 61% of Bank performance, and 59% of Borrower performance ratings were satisfactory or above).[4] This pattern changes slightly with the IEG reviews, where nearly 64% of the projects received a downgrading of ICR ratings from "satisfactory" to "moderately satisfactory." On the other hand, among 55 completed projects, 49 systems (89%) are operational (20 Treasury Systems + 29 FMIS solutions) mainly to support countrywide operations (27 fully functional and 22 pilot systems for one or more ministries), which suggests that, from the perspective of obtaining results and sustainability, many of these projects achieved their technical and operational targets. There were some significant delays, but mostly within the project budget. Comparisons to similar applications in the private sector are also provided to highlight parallel performance patterns.

Building from a previously prepared draft FMIS report in 2003 (Dorotinsky and Cho), this study reviews a broader set of projects and documents to analyze the performance and outputs of FMIS projects, with an in-depth analysis of the success and failure factors (the previous draft FMIS report focused on 31 projects from 24 countries, whereas the current report covers 94 projects from 51 countries). Based on the findings of the current study, the interventions of the World Bank in the design and implementation of FMIS solutions have been reasonably successful in most countries.

Findings

The design and implementation of effective FMIS solutions is challenging and requires the development of country specific solutions to meet a number of functional and technical requirements associated with the Public Financial Management (PFM) agenda. Based on the experiences of the last 25 years in World Bank funded FMIS projects, a number of useful conclusions can be drawn:

- The political commitment and ownership of the borrower matter.
- Success depends on adequate preparation.
- FMIS priorities and sequencing should be addressed carefully.
- A focus on developing internal client capacity early in the process is crucial.
- FMIS implementation is complex enough to deserve a dedicated project.
- The type of FMIS solution influences implementation.
- The presence of an ICT expert in the World Bank Team is important.
- The total number and complexity of procurement packages influence project duration.
- FMIS projects disburse late due to large ICT contracts, completed at later stages.
- ICT related risks need to be clearly identified during project preparation.

FMIS projects in which the preconditions for reforms were assessed properly and a time-bound action plan was developed with realistic sequencing of reform activities tend to produce more effective solutions in relatively shorter time. Success also depends on adequate preparation before the approval of the project (realistic functional and technical requirements, cost/time estimates, and procurement/disbursement plans).

An estimation of the cost of FMIS ICT solutions needs to be performed carefully during project preparation based on a detailed assessment of key "design parameters" (users, nodes, server performance benchmarks, network connectivity, etc.) and basic "system requirements" (FMIS application software functionality, workload estimates, data storage and transaction processing needs, etc.). In the absence of such design parameters and system requirements, it is not possible to have a realistic cost estimate during project preparation. This has lead to the acceptance of relatively large margins of error for FMIS ICT solutions, resulting in ICT costs much higher than market rates due to this initial uncertainty. Therefore, initial cost estimates should be verified based on the actual cost of similar solutions in other projects, using the FMIS Database and other sources to reduce the risk of cost overruns or the misappropriation of funds.

Comprehensive FMIS projects take a minimum of 6–7 years to complete (including the project design, procurement, development of information systems, and capacity building) and countries typically undergo at least one election cycle within this period. Elections may have a significant impact on such reform projects due to the changes in key management positions and priorities. Therefore, the continuity of the initial commitment of leaders is crucial to ensure the introduction of necessary changes in business processes and behaviors/mindsets within the project timeframe. Frequent changes in World Bank teams should also be avoided to ensure the consistency and continuity in advisory support and progress monitoring during project implementation.

The key elements of an FMIS enabling environment are referred to as "FMIS prerequisites." These prerequisites should be substantially completed before the contract signature with ICT solution provider(s) in order to reduce potential complications during system development and rollout. These elements are categorized in three groups:

Functional Aspects

- Improvement of budget classification
- Development of a unified chart of accounts, integrated with budget classification
- Improvement of treasury single-account operations
- Development of commitment control and monitoring mechanisms
- Establishment of cash management functions

Technical Aspects

- Establishment of a secure countrywide communication network
- Preparation of system/data centers

Human Resources

- Presence of a core team of ICT specialists within PFM organizations

In practice, country context will influence the degree to which these prerequisites should be met ex-ante. However, all of these prerequisites should be considered before any FMIS ICT implementation to minimize the risks of cost overruns, delays, and failure in meeting the design requirements and reform objectives.

Recommendations

Based on the lessons learned from earlier FMIS projects, there has been an attempt to define the basic steps in design and implementation of FMIS projects and apply this approach consistently in a number of new projects initiated since 2005. A checklist for the teams involved in FMIS project design and the simplified FMIS Questionnaire used in the design of several World Bank–funded projects are presented in Appendix B. The recommendations on how to improve the quality and performance in FMIS design and implementation are presented together with the suggestions on performance indicators, and quality and reliability of FMIS ICT solutions in this study.

Key suggestions on the design and implementation of FMIS projects include the following:

- Identify the PFM reform needs of the government first (What? Why?)

This includes assessing existing PFM capacity and needs; assisting in the development of a country-led PFM reform strategy (if not already available); identifying priorities and sequencing of country-specific reform actions; and developing of the Conceptual Design, covering the functional review of PFM organizations, the recommendations for improving the institutional capacity, and the definition of FMIS functional modules (business processes and information flows), together with necessary procedural and organizational changes needed.

- Develop customized solutions (How? Where? When?)

The next stage involves the assessment of existing ICT capacity; development of ICT modernization strategy and preparation of the System Design to define FMIS functional requirements, technology architecture, and implementation method, in line with the Conceptual Design. The preparation of a realistic cost/time estimate, procurement plan, disbursement schedule, and technical specifications (bidding documents), as well as the clarification of FMIS prerequisites, need to be completed during project preparation.

- Strengthen institutional capacity to manage project activities effectively (Who?)

The formation of a Project Management Group (PMG) composed of key managers from all stakeholder groups and the establishment of a Project Implementation Unit (PIU) within the client's organizational structure for building/strengthening institutional capacity for project preparation and implementation (based on existing country systems, if possible) are very important at early stages. The PIU is expected to provide administrative and procurement support to the PMG.[5] Proper mechanisms should be established for monitoring and evaluating project activities, and the measures of success for the project should be clearly defined in the PAD.

Images: JSCreations/FreeDigitalPhotos.net

On performance indicators used for FMIS projects, there is a need to:

- Improve the quality and reduce the number of performance indicators to better measure the progress and impact of FMIS projects on a government's ability to manage its finances.
- Consider the Public Expenditure and Financial Accountability (PEFA) Performance Measurement Framework as a vehicle through which to assess the enabling environment and perhaps in the future, the operational status of PFM information systems (with additional indicators).

Benefiting from the advances in technology, new FMIS projects are designed with better focus on the quality and security of information to minimize the risk of corruption and improve the reliability of systems. Widespread use of centralized Web-based ICT solutions available on high-speed countrywide networks has contributed substantially to the performance of FMIS projects since the early 2000s. In addition to these factors, simplification of the PFM procedures and supportive legislative framework are necessary for countries to benefit from advances in technology effectively.

The total number of procurement packages in FMIS projects affects the timely completion of activities, as it usually takes around 12–18 months to complete large International Competitive Bidding (ICB) procedures. FMIS ICT solutions can be implemented through one or two ICB packages to minimize the complexity of procurement.

Until the early 2000s, FMIS capabilities were implemented mostly through Locally Developed Software (LDSW) mainly because of the technical limitations of commercial packages (originally designed for private sector needs) and also because of the lack of adequate ICT infrastructure in many regions. Since the introduction of Web-based applications after 2000, a shift toward customized commercial off-the-shelf (COTS) software packages (tailored to public sector needs) began. Nevertheless, no single package can provide all the FMIS functionality needed for country-specific needs. Hence, most of the new FMIS solutions designed after 2005 integrate customized COTS packages with specific LDSW modules (including open-source software) to cover a broader spectrum of PFM functions.

Some of the instruments that can be used in FMIS projects to improve the reliability, cost effectiveness, and accountability of information systems include the following:

- Using Electronic Payment Systems (EPS) for all government payments
- Benefiting from digital/electronic signatures for all financial transactions
- Electronic records management
- Publishing the budget execution results and performance monthly on the web
- Interoperability and reusability of the information systems
- FMIS development and project management based on industry standards
- Using Free/Libre Open Source Software (FLOSS) in PFM applications

Other suggestions to the World Bank teams are presented below:

- The World Bank networks/sectors involved in the design and implementation of FMIS projects need to collaborate and coordinate more intensively. Project teams should possess practical experience in managing complex institutional changes and have a holistic understanding of the public sector results chain.

- The FMIS ICT costs (total and per user) presented in this study (also available in the FMIS Database) may provide useful feedback for the verification of FMIS design calculations.
- Options for FMIS application software development need to be clarified based on a detailed system design and realistic cost/benefit analysis (considering the total cost of ownership) during project preparation.
- Excessive use of external consultants to perform the tasks of government officials should be avoided (especially in low-capacity environments); and key PFM organizations should have a capacity building plan, starting from the preparation phase of FMIS projects, to assume the responsibility of running all daily operations through information systems.
- World Bank team involvement in reviewing and commenting on the consultant reports, FMIS design and cost estimates, competitiveness analysis, bidding documents, evaluation reports, contracts, and proposed amendments contributes substantially to the successful implementation of projects.
- Implementation teams should follow all procurement stages closely to avoid delays, especially in large ICB packages. Prompt publication of procurement notices and allocation of adequate time for the preparation of bids or proposals are very important to improve competition and timely completion of planned activities.
- It is always advisable to perform an ICT assessment (or information technology (IT) audit) before and after the FMIS implementation to improve IT governance structure and identify possible improvements in infrastructure, database integrity, and information security, based on various industry standards.

Conclusions

In general, "FMIS implementation is an art, not a science" —emblematic of complex systems that constantly evolve and expand, paralleling changes in PFM needs and advances in technology. As with the design and implementation of any complex system, leadership, collaboration and innovation are important to the process.

Grounded in lessons from more than 25 years of project implementation, this study suggests a methodology for the design and implementation of future FMIS projects, following a systematic approach to problem solving. This approach is expected to help clarify key "design parameters" through a simple questionnaire and identify "which solution fits which problem in what situation" during project design. If applied, such an approach may improve the quality and reliability of next-generation FMIS solutions.

The current focus of FMIS ICT solution providers and client countries is directed at the development of new open-source software and other innovative solutions to meet core FMIS requirements at a reasonable cost. Also, the improvement of knowledge sharing and learning among the client countries (through communities of practice and peer learning platforms) and within the World Bank is critical to the development of a common understanding of current challenges and priorities for FMIS reforms—promoting debates around emerging practices, innovative solutions, and sequencing in complementary PFM reforms.

It should be noted that the successful completion of FMIS projects depends on external factors as well. The adverse effects of country-specific political economy issues, global financial events, or a shifting political environment may have a substantial impact on any properly prepared project during its implementation and result in unexpected delays or failures.

Given the scope of this paper and the nature of project data available, it is not possible to address the many interesting and relevant questions about FMIS projects. The analysis is limited to the data and information within the Bank, not without recognizing the importance of other actors in this arena and the limitations of existing data. To that end, future studies might usefully explore:

- The impact of FMIS introduction on public financial outcomes (e.g., timely reporting, better decision making) in different types of countries.
- The significantly higher failure rate for projects in Africa.
- The costs of FMIS project implementation relative to total national annual budgets.
- The variation in procurement patterns among projects.
- Lessons from the implementation of such projects in developed countries.
- The correlation between notable changes in World Bank policies and/or technological advances and the outcomes of FMIS projects.
- Data and assessments from the operations of other development partners in this arena.

Notes

1. This number is based on actual + estimated budget of Treasury/FMIS related component activities in official project documents (55 completed and 32 active projects as of August 2010). See Table 2.1 for the details.
2. A number of reports and papers have been written to date about FMIS implementation, long-term sustainability, successes and failures—these include Schiavo-Campo and Tommasi (1999) and Diamond and Khemani (2005).
3. The World Bank FMIS Database (1984–2010), updated in August 2010.
4. Please refer to Table 3.3 for a description of the ICR performance ratings.
5. Given the procurement intensive nature of much of FMIS project implementation, a PIU is often the most time and cost efficient method of ensuring progress in implementation. This implementation mode should not undermine broader country systems.

## CHAPTER 1

Introduction

What is a FMIS?

Sound budgeting and financial management are based on the following principles: comprehensiveness, legitimacy, flexibility, predictability, contestability, honesty, transparency, and accountability. To achieve these principles, well-functioning accounting and financial systems are among the basics that underpin governmental capacity to allocate and use resources efficiently and effectively. *Financial management information systems (FMIS) can be broadly defined as a set of automation solutions that enable governments to plan, execute, and monitor the budget by assisting in the prioritization, execution, and reporting of expenditures, as well as the custodianship and reporting of revenues. Accordingly, FMIS solutions can contribute to the efficiency and equity of government operations.* Modern FMIS platforms help governments comply with domestic and international financial regulations and reporting standards and support decentralized operations through centralized Web-based solutions, providing access to a large number of authorized budget users at all levels.

Whenever FMIS and other PFM information systems (for example, payroll) share the same central database to record and report all daily financial transactions, offering reliable consolidated results for decision support, performance monitoring, and Web publishing, they can be referred to as an "integrated" FMIS, or IFMIS. IFMIS solutions are rare in practice, and, to avoid unrealistic expectations, the term should not be used as a synonym for core FMIS functionality. In some projects, core Treasury systems are called FMIS or IFMIS, and this is also misleading. In this document, FMIS will be used to denote the core budget preparation and execution systems in general. The term "Treasury/FMIS" (T/F) will be used when there is a need to distinguish between Treasury projects (primarily dealing with budget execution) and FMIS projects (covering budget preparation and execution) during data analysis (Figure 1.1).

In addition to those mentioned above, some of the positive spillover effects of automated FMIS solutions include improved efficiency and transparency through direct payments to suppliers/contractors. It may also lead to a reduction in prices as a result of gains based on the time value of money, as well as the comparative analysis of market rates. FMIS solutions improve interactions across the various organizational units within government in terms of execution, reporting, and accuracy of budget transactions. More recently, open budget initiatives have led to an increase in the provision of public sector financial information for the general public, and such systems facilitate this information exchange. In sum, FMIS offers a great potential for increasing predictability, participation, transparency, and government accountability.

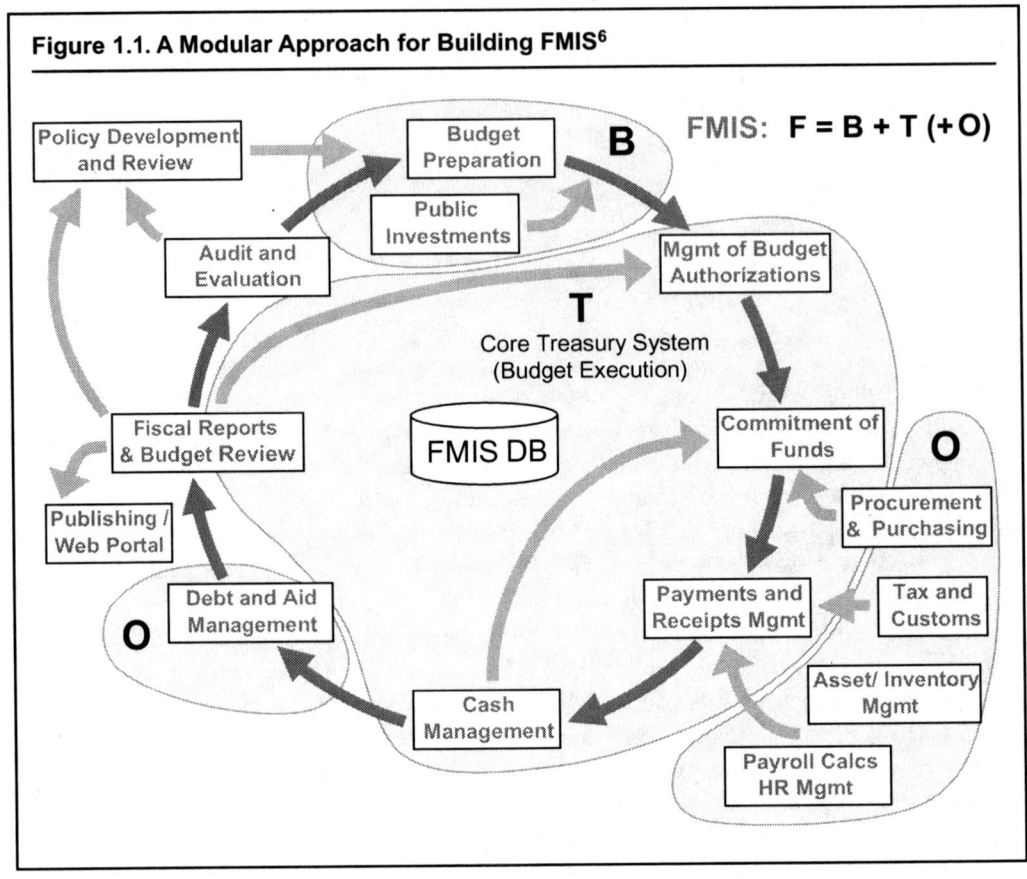

Figure 1.1. A Modular Approach for Building FMIS[6]

However, implementing FMIS solutions is no easy task, and its introduction entails the allocation of significant resources and substantial capacity building efforts. This study sheds light on the challenges involved in the design and implementation of FMIS projects. Financial management information systems can be powerful tools, if designed to meet the specific user requirements and in line with a well-defined PFM strategy and realistic action plan. Moreover, the development of a countrywide FMIS solution and infrastructure will be more useful, when it is an integral part of a coherent and realistic national ICT or e-government strategy. The risks of supply or market driven choices of FMIS solutions are high and must be counterbalanced with significant attention to the design of a tool that is adaptive and responsive to the needs of its ultimate users. These systems are no replacement for good management and robust internal controls and will not be very useful if budget coverage itself is limited or budget planning/execution practices are not well established.

Since the late 1980s, the World Bank and other development agencies have been active in funding Treasury and FMIS projects. In particular, the World Bank has financed 87 completed/active projects in 51 countries, totaling over US $2.2 billion. In fact, the total amount allocated for these projects is around $3.5 billion, including the borrower co-financing and other donor funds, and the total cost of FMIS-related ICT solutions is nearly $938 million.[8] Despite the high levels of financing by the World Bank in this area with frequently limited co-financing from the recipient country (only 11% of completed and active projects have government co-financing of 25% or above), little is known about the achievements and the lessons learned across projects over time.

Based on findings from a preliminary draft report that focused on 31 of these projects completed by 2003, World Bank experience with FMIS reforms is mixed.[2] The current report attempts to review all of the 55 completed Treasury/FMIS projects using project-level data and improved access to information available in the World Bank databases and archives. Several key questions are addressed in this study:

1. What historical patterns emerge from World Bank financed FMIS projects?
   a. How much does it cost to implement a FMIS solution?
   b. How long does it take to implement on average?
   c. What types of software packages have been used (commercial or locally developed)?
   d. How have these projects been designed and sequenced?
2. How have FMIS projects performed according to various criteria?
3. What are the key factors that contribute to the success and failure of projects?
4. What have we learned that could be useful for future projects?

The findings of this study are based on a comprehensive database of 55 closed and 32 active Treasury/FMIS projects[3] implemented between 1984 and 2010 (7 pipeline projects were also analyzed in some sections). The data presented here was gathered from individual project Implementation Completion Reports (ICRs), PADs, the IEG reports, and complemented with interviews with task team leaders and relevant public sector/informatics specialists.

This study is dived into five chapters. The introduction covers the definitions used and methodology applied in reviewing projects. Chapter 2 provides descriptive characteristics of the sample data drawn from Bank databases and describes general patterns in duration, regional distribution, costs, and ICT solutions implemented, among other aspects. Chapter 3 analyzes the performance of the projects, differentiating between ratings of the ICRs and the IEG reports, as well as the factors contributing to the success and failure of projects and individual components. A detailed analysis of country case studies from Mongolia, Turkey, Albania, Guatemala, and Pakistan are presented in chapter 4. In conclusion, chapter 5 synthesizes the main lessons learned and prerequisites necessary for an effective FMIS project.

Definitions

A core FMIS generally refers to automating the financial operations of both the budget and treasury units. The system tracks financial events and records all transactions; summarizes information; supports reporting and policy decisions; and incorporates the elements of ICT, personnel, procedures, controls, and data. An FMIS is usually built around a core treasury system that supports key budget execution functions, such as accounts payable and receivables, commitment and cash management, and the general ledger and financial reporting, combined with budget formulation (multi-year), debt management, and public investment management modules. The non-core systems sometimes linked with FMIS solutions are personnel management/payroll, revenue administrations (tax and customs), public procurement, inventory and property management, and performance management information.[4] Financial control is not the only reason for developing FMIS. More importantly, FMIS solutions are used to support informed decisions on policies and programs, and publish reliable information on budget performance.

For the purposes of this report, FMIS (F) is defined narrowly to include mainly core Budget (B) and Treasury (T) systems. Through a process of coding all projects by their components (described below), only the FMIS projects designed and implemented with a focus on core budget and/or treasury systems were included in the database. Projects with a secondary focus on non-core systems were listed separately and excluded from in-depth analysis.

Methodology

The World Bank–funded projects were selected from internal databases hosted in the operations portal and business warehouse. The initial selection of FMIS projects involved identifying all 55 projects completed between 1984 and 2010, coded under the Poverty Reduction and Economic Management (PREM) network. Most of these projects are mapped to the PREM Public Sector Governance (PSG) sector board. Several others were identified under the Economic Policy (EP) and Financial Management (FM) sector boards, as well as the Financial and Private Sector Development (FPD) network. Selected projects are mainly investment (INV) operations, using Specific Investment Loans (SIL) or Technical Assistance Loans (TAL) as lending instruments. From that initial selection, each project's Implementation Completion Report (ICR) was reviewed to identify the type of FMIS solution by coding project components (corroborated by project objectives, activities and the total amount of FMIS investment).[5] The coding of FMIS projects can be seen in Table 1.1.

Figure 1.1 provides an explanation of how the coding of the projects is mapped to the PFM cycle, and shows the distinction between core (**B** and **T**) and non-core (**O**) FMIS modules in graphic form.

The quantitative methods employed in this study consist mainly of descriptive statistics of the sample contained within the FMIS Database.[7] The database will be open to further analysis (including econometric studies) in the near future. To complement these methods, a number of interviews were conducted with more than 25 Task Team Leaders (TTLs) and Public Sector/ICT specialists, closely involved in the projects included in the database to cross-check information and develop a richer understanding of the context in which these projects were implemented.[8] Moreover, a selection of country case studies is presented to illustrate the key elements of FMIS implementation.

The primary unit of analysis in this study is the individual *project* due primarily to the way the World Bank documents and implements its work. However, FMIS can be implemented through a project focused on T/F solutions only, or as a component of a broader project. Hence, some of the data can be misleading when analyzed only at the project level.

Most countries have implemented more than one project—sometimes up to four separate projects. A holistic approach would consider the sequence of projects and the way in which they build on one another. While this is difficult to do with the dataset, a case study analysis lends itself well to such considerations. Nonetheless, to address this issue within the dataset, a typology of projects was created to improve the ability to compare projects to one another.

Table 1.1. Coding of FMIS Project Components

Code	FMIS Project Components
B	Budget systems (budget planning + preparation) including: ▤ budget planning/formulation ▤ medium-term frameworks (e.g. MTFF, MTBF, MTEF) ▤ public investment management ▤ program-based budgeting and/or performance-informed budgeting
T	Treasury systems (budget execution) supporting: ▤ management of budget authorizations/releases ▤ commitment of funds ▤ payment/revenue management (mostly based on treasury single accounts (TSAs)) ▤ cash forecasting and management ▤ accounting and reporting
F	Financial Management Information System (FMIS): ▤ a combination of Budget and Treasury systems ($F = B + T$)
O	Other FMIS components one or more of which may be present in FMIS ($F = B + T + O$): ▤ revenue collection (mainly interfaces with tax and customs systems) ▤ debt management (covering both domestic and external debt) ▤ procurement/purchasing (tracking all payments after contract signature) ▤ asset and inventory management ▤ Human Resources Management Information System (HRMIS) + payroll
P	Preparatory work (advisory support/training) for Treasury or FMIS implementation: ▤ accounting/financial reporting reforms, including compliance with International Public Sector Accounting Standards (IPSAS) ▤ budgeting and macroeconomic forecasting in the Ministry of Finance/Economy ▤ establishment of TSA ▤ improvement of budget classification (BC) and unified chart of accounts (CoA)

World Bank–funded projects are grouped along the following five dimensions (T/F Type):

1. Comprehensive FMIS projects (new system implementation);
2. Incremental expansion of existing comprehensive FMIS;
3. Emergency operations in fragile states;
4. Incremental expansion of systems implemented through emergency operations; and
5. Ex-post intervention by the World Bank.

Most of these categories are self-explanatory, with the exception of "ex-post intervention by the World Bank." This category refers to the improvement or expansion of an existing FMIS solution, which was previously implemented by the government and/or other development partners.

In order to provide public access to the summary of 94 FMIS projects in 51 countries, the FMIS Data Mapper application is available on Google Maps (Appendix M).

Basic information for each project is displayed in an information box, and related project documents can be displayed or downloaded from the World Bank external Web site using the link provided.

This study does not include a detailed description of basic PFM concepts or the importance of FMIS or ICT in general, which are well documented in literature.[9,10] Instead, it presents the World Bank's experience on what works and what doesn't in FMIS reforms, based on a comprehensive database of 94 projects, in order to share the lessons learned and provide practical guidelines for teams involved in the design and implementation of FMIS projects. The literature on FMIS is replete with individual country case studies, but has to date not relied on systematic data analysis as a basis upon which to draw conclusions and lessons for future implementation.[11]

Notes

1. This number is based on actual + estimated budget of Treasury/FMIS related component activities in official project documents (55 completed and 32 active projects as of August 2010).
2. William L. Dorotinsky, Junghun Cho, "World Bank's Experience with Financial Management Information (FMIS) Projects," Draft Report, 2003.
3. The World Bank FMIS Database (1984–2010)—updated in August 2010.
4. The linkage between FMIS and other financial systems such as payroll and procurement is a very important issue, but is beyond the scope of the present report.
5. The observations presented in this report are based on the information available in the World Bank operations portal, archives and business warehouse. Although more than 80% of the project related data was verified through interviews and meetings with task team leaders/members, due to the dynamic nature of operations portal, some of the details on recently completed/active projects may not be present (if the ICRs are not available yet or the progress is not updated within the report preparation period). Nevertheless, a substantial amount of the information presented here is based on reliable and verified project data.
6. Updated version of the FMIS diagram included in Cem Dener's presentation posted on the PFM Reform Database.
7. The FMIS database is available from: http://connectprem.worldbank.org/psg/pf/fmis. Currently this database is only available to World Bank users. An external version is expected to be available in 2011.
8. Future studies could usefully survey client countries for their views on current operational status.
9. Salvatore Schiavo-Campo and Daniel Tommasi, "Managing Government Expenditure", Asian Development Bank Report, April 1999.
10. Richard Allen and Daniel Tommasi, "Managing Public Expenditure—A Reference Book for Transition Economies", OECD-SIGMA Report, 2001.
11. "Review of PFM Reform Literature", DFID Report, January 2009.

## CHAPTER 2

Descriptive Data Analysis

What Historical Patterns Emerge from World Bank–Financed Treasury/FMIS Projects?

As of August 2010, the WB FMIS Database contains 94 projects (with a substantial ICT component), of which 55 are completed, 32 are active, and 7 are in development (pipeline). These projects cover 51 countries and span 1984–2010. This chapter provides the descriptive statistics drawn from the FMIS project-level database. The summary data analysis is structured in three sections: (i) project duration, (ii) regional distribution, and (iii) project characteristics (in terms of objectives, scope, costs, and ICT solutions). In order to reveal some of the underlying patterns, the data is disaggregated according to project, country, region, and type at various points in the project cycle (pipeline, active, completed).

Duration

The first two World Bank FMIS projects included in the database are Brazil and Ecuador, which began in 1984. The bulk of the projects span the 1990s up to 2010. On average, it took 7.9 years to complete an FMIS project with a range of 5–10 years for most projects, with the exception of an Emergency Public Administration Project in Afghanistan (3.6 years) and an institutional development project in Malawi (13.4 years). Figure 2.1 shows the total (actual) duration of 55 completed projects included in the database.

If viewed from a country perspective, rather than an individual project perspective, the time required to implement such systems may be considerably longer. The majority

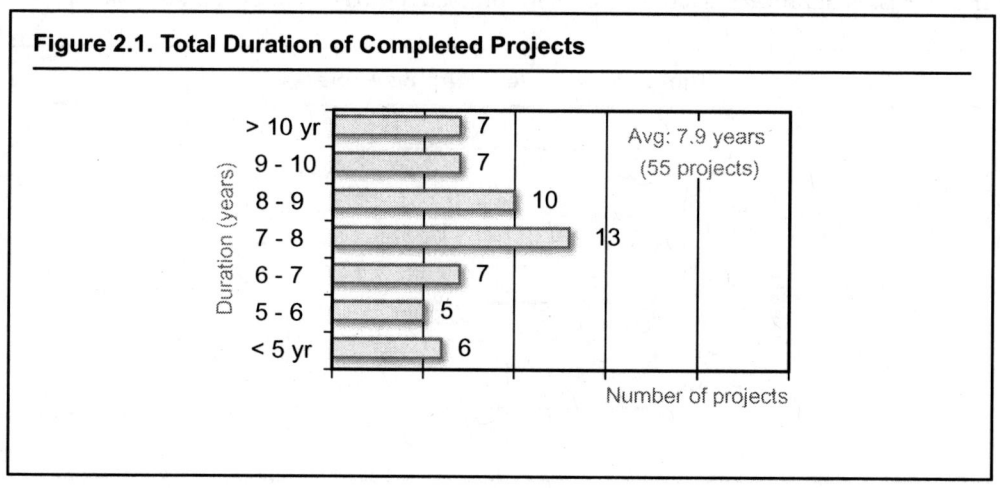

Figure 2.1. Total Duration of Completed Projects

of countries have more than one project back-to-back. In the case of Ecuador, three separate projects spanned across 23.1 years. Guatemala had three projects in 16.5 years, and Nicaragua had four projects in 17 years (Appendix E). Argentina had two overlapping projects which lasted for 19.1 years.

Appendix I contains a detailed timeline for all completed projects included in the database, grouped by country and region. This includes information for each project on (i) the preparation period, defined as the time between the concept note and the board approval; (ii) the effectiveness period, defined as the time between the board approval (not the signature of the loan agreement) and the start of the project; (iii) the implementation period, defined as the time between when the project began and its actual closing date; and (iv) the extension period, defined as the period between the original closing date and the actual closing date.

Next we turn to analyzing the sample of projects to get a better sense of the average length of each of these stages. During the preparation/design period typically, the legal basis for the reforms, the institutional landscape and capacity of various actors, the business processes and the use of ICT systems are assessed. With these inputs, a detailed preparation plan is then created with clear reform actions and deadlines, realistic implementation and procurement plans, and a disbursement schedule.

Often, other PFM assessments are performed in tandem, such as PEFA assessments, Public Expenditure Review (PER) or the Country Financial Accountability Assessments (CFAA). Due to the number of inputs required to properly design a program, the preparation period is quite long. For both active and completed projects, preparation took on average 16 months among 87 projects (Figure 2.2).[1] In a few cases, changes in political leadership and the design of complex and independent components led to a substantial lengthening of the preparation period (mainly in the Africa region).

The effectiveness period—the time between board approval and the actual start date—was six months on average for completed and active projects (Figure 2.3). This delay often occurs because once the World Bank's Board of Directors approves a project, the government is then required to sign the loan agreement and ratify it through Parliament or a similar body. Bureaucratic procedures, or in some cases changes in government, often delay the signing or ratification of the loan.

Implementation took up the bulk of time, averaging six years for completed projects. The extension of projects is also common in completed projects. Out of 55 projects, 44 proj-

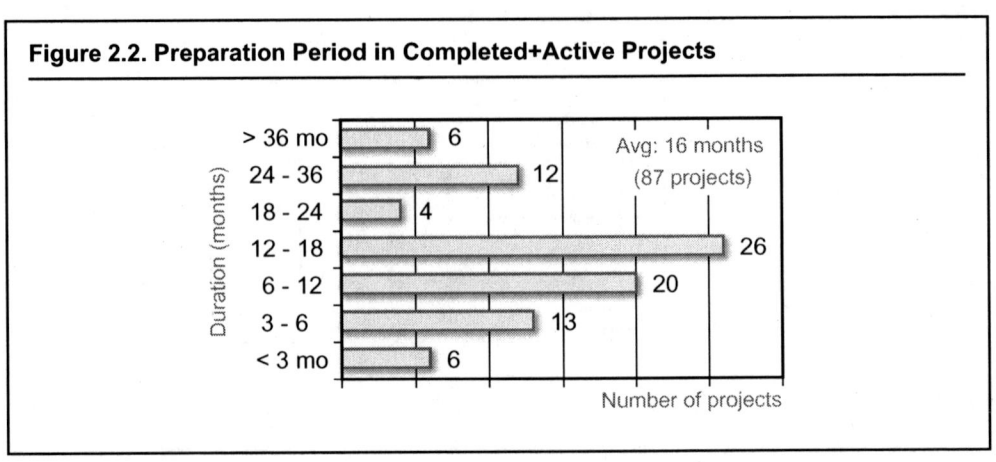

Figure 2.2. Preparation Period in Completed+Active Projects

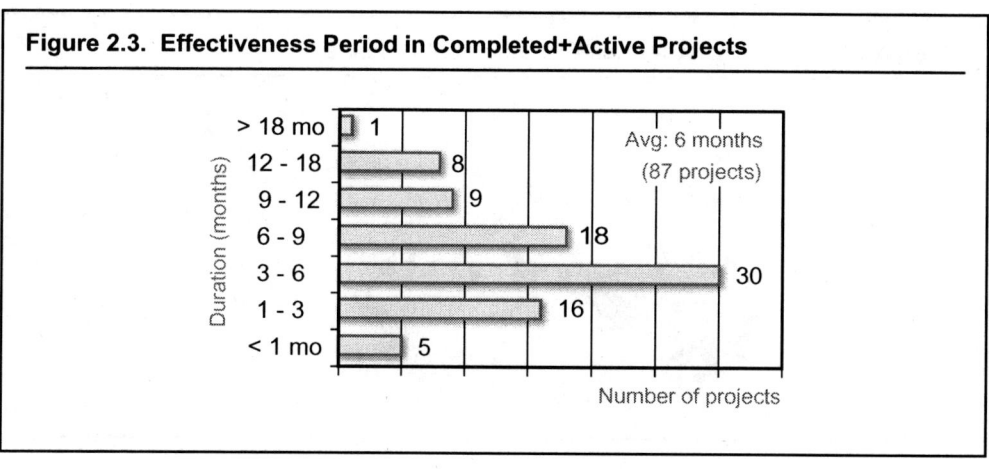

Figure 2.3. Effectiveness Period in Completed+Active Projects

ects (80%) were extended on average by 2.2 years (Figure 2.4). Extensions happen for a number of reasons, including earlier delays in the preparation, effectiveness, or implementation of the project. The restructuring of projects due to a change in scope or components (which occurred in 22 out of 55 projects) often leads to extension. Moreover, a relatively long procurement period for ICT solutions (18–24 months) contributes to this rate of extension.

Among completed projects, it takes 2.2 years to procure FMIS solutions, on average, because of the selection of suppliers and contract signatures required. This duration also depends on the complexity of the project and the number of procurement packages needed. The time required to specify the details of ICT solutions also takes a long time, particularly for FMIS with many components. Among completed projects, it took on average 2.5 years to implement ICT solutions. If the contracting for required ICT solutions does not take place 2–3 years before the closing date, this invariably leads to an extension.

Regional Distribution

The regional patterns that emerge from the database are quite striking. The Latin America and the Caribbean (LCR) regions stand out with the largest number of completed projects (25), and Africa (AFR) has the second-largest number of completed projects (13). Europe and Central Asia (ECA), South Asia (SAR), East Asia and the Pacific (EAP), and the Middle East and North Africa (MENA) have 7, 5, 3, and 2 completed projects, respectively (Figure 2.5).

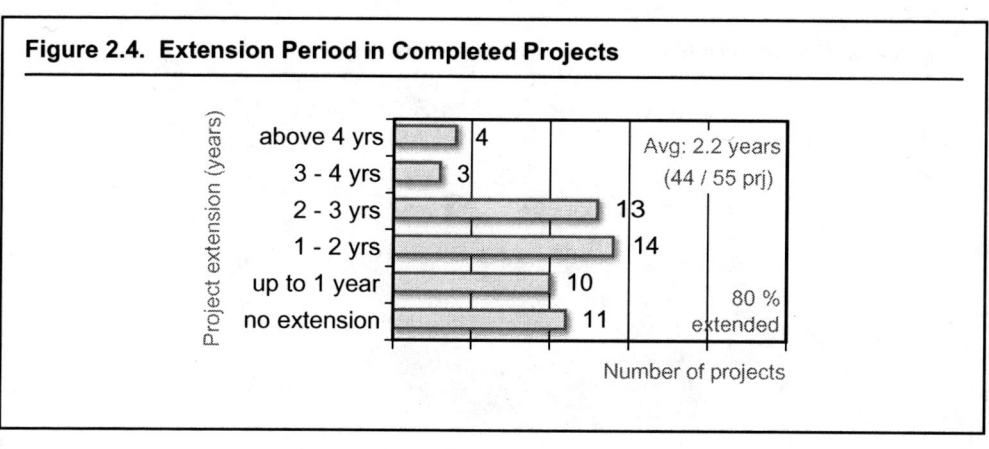

Figure 2.4. Extension Period in Completed Projects

Figure 2.5. Regional Distribution of Completed Projects

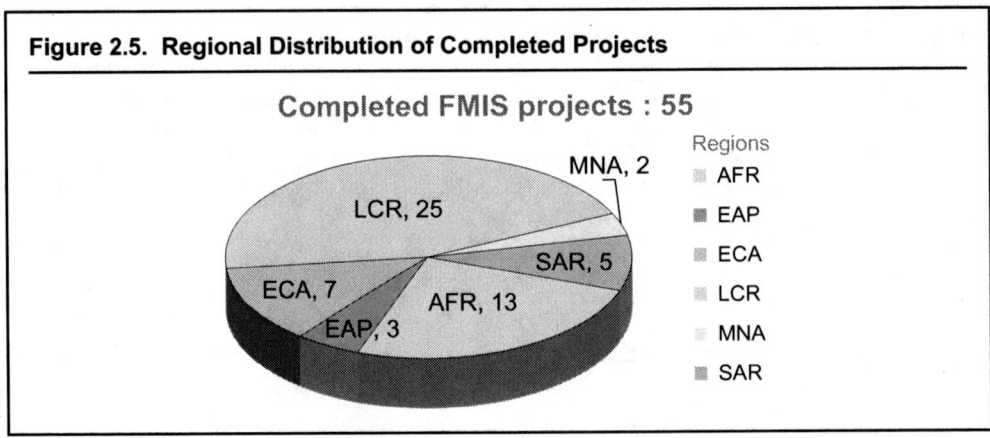

Completed FMIS projects : 55

Among active projects, the distribution is more even. AFR has 12, ECA has 7, EAP has 7, and SAR has 2, while LCR only has 4 active projects. MNA has no active FMIS project. The initial push for FMIS implementation was strongest within LCR. The LCR region was an early adopter of these systems because of the relatively early establishment of the treasury organizations (ranging from 1927 in Chile to 1995 in Honduras). By the late 1990s the region was well positioned to take advantage of the technological advances within the industry.

In Africa, an urgent need to improve PFM practices and a substantial increase in the influx of development funds beginning in the late 1990s are likely the main drivers for most of the ambitious FMIS projects. These FMIS projects were based on relatively complex information systems to cover a large number of PFM functions—at times without an adequate focus on capacity building and the necessary process improvements. In total, there are 87 completed and active projects residing primarily in the regions of LCR, AFR, ECA, and EAP (Figure 2.6).

Project Characteristics

This section explores the types of projects included in the database and the sectoral mapping assigned to projects by the World Bank. In order to accurately compare projects, individual PADs were reviewed to further disaggregate projects by the type of FMIS

Figure 2.6. Regional Distribution of Completed+Active Projects

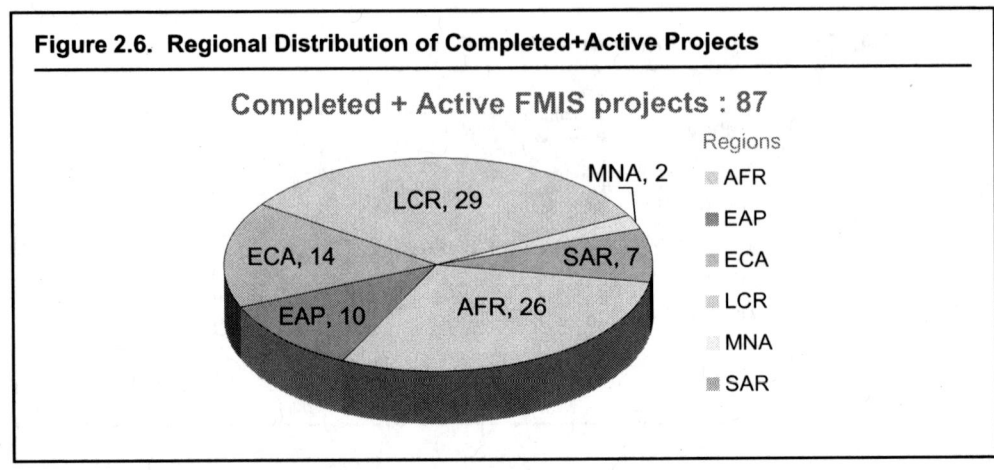

Completed + Active FMIS projects : 87

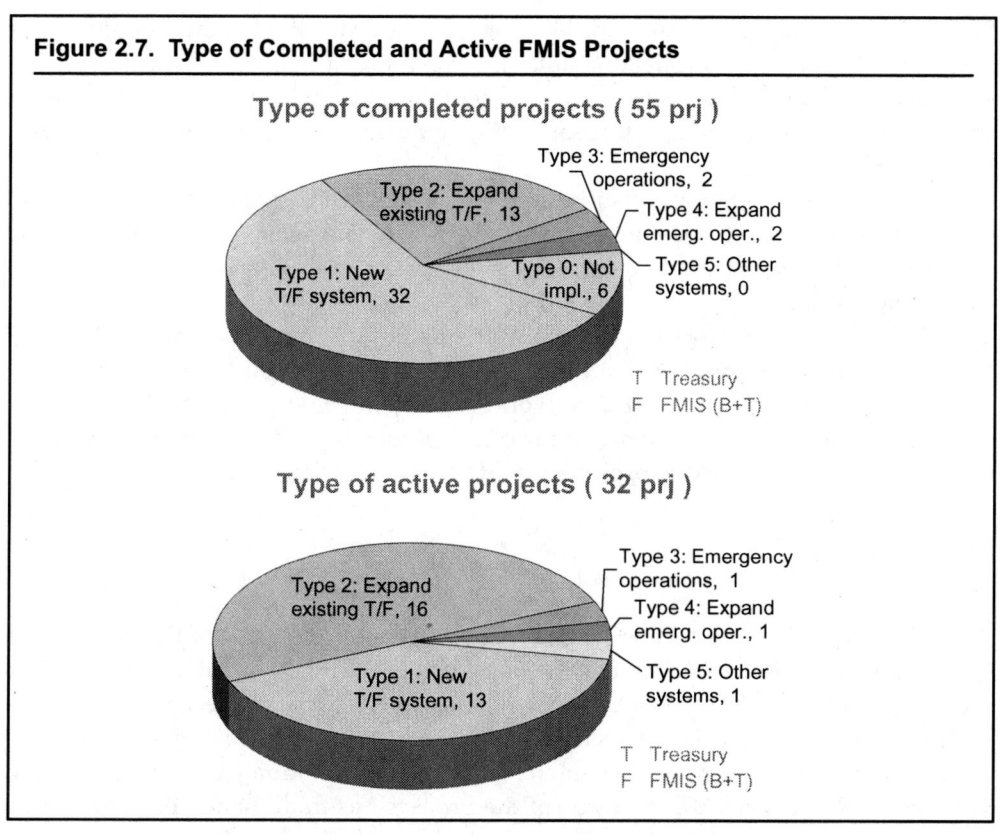

Figure 2.7. Type of Completed and Active FMIS Projects

Type of completed projects (55 prj)

Type 2: Expand existing T/F, 13
Type 3: Emergency operations, 2
Type 4: Expand emerg. oper., 2
Type 1: New T/F system, 32
Type 0: Not impl., 6
Type 5: Other systems, 0

T Treasury
F FMIS (B+T)

Type of active projects (32 prj)

Type 2: Expand existing T/F, 16
Type 3: Emergency operations, 1
Type 4: Expand emerg. oper., 1
Type 1: New T/F system, 13
Type 5: Other systems, 1

T Treasury
F FMIS (B+T)

project. As noted earlier, the categories are (i) World Bank–funded new FMIS projects, (ii) an expansion of existing FMIS projects, (iii) emergency operations in fragile states, (iv) an expansion of emergency operations, and (v) the ex-post intervention by the World Bank to improve FMIS solutions developed by others.

Among the 55 completed FMIS projects, just over half of projects are new FMIS projects (32), whereas 13 projects were an expansion of existing systems (Figure 2.7).

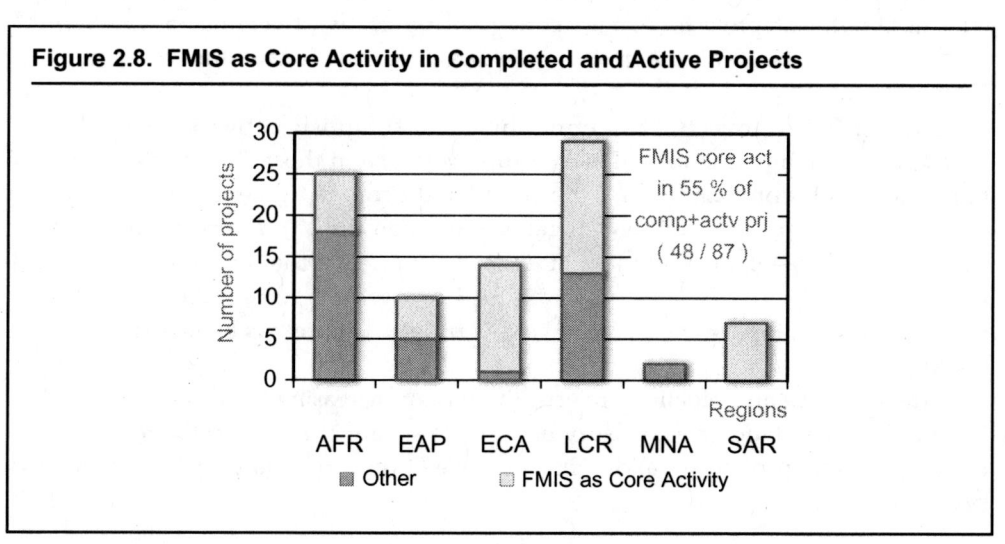

Figure 2.8. FMIS as Core Activity in Completed and Active Projects

Number of projects

FMIS core act in 55 % of comp+actv prj (48 / 87)

AFR   EAP   ECA   LCR   MNA   SAR

Regions

■ Other   ☐ FMIS as Core Activity

Six projects were not implemented. Most of the new FMIS include large-scale, countrywide ICT solutions (application software, servers, data storage, field hardware, engineering systems, and network equipment) implemented through comprehensive (or "turn-key") contracts to reduce the complexity of system integration and management.

Among active projects, the distribution between new and expanded systems is even. Overall, the World Bank engages to a lesser degree in emergency operations and their expansion. The majority of ongoing projects are either a new FMIS or an expansion of existing systems.

Most of the FMIS projects included in the database are mapped to the PSG sector board, with a few mapped to other units such as Financial Management (FM), Economic Policy (EP) and the FPD network. With an increasing demand for the modernization of information systems in parallel to second and third generation reforms in various sectors, the FMIS projects initiated by other Bank units are expected to increase.

Objectives

All ICRs and PADs were reviewed to determine whether the focus of the project was on implementing FMIS or whether it was a relatively small part of a larger project focused on other goals such as broader public sector reforms or decentralization. In 55% of completed and active projects, the implementation of FMIS is considered a core activity (Figure 2.8). There is some interesting regional variation with respect to these numbers. In ECA and SAR, the focus of the projects has traditionally been on developing a core FMIS solution. Conversely, in Africa, only 7 out of 25 projects focused specifically on a core FMIS. LCR with the largest numbers of projects (29) has 16 projects with FMIS as core activities and 13 as a relatively small part of broader activities. The additional component most often included in these projects is a medium-term budgetary framework (MTBF) or medium-term expenditure framework (MTEF)—29 out of 55 completed projects included this component. Other core components include performance-based budgeting (PBB) in16 out of 55 projects, human resource management information systems (HRMIS) in 17 out of 55 projects, and debt management systems in 11 out of 55 projects. To a lesser degree, public investment management (PIM) systems, payroll, tax, and customs components were included as other components of FMIS projects.

Among FMIS projects, it is important to distinguish between those that focused solely on implementing the Treasury system, and those that implemented an FMIS (B+T) solution. Comparing the completed projects across the regions, about 60% more FMIS projects (35) have been undertaken than Treasury projects (20), as shown in Figure 2.9. The regional pattern that emerges is that LCR and AFR mostly focused on FMIS, while EAP, ECA, and SAR focused on getting the Treasury systems in place first. However, among active projects, there has been a further shift towards FMIS.

Among active and pipeline projects, there is an increasing focus on implementing FMIS rather than standalone Treasury projects. There are 26 active FMIS projects versus 6 active Treasury projects (in addition, 7 pipeline FMIS versus only 2 planned Treasury systems).

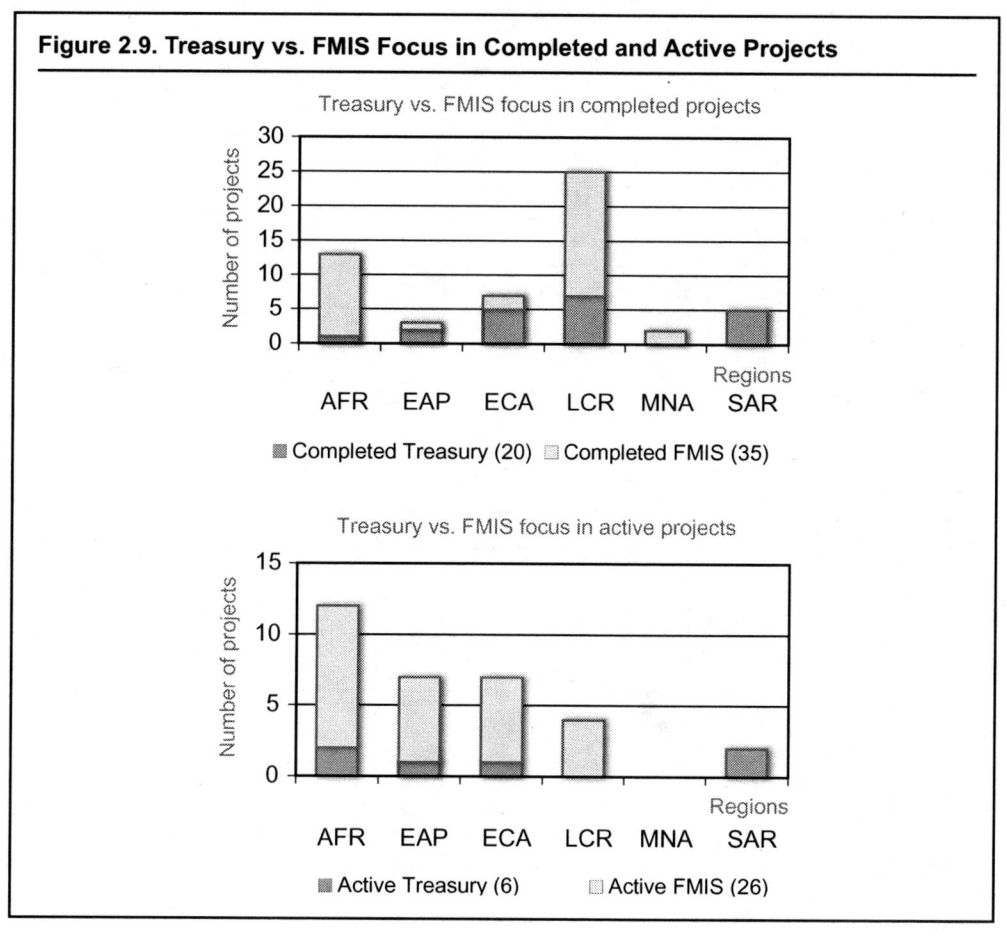

Figure 2.9. Treasury vs. FMIS Focus in Completed and Active Projects

Scope

An important consideration in assessing FMIS solutions is whether they cover only central units (Treasury, Ministry of Finance (MoF), and Line Ministries) or both central and local (defined here as the regional and/or district level offices of Treasury/MoF).[2] When the focus is on the central level, the project is less complex, but if you start to expand beyond the central level to regional and district level offices the project becomes much more challenging. Nevertheless, projects successfully completed in 21 countries (out of 38) cover the needs of both central and local units.

Among 55 completed projects, 49 are currently fully or partly operational. Among operational projects, 47% (or 23 out of 49 projects) covered central and local units (Figure 2.10). In AFR, the focus tends to be on central units, which may reflect the lack of capacity and/or ICT infrastructure at subnational levels of government. ECA is the reverse, and all of the completed projects focused on FMIS implementation at both the central and local levels. The LCR, EAP, and SAR regions are split among central and central + local focused projects.

Among active projects, a different pattern emerges: 78% of all projects focus on the implementation of FMIS in both central and local units. This is because almost half of the active projects are an expansion of an existing FMIS solution.

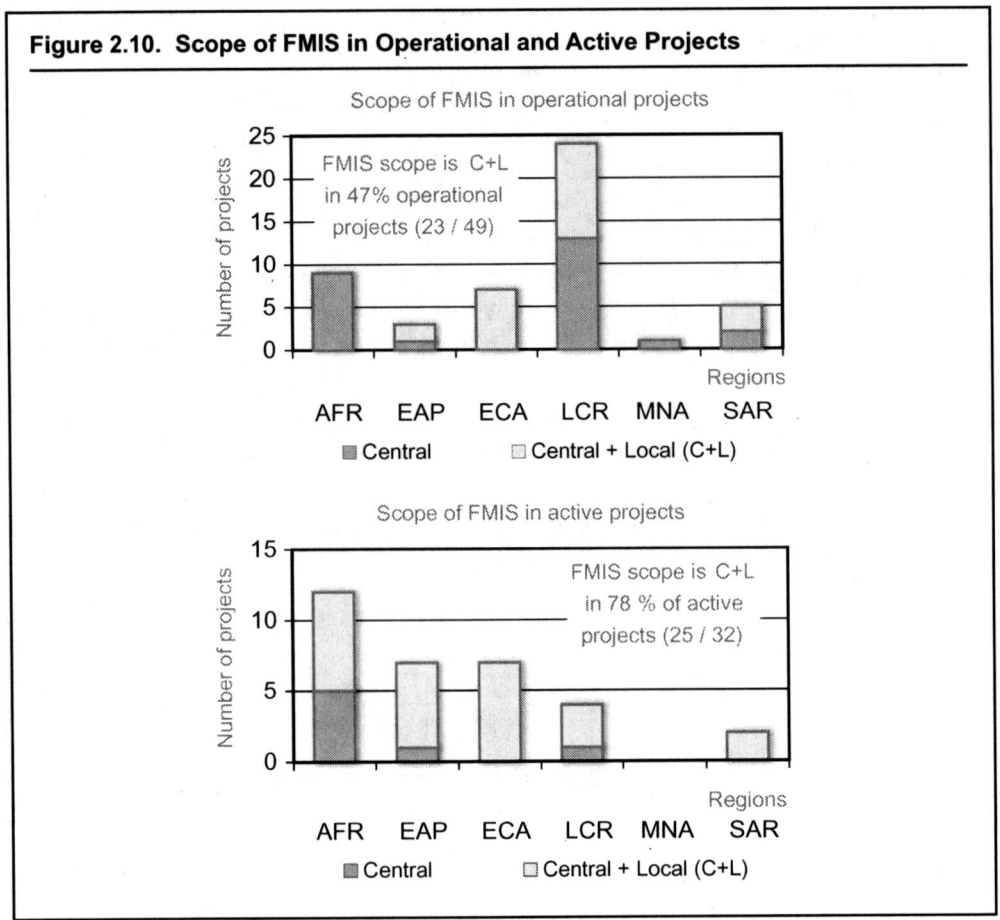

Figure 2.10. Scope of FMIS in Operational and Active Projects

Scope of FMIS in operational projects

FMIS scope is C+L in 47% operational projects (23 / 49)

AFR   EAP   ECA   LCR   MNA   SAR   Regions

■ Central   □ Central + Local (C+L)

Scope of FMIS in active projects

FMIS scope is C+L in 78 % of active projects (25 / 32)

AFR   EAP   ECA   LCR   MNA   SAR   Regions

■ Central   □ Central + Local (C+L)

Project Funding

The cost of the FMIS-related ICT solutions was captured from the operations portal (via signed contracts) and ICRs (which documented the actual cost of each activity) and includes the total spending of all ICT work—Budget, Treasury, FMIS, and other components (B/T/F/O, as described in the methodology section), as well as other key ICT activities such as establishment of countrywide network or rehabilitation of offices and data centers, including government contributions.

Of the 55 completed projects included in the database, 75% of the total cost of all projects was funded by the World Bank. The share of the total spending dedicated to the ICT components was 44%. Further disaggregating this, the total percentage spent on FMIS ICT solutions was 23% across all completed projects. This pattern seems to be changing in active projects, with more government contributions and an increased share of spending on ICT solutions.

The total amount of the actual World Bank financing in 87 completed/active projects in 51 countries is over $1.4 billion (Table 2.1). The total cost of ICT solutions in completed projects is around $612M (Total ICT spending), and out of this amount $324m has been spent specifically on FMIS ICT solutions (Total T/F ICT systems). It should be

Table 2.1. Funding and ICT Costs of FMIS Projects

Completed Treasury/FMIS Projects (55)			
	Estimated ($ M)	**Actual ($ M)**	**%**	
Project cost	1,363	1,399	103%	Actual/Estimated
WB funding	1,102	1,056	75%	WB funds/Prj cost
Total ICT spending		612	44%	Total ICT/Prj cost
Total T/F ICT systems		324	23%	T/F ICT/Prj cost

Completed + Active Treasury/FMIS Projects (87)			
	Estimated ($ M)	**Actual ($ M)**	**%**	
Project cost	3,419	3,596	105%	Actual/Estimated
WB funding	2,267	1,426	40%	WB funds/Prj cost
Total ICT spending		1,794	50%	Total ICT/Prj cost
Total T/F ICT systems		938	26%	T/F ICT/Prj cost

Note: Above figures include ECA RF TDP funding/costs as well.

noted that the total ICT spending includes both the WB funding and the government/other contributions for the implementation of all ICT solutions in the project (including FMIS and other activities). However, total T/F ICT systems cost is the spending on FMIS solutions only. Major FMIS ICT investments are mainly funded by the Bank and the procurement of all goods and services is performed according to World Bank procurement guidelines.

Disaggregated by region, the pattern is slightly different for completed projects (Table 2.2). The ECA and SAR regions spent more than 40% of the total project cost for FMIS ICT solutions, whereas LCR, AFR, and EAP spent between 14–22%. On average, total spending on FMIS ICT solutions ($324.4m) was less than 25% of the total project budget in most projects.

Overall ICT spending ($612.4m), which include FMIS solutions and other project ICT needs, goes up to 45% of the total project cost. This indicates that a substantial amount of total project budget (more than 55%) is used to fund PFM reform related

Table 2.2. Regional Distribution of Completed FMIS Project Funding and ICT Costs

Total vs. ICT Cost of Completed Treasury/FMIS Projects (55)						
Region	**# Prj**	**Prj Total ($ M)**	**WB Disb ($ M)**	**ICT Cost ($ M)**	**T/F ICT ($ M)**	**% T/F**
AFR	13	384.2	305.2	128.3	52.6	14%
EAP	3	105.8	71.6	66.7	16.3	15%
ECA	7	160.8	107.4	125.4	70.0	44%
LCR	25	595.6	441.8	222.9	131.3	22%
MNA	2	51.0	37.5	20.8	12.6	25%
SAR	5	101.4	92.5	48.4	41.6	41%
Totals	**55**	**1,398.7**	**1,056.0**	**612.4**	**324.4**	**23%**

advisory support, capacity building, change management and training needs, as well as project management activities.

Another aspect of project funding is the contributions from other development partners and government co-funding. In 13 of the 55 completed projects (24%), co-financing from other development partners supported implementation of FMIS projects. 54% of these multi donor funded projects received low performance ratings (three out of six failed projects are among those). The AFR region stands out with the largest number of donor funded projects (5), together with the LCR (5). The European Union (EU), UK Department for International Development (DFID), Inter-American Development Bank (IDB) and US Agency for International Development (USAID) are the key development partners involved in completed FMIS projects. The IMF is also involved primarily in the preparation phase of these projects, laying the groundwork necessary to develop a well-functioning system. Also, there was government co-funding (more than 25% of project cost) only in 6 of the 55 completed projects (10.9%).

The donors supporting the implementation of FMIS projects increased considerably since the early 2000s. Currently, 12 of the 32 active FMIS projects (38%) are being supported by twelve development partners. In all of these projects, the World Bank is the lead agency supervising the design and implementation of FMIS solutions. The AFR, ECA, and EAP regions have 5, 4 and 3 active FMIS projects funded by multiple donors, respectively. In addition to the EU, DFID, IDB, and USAID, Japan, the Netherlands, Germany, Sweden, Canada, Switzerland, Norway, Finland, and Australia are among the donors supporting the FMIS projects. Government co-funding (more than 25% of project cost) exists in 4 of the 32 active projects (12.5%).

Lending Instruments

In general, FMIS projects are designed as long-term (5–10 years) investment operations that finance goods, works, and services to support economic and social development. There are several types of investment loans suitable for FMIS projects: SILs, TALs, and adaptable program loans (APLs). Other options include emergency recovery loans (ERL) and financial intermediary loans (FIL) in some exceptional cases. Development policy operations, which typically run from one to three years and provide quick-disbursing external financing to support government policy and institutional reforms, are not suitable for FMIS design and implementation activities.

Among 55 completed projects, there are 41 TAL, 11 SIL, 1 APL, and 2 other instruments (Figure 2.11). This pattern has changed slightly within the last decade. Among 32 active projects, lending instruments are selected as follows: 14 TAL, 9 SIL, 6 APL and 3 other.

This trend is similar to other sectors in the Bank, where SIL is the dominant instrument, followed by APL and TAL as the derivatives of SIL. 86% of FMIS projects are designed as a long-term SIL or TAL, with longer preparation times and close supervision needs compared to other instruments. Such activities usually include lengthy procurement processes which result in late disbursement of funds.

There are two active FMIS projects (Albania, Georgia) designed as a technical assistant grant (TAG), as a part of TAL products, and funded through a multi-donor trust fund (MDTF). When funding is provided through a grant, usually there is more than one beneficiary and such projects support a number of reforms in parallel, result-

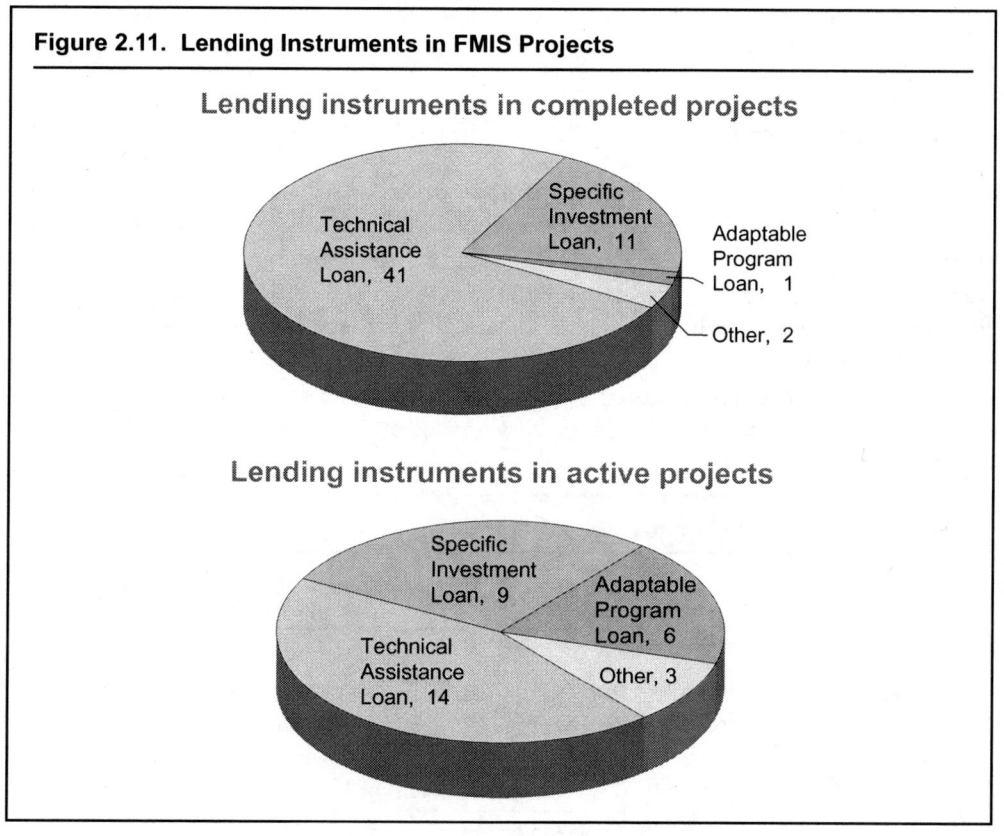

Figure 2.11. Lending Instruments in FMIS Projects

Lending instruments in completed projects

- Technical Assistance Loan, 41
- Specific Investment Loan, 11
- Adaptable Program Loan, 1
- Other, 2

Lending instruments in active projects

- Specific Investment Loan, 9
- Adaptable Program Loan, 6
- Technical Assistance Loan, 14
- Other, 3

ing in delays due to changes in priorities and difficulties in project management and coordination.

In recent years, there has been an interest in APLs due to the need to establish the enabling environment (capacity building, procedural and legislative changes, technical infrastructure) before the development of FMIS ICT solutions. Such FMIS projects are usually designed as two-stage APLs, and the implementation of FMIS ICT solutions is included in the second stage based on the successful completion of certain triggers in the first stage. Despite obvious advantages of the APL approach, there seems to be a need to develop more flexible, results-oriented, and adaptable products for the next generation of PFM reforms in which the expansion of FMIS capabilities and their integration with other e-government systems is expected within a relatively shorter period of time (less than 5 years).

The World Bank is currently working on a new results-based lending (RBL) product that would support a government's program in particular sectors with a clearly defined results framework, as a part of ongoing investment lending reform process. Under the RBL, disbursements for expenditures and investments would be made against intermediate and monitorable results or indicators that are judged to contribute to final outcomes and are largely within the control of the government. Similar products are available in other donor funded FMIS projects, especially in Latin America and the Caribbean region. The IDB has a policy-based loan (PBL) to support FMIS related investments in relatively shorter periods. The average disbursement period in 20 PBLs in 10 countries is around 18 months (ranging from a few months to three years); however, a detailed as-sessment of the results achieved in these PBLs related with FMIS activities is not publicly available yet.

Cost of FMIS ICT Solutions

In the case of 49 operational T/F systems, the average cost of FMIS ICT solutions was $6.6m (Figure 2.12). Twenty projects implemented T/F systems under $4M and another twenty projects ranging from $4M to $12M. Using an average annual index[3] for the varia-tion in the buying power of the U.S. dollar, the average cost (present value) of ICT solu-tions is $7.7 M (corresponding to an increase of 15.8% in the actual investment amount for the period from the closing year to today).

A number of reasons explain the range in costs of these systems: (i) the variation in size of countries; (ii) the number, scope and type of project components (e.g., PIM, HR-

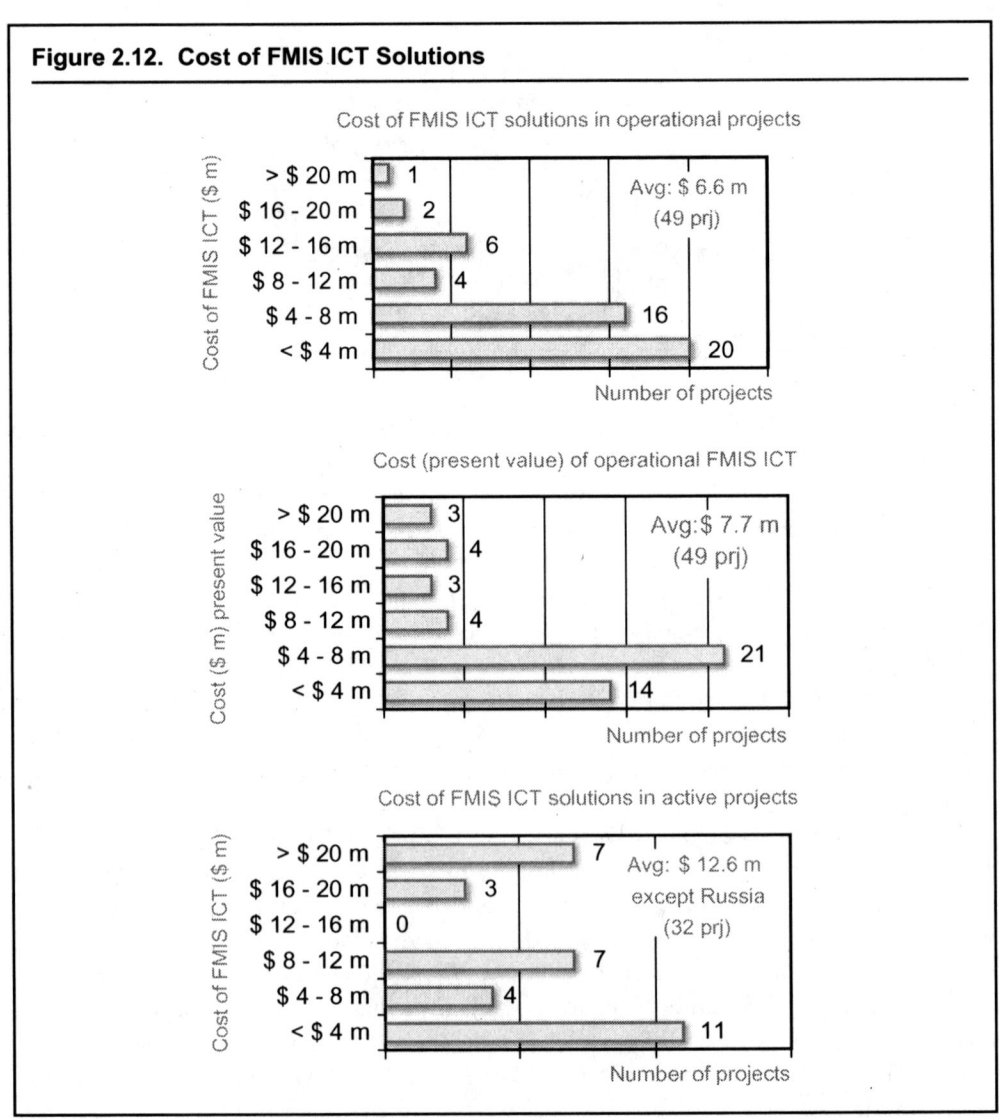

Figure 2.12. Cost of FMIS ICT Solutions

MIS modules); and (iii) whether the T/F system is implemented only at the central level or at the central and local levels. Another variation comes from the use of COTS versus LDSW. Therefore, it is not practical to compare the total ICT investment in individual projects directly, since the scope of FMIS ICT solutions vary. A more realistic comparison can be made based on the total FMIS ICT costs (considering the differences in between COTS and LDSW solutions) versus the number of FMIS users.

Among active projects, the picture is slightly different. The average cost of a T/F ICT system among 32 projects was $12.6M, with the exception of Russian Federation Treasury system for $576M,[4] an outlier in the sample. Typically, the range of costs is between $610k (Cape Verde) to $12M on average. This broad range reflects the differences in the focus of the systems (Treasury vs. FMIS), as well as differences in the size and complexity of projects. Generally, the average total cost of completed projects (including advisory support, training, project management, etc.) was roughly $25M—although this figure is muddled by the differences in scope of the projects included in the database.

Interestingly, cost overrun is not a pattern which emerges from the data (Figure 2.13). A comparison of the actual versus the estimated cost of projects shows that the actual cost of 23 projects (42%) matched estimated costs by ±5%. Only 10 projects out of 55 (18%) exceeded their estimated costs, while 22 (42%) under-ran. This finding differs, in terms of cost overruns, from the earlier observations of Diamond and Khemani that FMIS introduction typically cost much more, took much longer, and experienced more problems than originally anticipated.[5] One of the reasons seems to be the selection of relatively large margins of error (or contingency) while estimating the budget of FMIS ICT solutions in earlier projects, in the absence of detailed system design and realistic cost estimates during project preparation. Such projects tend to be completed within budget at the risk of paying more than market rates due to high initial uncertainty. The comparison of selected FMIS project costs presented below shed some light on this. Another aspect is improved focus on detailed cost estimates during project preparation, by learning from the previous projects. More realistic design and better cost estimates are visible in many active FMIS projects prepared within the last decade.

Due to the lack of reliable detailed information on FMIS ICT costs (based on the number of sites, system users, and cost of individual ICT components), it was only possible to

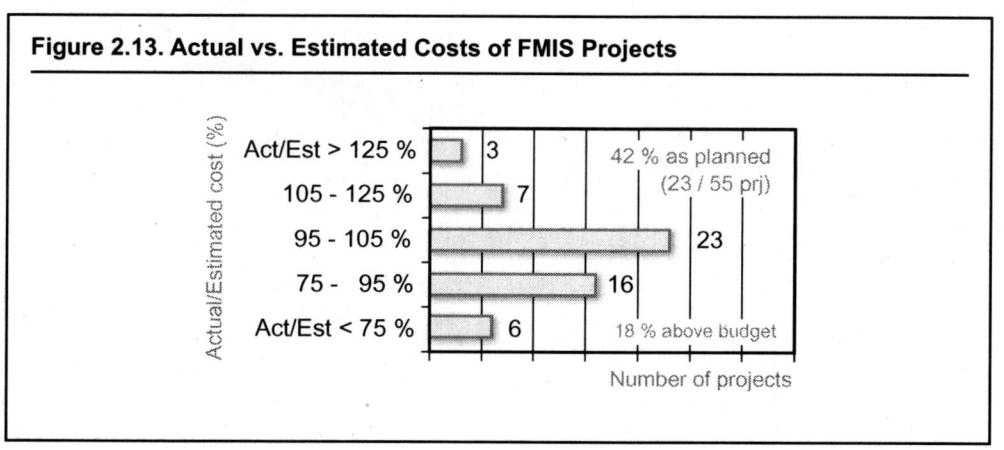

Figure 2.13. Actual vs. Estimated Costs of FMIS Projects

compare 27 of 45 new T/F projects (Type 1) completed/active in 20 countries. Nevertheless, a comparison of FMIS ICT costs versus FMIS users for 17 COTS-based and 10 LDSW
solutions reveals some useful trend lines that may help in the estimation of FMIS ICT
costs when designing new projects. Figure 2.14 presents the trend lines for 17 FMIS solutions based on COTS (9T + 8F), together with 10 LDSW solutions (2T + 8F) in two parts,
for large- and small-scale projects.[6] As expected, COTS solutions tend to cost much more
than LDSW as the number of users increase. However, this figure should be interpreted
with *caution* for two reasons. First, the cost of LDSW solutions may be understated here
and in the data due to the in-house and noncontractual nature of system development.
Second, the definition of system users differs in FMIS solutions. In earlier projects, the
system users were defined as the total number of named users. In Web-based solutions,
concurrent system users are considered a more appropriate measure of FMIS users.

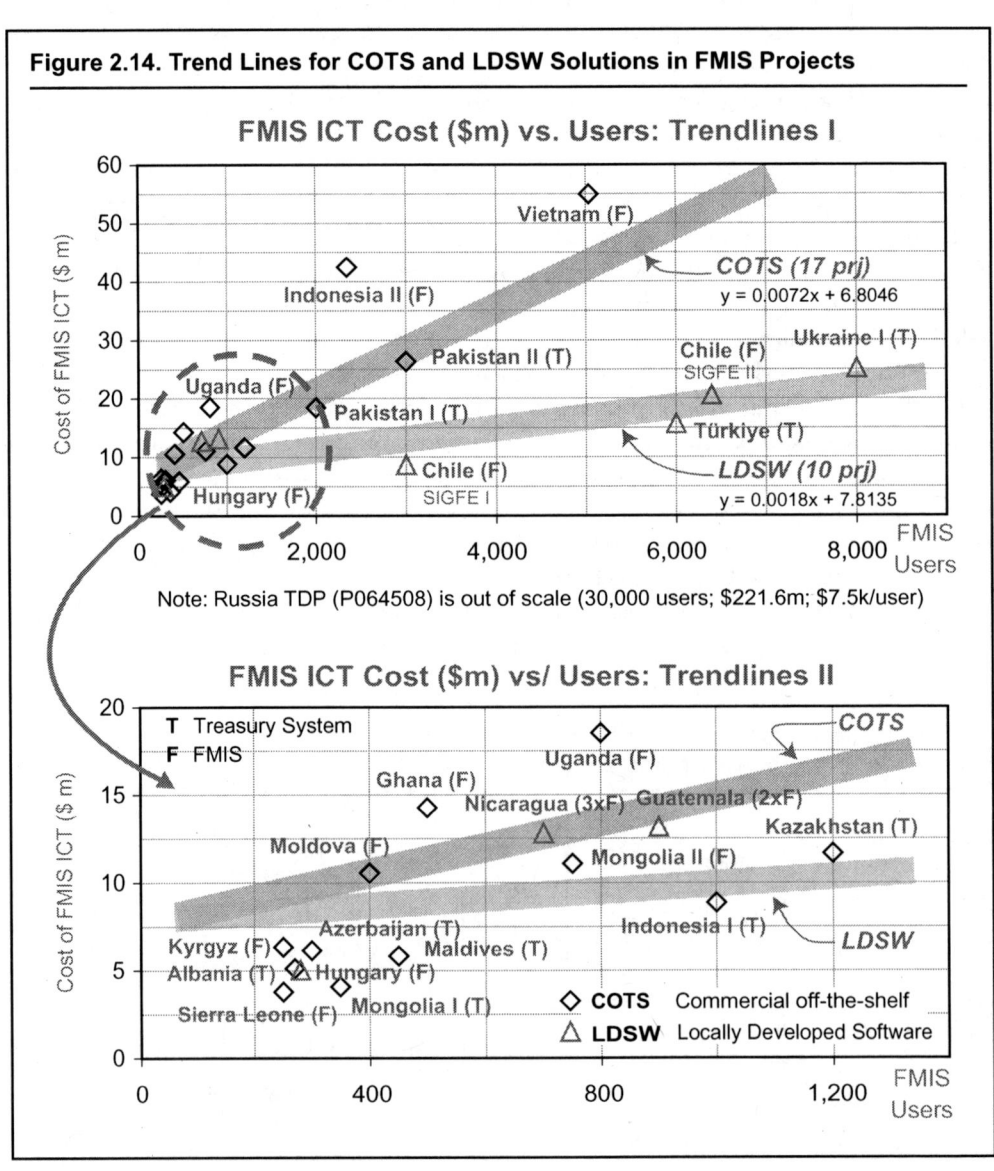

Figure 2.14. Trend Lines for COTS and LDSW Solutions in FMIS Projects

FMIS ICT Cost ($m) vs. Users: Trendlines I

Note: Russia TDP (P064508) is out of scale (30,000 users; $221.6m; $7.5k/user)

FMIS ICT Cost ($m) vs/ Users: Trendlines II

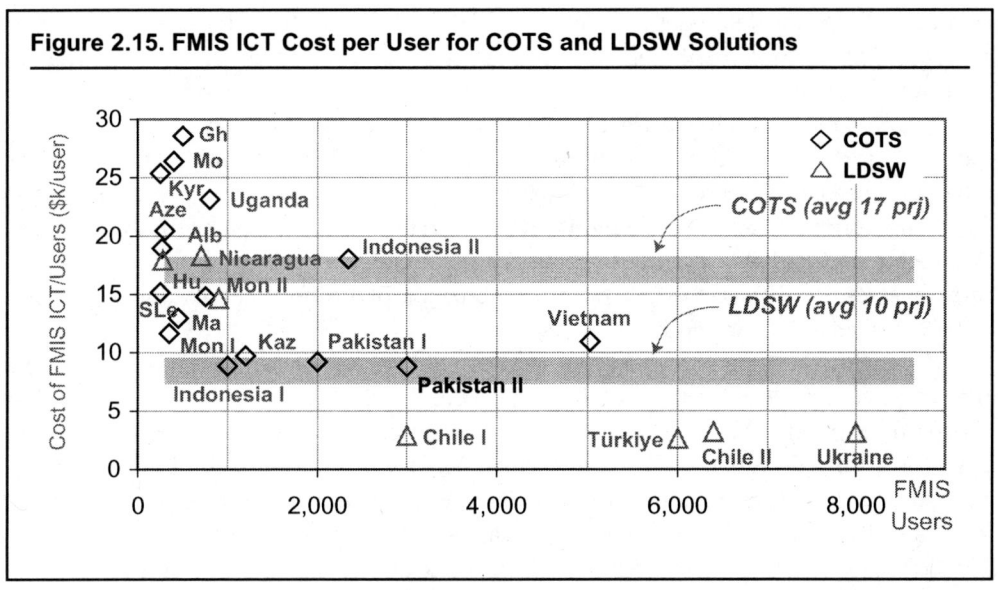

Figure 2.15. FMIS ICT Cost per User for COTS and LDSW Solutions

The cost of FMIS ICT solutions per user tends to go down as the number of users increases. Average FMIS ICT cost/user in 17 COTS-based solutions is around $15.9k per user, whereas this drops to around $9k/user for LDSW-based solutions (Figure 2.15). It should be noted that the average cost of LDSW solutions is much lower (around $3k/ user) in large projects (Chile, Ukraine, Turkey), and relatively higher (above $15k/user) in smaller projects (Nicaragua, Guatemala, Hungary). In small-scale projects where the FMIS users are less than 250 in total, total cost of FMIS ICT solutions based on COTS and LDSW are comparable.

Obviously, the selection of proper FMIS application software solution should be based on a detailed system design and realistic cost/benefit analysis, considering the total cost of ownership. The figures below may provide useful feedback for the verification of such detailed calculations, as well as the reduction of risks for corruption or extreme variations in FMIS ICT cost per user. Nevertheless, given the small sample size and lack of a full picture of LDSW costs, it is important to interpret these figures with caution.

Information and Communication Technology Solutions

The type of ICT solution selected for FMIS projects plays a considerable role in project implementation. Until the early 2000s, most countries developed their FMIS ICT solutions as distributed database applications based on a client-server model, with application software, database, and servers installed in every office. FMIS applications run locally (offline) and the consolidation of data is achieved by replicating all databases at a central location on a daily basis through a network. This approach was abandoned after 2000, with the advent of centralized Web-based solutions.

Starting in the early 2000s, FMIS projects were designed as centralized database applications based on Web-based solutions in parallel to the advances in telecommunications infrastructure and the expansion of broadband networks. In Web-based systems, application software, database, and servers are located centrally, and online access is provided to all users through a countrywide network. A backup center is established to replicate all central databases automatically. Web-based solutions reduce the duration and cost of FMIS implementation, providing effective centralized systems supporting decentralized operations.

The data presented in Figure 2.16 reflects a historical shift from client server to web-based platforms in FMIS ICT solutions. Among the 49 operational projects, 32 systems (65%) are based on client server model, while 17 systems (35%) were built on a web-based platform. Compared across the regions, ECA opted for web-based platforms, while LCR, AFR, SAR, and EAP went with the client-server model. Among active projects, the pattern reverses—28 projects (87.5%) use a Web-based platform, whereas only 4 projects (12.5%) use client-server model.

Regarding the type of application software (ASW) developed for FMIS needs, two main types of solutions exist. Until the early 2000s, FMIS capabilities were implemented mostly through LDSW, mainly because of the technical limitations of commercial packages (originally designed for private sector needs) and also the lack of adequate ICT infrastructure in many regions. Since the introduction of Web-based applications after 2000, a shift toward customized COTS packages (tailored to public sector needs) began. Nevertheless, no single package can provide all the FMIS functionality needed for country-specific needs. Hence, most of the new FMIS solutions designed after 2005 integrate

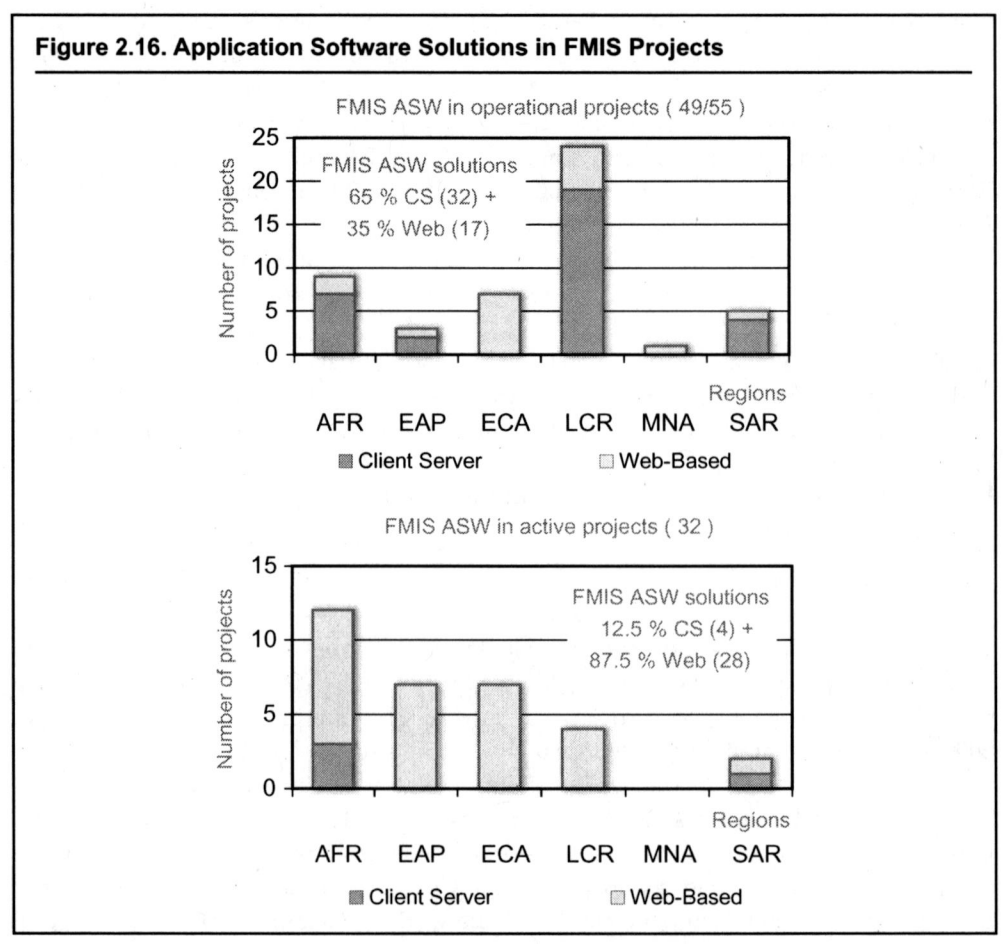

Figure 2.16. Application Software Solutions in FMIS Projects

FMIS ASW in operational projects (49/55)

FMIS ASW solutions
65 % CS (32) +
35 % Web (17)

Number of projects

AFR   EAP   ECA   LCR   MNA   SAR

Regions

■ Client Server   □ Web-Based

FMIS ASW in active projects (32)

FMIS ASW solutions
12.5 % CS (4) +
87.5 % Web (28)

Number of projects

AFR   EAP   ECA   LCR   MNA   SAR

Regions

■ Client Server   □ Web-Based

Table 2.3: Regional Distribution of the Type of T/F ASW Solutions

T/F Application Software (Operational)					T/F Application Software (Active)				
Region	# Prj	COTS	LDSW		Region	# Prj	COTS	LDSW	? *
AFR	9	9	–		AFR	12	10	–	2
EAP	3	2	1		EAP	7	6	–	1
ECA	7	4	3		ECA	7	4	–	3
LCR	24	1	23		LCR	4	1	3	–
MNA	1	–	1		MNA	–	–	–	–
SAR	5	5	–		SAR	2	2	–	–
Totals	**49**	**21**	**28**		**Totals**	**32**	*23*	*3*	*6*

(*) ASW not designed/procured yet

customized COTS packages with specific LDSW modules (including open-source software) to cover a broader spectrum of PFM functions (Table 2.3).

Among 49 operational FMIS projects, LDSW (28) was used slightly more often than COTS (21). Analyzed by region, LCR selected LDSW, while AFR and SAR mostly selected COTS solutions. The EAP and ECA regions are split between the two types. As most of the LDSW solutions implemented in LCR were built on commercial relational databases, the distinction is not entirely neat.

There has been a shift from LDSW to customized COTS packages among 32 active projects. The regions driving the selection of COTS are AFR, EAP, and ECA with 10, 6, and 4 FMIS solutions, respectively. Therefore, among 81 completed and active projects, COTS (44) is used more than LDSW (31). Part of the reason for this shift from LDSW to COTS in active projects may be due to decreasing costs and improved capabilities (MTBF, PIM, payroll, procurement, and debt management) of commercial software packages; the industry faced a steep learning curve for adopting the software for public sector use at the onset of such projects. Over time, the firms have improved the usability of their software packages significantly. Nevertheless, many capable countries have the skills to rely on LDSW and have continued to do so.

Procurement Packages and Contracts Signed

The total number of procurement packages in FMIS projects plays an important role in the timely completion of activities, as it usually takes around 12–18 months to complete large CB procedures for ICT solutions. Based on the data available from the operations portal[7] on 52 completed FMIS projects, the average number of procurement packages was 46 (Figure 2.17). Only 14 out of 52 projects were implemented with less than 20 procurement packages in total, and there was no or minor (less than 9 months) extension in 70% of these projects. Longer extension periods were observed (more than 18 months) in completed FMIS projects with more than 20 procurement packages. The regional patterns that emerge from the number of procurement packages in completed projects are quite different. The LCR region stands out with the largest number of procurement packages and contracts signed in completed FMIS projects (14 out of 22, or 64%, of the LCR projects include more than 40 packages). Other regions have less than 40 procurement packages in general.

The total number of contracts signed in completed FMIS projects was different than the number of packages (Figure 2.18) due to rebidding, cancellation of bids, or other

Figure 2.17. The Number of Procurement Packages Processed in Completed Projects

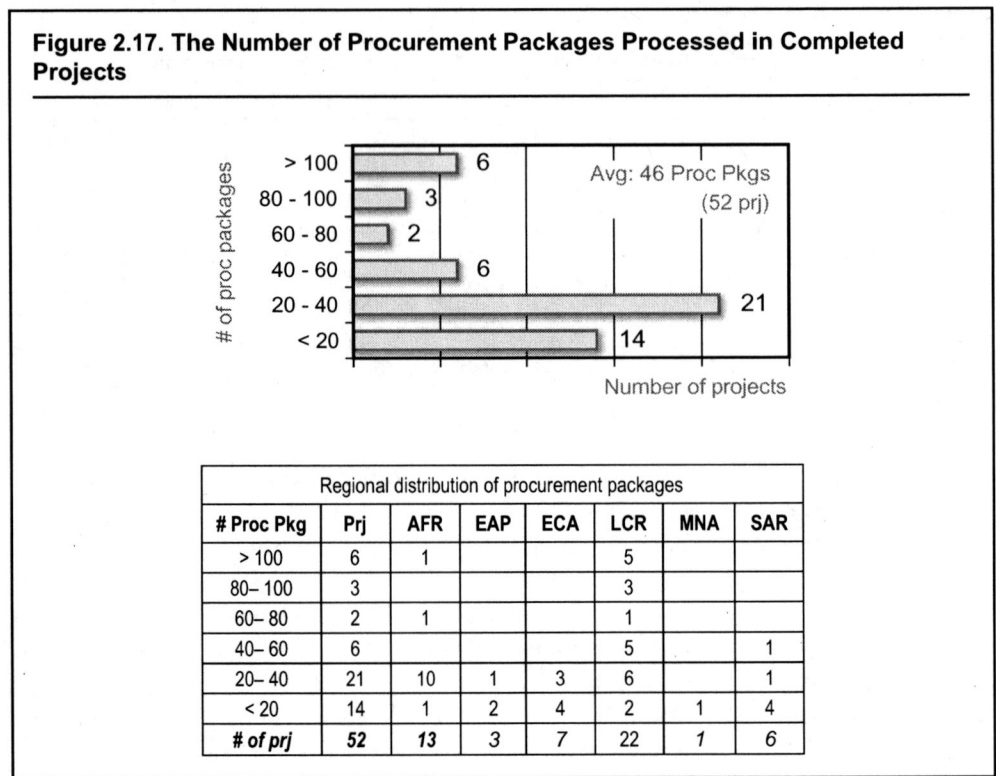

Regional distribution of procurement packages							
# Proc Pkg	Prj	AFR	EAP	ECA	LCR	MNA	SAR
> 100	6	1			5		
80– 100	3				3		
60– 80	2	1			1		
40– 60	6				5		1
20– 40	21	10	1	3	6		1
< 20	14	1	2	4	2	1	4
# of prj	52	13	3	7	22	1	6

Figure 2.18. The Number of Contracts Signed in Completed Projects

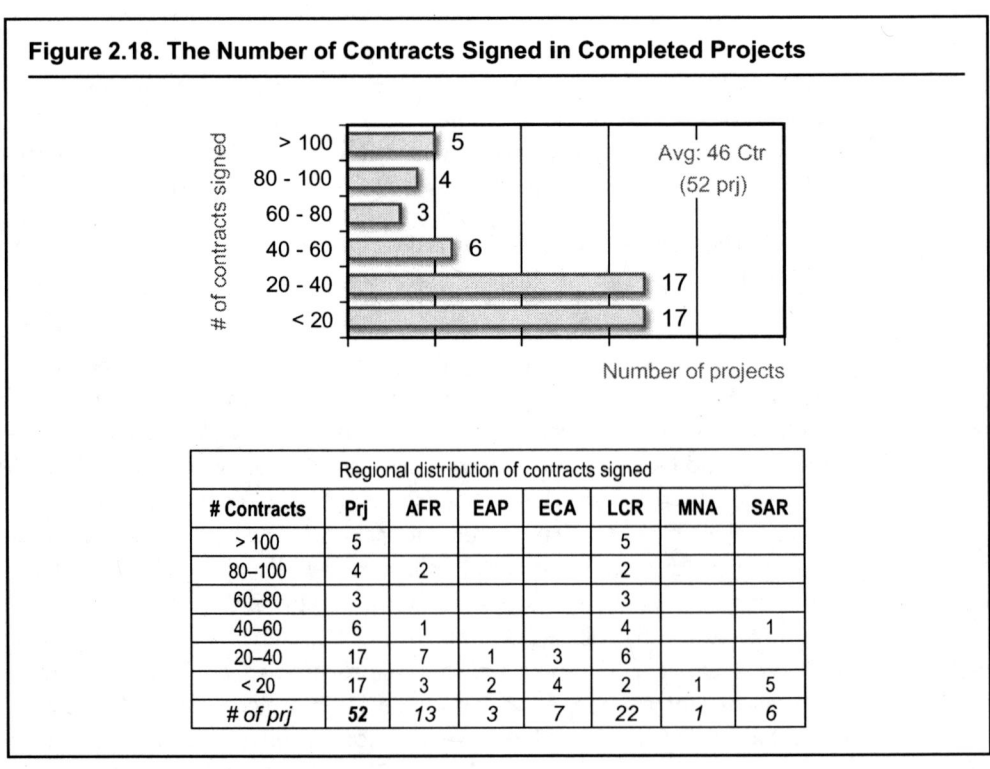

Regional distribution of contracts signed							
# Contracts	Prj	AFR	EAP	ECA	LCR	MNA	SAR
> 100	5				5		
80–100	4	2			2		
60–80	3				3		
40–60	6	1			4		1
20–40	17	7	1	3	6		
< 20	17	3	2	4	2	1	5
# of prj	52	13	3	7	22	1	6

activities that do not generally require a contract signature (e.g., study tours, training). Basic information about most of the major contracts related to the development of FMIS ICT solutions or advisory support activities are published on the web (operations portal). However, amendments to these contracts and related price changes are not listed. Hence, available information about the total number of contracts and final cost figures need to be validated for more detailed analysis, when necessary.

Implementation Resources

Based on the information available in the ICRs, the staff time (in weeks) and the World Bank budget (BB) allocated for the preparation and implementation of FMIS solutions were analyzed to see regional variations and their impact on the duration and successful completion of projects. The distribution of staff weeks[8] for 54 completed projects (one ICR is in progress) is shown in Figure 2.19. On average, 188 staff weeks have been spent during the design and implementation of FMIS solutions. 33 out of 54 projects (61%) were completed with less than 200 staff weeks of input from the task teams.

The regional distributions of the task team inputs indicate that the amount of time spent on FMIS projects was much less in the EAP, ECA, and SAR regions (12 of 15, or 80%, of projects were completed with less than 200 staff weeks) and this didn't have a negative impact on the performance of the projects in general. In the AFR region, more than 200 staff weeks of task team input was required in 69% of the projects. However, the outcomes of these interventions are mixed. The LCR has a similar pattern, with 36% of the projects having more than 200 staff weeks of task team input, but the performance of 25 completed projects seems to be better comparatively.

Figure 2.19. Distribution of Staff Weeks Devoted to Completed Projects

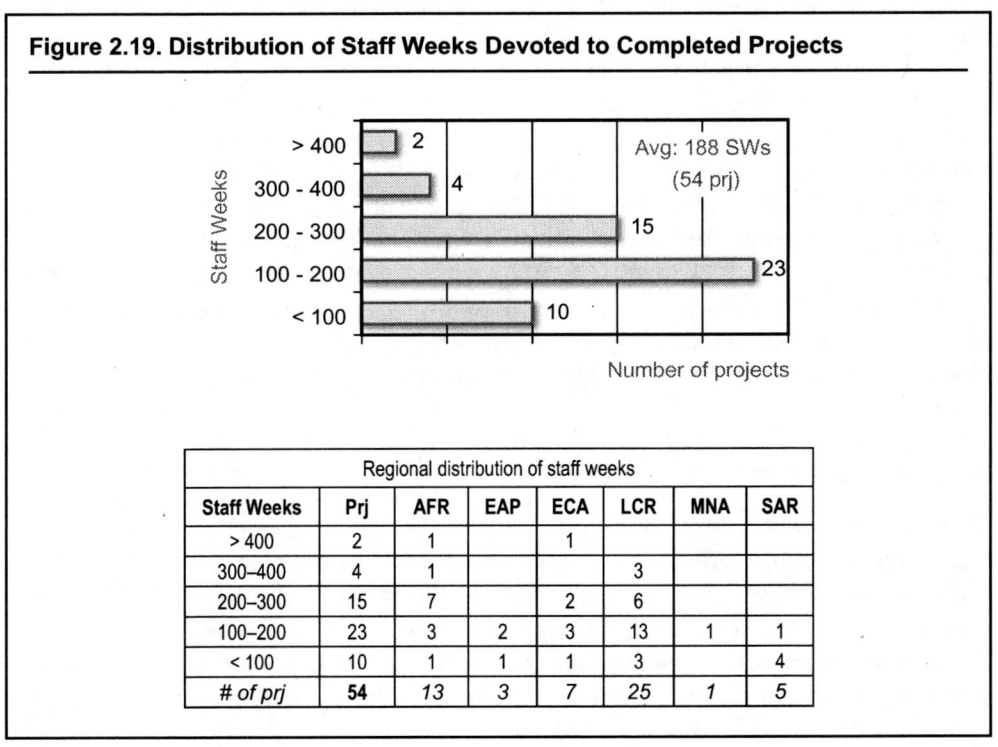

Regional distribution of staff weeks						
Staff Weeks	Prj	AFR	EAP	ECA	LCR	MNA	SAR
> 400	2	1		1			
300–400	4	1			3		
200–300	15	7		2	6		
100–200	23	3	2	3	13	1	1
< 100	10	1	1	1	3		4
# of prj	54	13	3	7	25	1	5

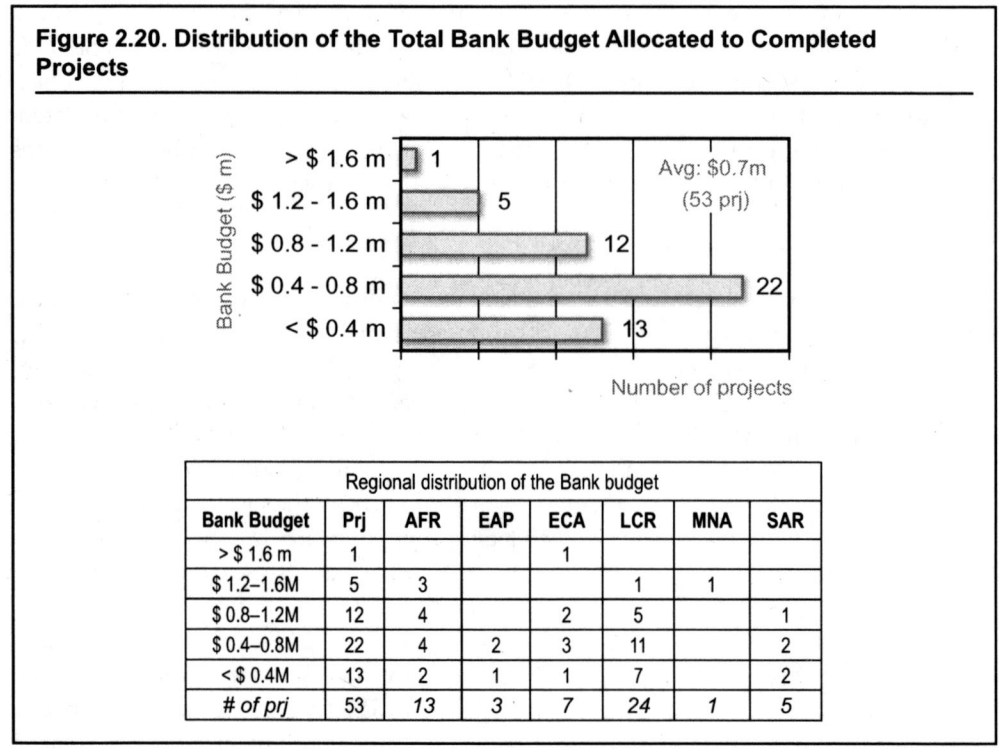

Figure 2.20. Distribution of the Total Bank Budget Allocated to Completed Projects

Bank Budget	Prj	Regional distribution of the Bank budget					
		AFR	EAP	ECA	LCR	MNA	SAR
> $ 1.6 m	1			1			
$ 1.2–1.6M	5	3			1	1	
$ 0.8–1.2M	12	4		2	5		1
$ 0.4–0.8M	22	4	2	3	11		2
< $ 0.4M	13	2	1	1	7		2
# of prj	53	13	3	7	24	1	5

The BB allocated for the preparation and implementation of FMIS projects varies considerably, and the average cost is around US $708,000 for completed projects (Figure 2.20).

Based on the information available in the ICRs of 53 completed FMIS projects, 66% of the projects (35 of 53) were completed with less than $800k BB, and 50% of these projects had no or minor (less than 9 months) extensions. The regional patterns emerging from available data indicate that 54% of the projects (7 of 13) in the AFR region had more than $800k BB. The total BB allocated to FMIS projects is usually below $800k in all other regions.

Average annual BB for the preparation and implementation of 53 completed FMIS projects is around US $92k (Figure 2.21). Around 60% of the completed projects (32 of 53) have been completed with less than $100k BB per year. The regional distributions indicate that the AFR region had more projects (54%) completed with an annual BB of more than $100k. Annual BB allocated for the completed FMIS projects in other regions was less than $100k in general.

Disbursement Rates

Comprehensive FMIS projects (Type 1) include substantial amounts of ICT investment, and the design, procurement, and implementation of these solutions take time. Moreover, these solutions need to be aligned with other PFM reform activities and a considerable amount of prior advisory support activities is required to improve selected business processes, the legal and operational framework and other parameters, which are prerequisites for FMIS implementation. Therefore, FMIS projects are slow disbursing operations with a typical disbursement curve as shown below (Figure 2.22):

Figure 2.21. The Bank Budget/Year Allocated to Completed Projects

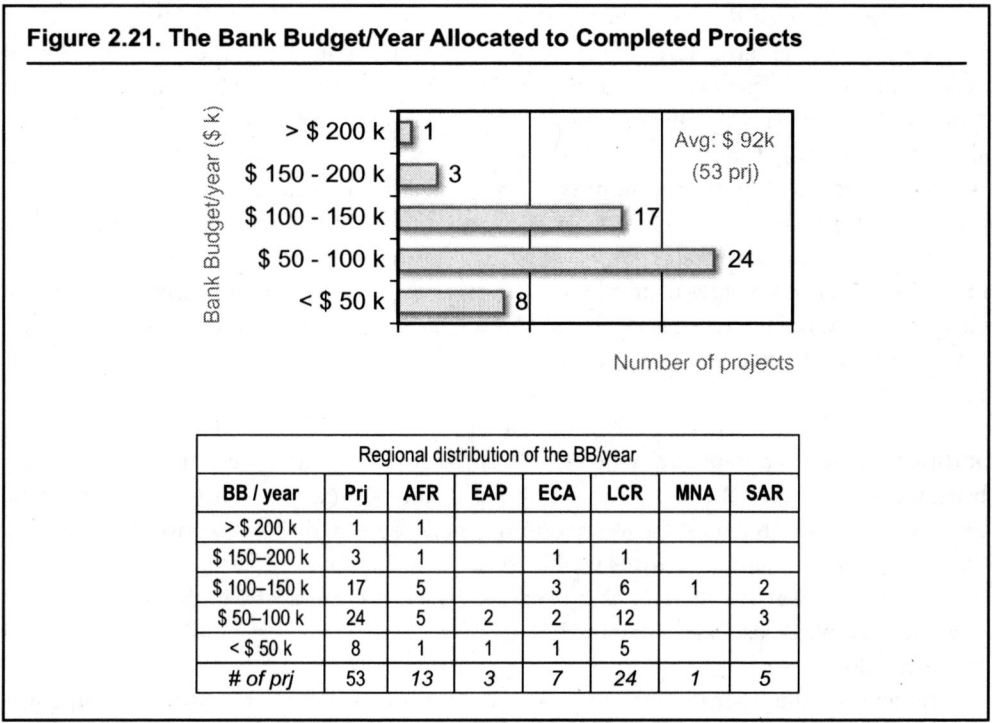

BB / year	Prj	AFR	EAP	ECA	LCR	MNA	SAR
> $ 200 k	1	1					
$ 150–200 k	3	1		1	1		
$ 100–150 k	17	5		3	6	1	2
$ 50–100 k	24	5	2	2	12		3
< $ 50 k	8	1	1	1	5		
# of prj	53	13	3	7	24	1	5

Regional distribution of the BB/year

Figure 2.22. Typical Disbursement Profile of FMIS Projects

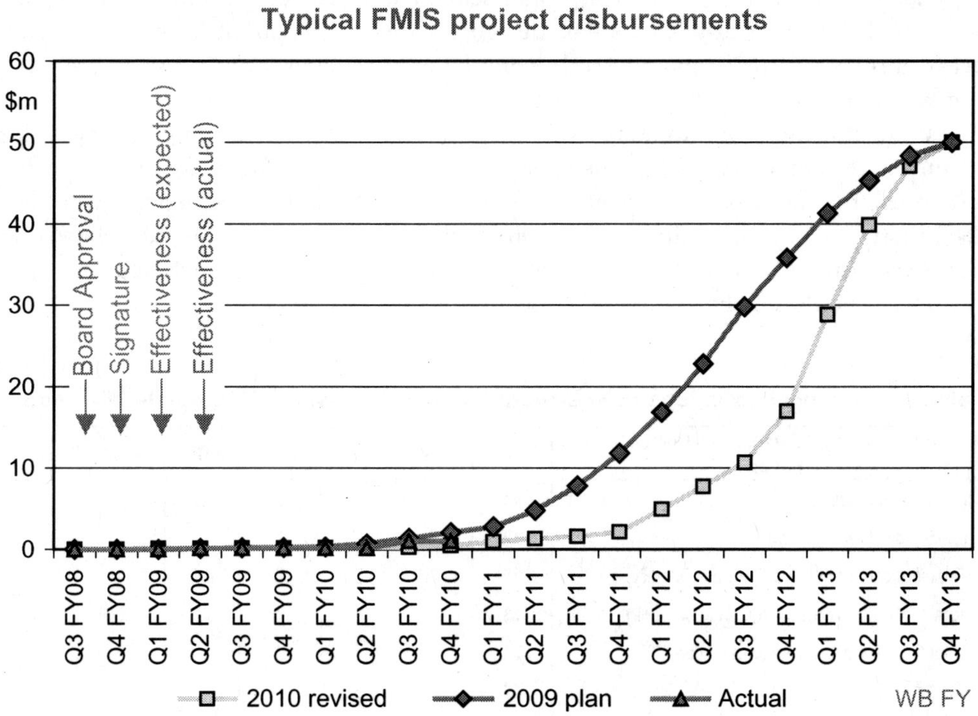

Typical FMIS project disbursements

Legend: 2010 revised, 2009 plan, Actual   WB FY

The start date of the "original" disbursement estimate is the Board approval date. However, disbursements normally start after the project effectiveness date. As the initial version of the disbursement schedule is finalized during negotiations and taken as the "original" estimate for the disbursement graphs used in the operations portal, task teams should consider the time needed for signature of the agreement and effectiveness, which is expected to occur within 3 months after the signature, to avoid unrealistic expectations. It is not possible to accurately predict any potential delay in effectiveness period (mainly due to the ratification process) and the initial disbursement estimates need to be revised at critical stages of implementation (effectiveness, restructuring, extension of closing date) to reflect necessary changes. Hence, all disbursement curves usually have at least one "revised" version, and the "actual" values are automatically updated to monitor progress.

The disbursement curves of 55 completed projects are presented in Appendix G, with additional notes to demonstrate the effect of project restructuring and extensions on disbursements (see Table 2.4 for the regional distributions). There seems to be a systematic and persistent discrepancy between original and revised disbursement projections in these projects. The same pattern is visible in some of the active projects as well. This may be due to optimistic disbursement projections based on unrealistic implementation and procurement plans, as well as relatively large margins of error (or contingency) in initial cost estimates.

In general, the restructuring of projects (22 out of 55) contributed to the improvement of disbursement rates and implementation performance. In 16 of the 22 restructured projects (73%), changes in project scope and activities resulted in rapid improvements in disbursement rates. The impact of restructuring is less visible in the remaining 6 projects (27%), as the changes in project scope and activities were made rather late, near the closing date, or were not well designed. Similarly, 44 out of 55 completed projects were extended (80%) mainly for the completion of remaining project activities, without substantial increases in project budget.

While it is important to monitor the disbursement rates (which indicate the funds disbursed over time to the designated bank accounts of the beneficiary for project related expenses), the status of actual payments made by the Bank or the beneficiary (to track the duration of payments after submission of invoices submitted against completed and approved activities) as well as the total amount of commitments (included in signed contracts) should also be monitored closely.

Table 2.4. Regional Variations in Restructuring and Extension of Completed Projects

Restructuring & Extension of Completed Projects	Prj	AFR	EAP	ECA	LCR	MNA	SAR
FMIS project extensions	44	11	2	6	20	2	3
FMIS project restructuring	22	7	1	2	10	1	1
Total # of comprehensive FMIS projects (Type 1)	32	6	3	7	14	1	1
Total # of countrywide implementation (C+L)	23	0	2	7	11	0	3
Total # of central level implementation (C)	26	9	1	0	13	1	2
Total # of operational FMIS	49	9	3	7	24	1	5
# of projects	55	13	3	7	25	2	5

Table 2.5. Regional Variation of FMIS Implementation Approach

Treasury/FMIS project design and implementation: Regional approach								
Region	# Cnty	# Prj	T/F	Scope	ASW	T/F Core	T/F #PP	ICT in TT
LAC	13	29	T >> F	C >> C+L	LDSW	Mixed	> 3	TT+Cons
ECA	12	14	T >> F	C+L	COTS+LDSW	Yes	< = 3	TT
AFR	14	25	F	C	COTS	No	> 3	Cons
MNA	2	2	F	C	COTS	No	> 3	Cons
EAP	7	10	T	C+L	COTS	Mixed	< = 3	TT+Cons
SAR	3	7	T	C+L	COTS	Yes	< = 3	Cons
Totals	51	87	< Completed + Active projects					

Regional Variation in Design and Implementation

Table 2.5 summarizes the design and implementation approaches taken by different regions. The table provides information by regions on the number of countries (# Cnty), number of projects (# Prj), the focus on Treasury versus FMIS (T/F), the scope of the system in terms of central (C) versus central and local (C+L), the ASW solution selected, whether the focus on FMIS was a core component of the project or a relatively small part (T/F core), the number of T/F related procurement packages for ICT solutions (T/F #PP), and finally the presence of an ICT expert within the World Bank task team (TT) or a consultant (Cons).

With the largest number of completed/active projects (29), LCR stands out from the other regions in terms of developing projects focused on Treasury rather than FMIS, a 'central first' approach, and the use of LDSW. Generally, the overall direction of LCR projects was mixed, with some projects dedicated to getting the T/F systems running, and others focused on MTEF, tax, or customs, for example. The number of procurement packages needed was quite high (well above 3) and technical expertise was available within the World Bank task team and through consultants.

With the second largest number of projects (25), the AFR approach was to develop FMIS at the central level, although the overall focus on these projects was not just on an FMIS. For these systems, commercial off the shelf software was preferred and in general, more than three procurement packages were needed. Expertise in ICT development was provided through consultants and not the World Bank staff. Both AFR and LCR have had about two projects per country to date.

In ECA, 14 projects were implemented with an overall focus on T/F systems, and specifically treasury systems at both the central and local levels. A mix of COTS and LDSW were used for these systems and, in general, one or two procurement packages were needed. An ICT specialist experienced in the design and implementation of PFM reform and capacity building projects was present in the task teams.

The overall approach in EAP has been a mixed, with some projects prioritizing T/F systems and others not. The type of systems selected were COTS treasury systems at the central and local levels. Similar to ECA, the number of procurement packages was low. ICT expertise was available in both the task team and through consultants.

Quite similar in approach to EAP, SAR focused on developing treasury systems at the central and local level with COTS, but in contrast, the overall focus of these projects has been on the actual T/F system. The number of procurement packages has also been relatively low and consultants were used for their ICT expertise.

Finally, MNA, with the fewest projects of any region (2), chose to design projects with a combination of objectives, of which one is a T/F system. The focus of these systems has been on an FMIS at the central level, implemented with COTS. The number of procurement packages needed was typically high, and ICT expertise existed in the task team and through the use of consultants.

The diversity of these regional approaches suggests that the World Bank task teams responded to different regional/country specific needs with a variety of solutions that were very effective in some regions/countries. Several ambitious projects failed mainly in Africa due to a broad focus on PFM reforms before the establishment of basic infrastructure and institutional capacity. However, most of these projects resulted in operational PFM systems, of which many are still in use.

A summary of the FMIS projects implemented through International Development Association (IDA) funding is presented in Appendix F. Out of 55 completed FMIS projects, 23 were in IDA countries (12 completed in Africa). Similarly, 23 out of 32 active projects are being implemented in IDA countries (12 active in Africa). Almost 66% of the IDA funding ($747M out of $1,133M) has been allocated to Africa in completed/active FMIS projects so far. In spite of these investments, Africa has the highest rate of failure in FMIS projects (4 out of 12 completed projects did not result in any operational PFM system), mainly due to initial attempts to implement ambitious FMIS solutions without adequate consideration of the limitations in capacity and infrastructure.

Notes

1. Among the 32 active projects, the preparation period is slightly lower—14 months on average.
2. Sub-national government and municipalities are not included here.
3. Variation in the buying power of the US Dollar was calculated from http://www.usinflationcalculator.com/
4. The Russian Federation (RF) Treasury Development Project (TDP), expected to be completed in mid-2012, is the largest Treasury system implementation funded by the Bank with $576m ICT investment in total ($196m from the WB + $380m from the RF).
5. Jack Diamond and Pokar Khemani, "Introducing Financial Management Information Systems in Developing Countries," IMF Working Paper, October 2005.
6. Data on FMIS ICT costs and number of users were obtained from FMIS Database and project documents.
7. The information available from the operations portal on ongoing procurement activities or signed contracts may be incomplete for some of the projects, or the type of procurement packages may be indicated differently sometimes. Hence, the actual FMIS ICT cost may be higher than indicated amounts in some of the projects, if all ongoing activities or signed contracts are not posted on the portal yet.
8. The staff weeks indicated in the ICRs may be less than the actual time spent on the preparation and supervision of FMIS projects, since these figures may not take into account the contributions from all project team and overtimes.

Project Performance

How Have FMIS Projects Performed According to Various Criteria?

What Are the Key Factors That Contribute to the Success and Failure of Projects?

This section provides a multidimensional perspective on the performance of completed FMIS projects included in the database. Analyzing success and failure is contested ground and often two perspectives on a similar project yield significantly different interpretations. To gain a richer understanding of project performance, this section presents various criteria upon which to analyze success and failure during the design and implementation phases—beyond indicators traditionally included in project documentation.

Using a combination of PADs, ICRs, and Independent Evaluation Group (IEG) ratings, projects are analyzed along a number of dimensions, including whether the FMIS became operational at closure, as well as project sustainability and outcomes. The first part focuses on ICR performance ratings, the second part looks at IEG ratings, and the third section considers additional criteria such as the operational status of the FMIS solutions developed. The remaining sections cover frequently cited factors identified in ICRs leading to the success and failure of individual components or the project as a whole, general patterns across projects, and comparisons in performance with private sector implementation.

ICR Ratings

The ICR is a critical step in the self-evaluation by the Bank and the borrower of project performance. It typically occurs within six months of project closure. The ICR details what was achieved by the project against what was planned (documented in the PAD) and reflects on lessons learned regarding the design, implementation, and results of the projects. Three main stakeholders are involved in the ICR completion. The task teams and consultants complete reporting for all Bank-financed projects. The borrower contributes to the completion report and prepares its own final evaluation report. The IEG carries an independent ex-post evaluation of all ICRs. Table 3.1 provides the definitions of the ratings included in the ICRs.[1]

The ICR ratings for project implementation performance, project outcomes, sustainability, and other aspects were reviewed in this study. All ratings, with the exception of "sustainability" and "development impact," range from highly satisfactory (HS) to highly unsatisfactory (HU) on a six-point scale (HS, S, MS, MU, U, HU).[2] Fifty-four out of 55 completed projects are included in this analysis.[3] The key pattern which emerges is that the majority of projects fall in the "satisfactory" (S) range along most dimensions

Table 3.1. Definitions of ICR Ratings

ICR Ratings	Definitions
Project Development Objective	The extent to which the operation achieved its development objectives.
Implementation Performance (in ISR)	The extent of overall implementation progress, project management, financial management, procurement, monitoring, evaluation, and counterpart funding.
Sustainability	The probability of its maintaining the achievements generated or expected to be generated in relation to its objective over the economic life of the project.
Institutional Development Impact	The extent to which a project has improved an agency's or a country's ability to make effective use of its human and financial resources.
Outcome	The extent to which the operation's major relevant objectives were achieved, or are expected to be achieved, efficiently.
Risk to Development Outcome	The risk, at the time of evaluation, that development outcomes or expected outcomes will not be maintained (or realized).
Bank Performance	The extent to which services provided by the Bank ensured quality at entry of the operation and supported effective implementation through appropriate supervision (including ensuring adequate transition arrangements for regular operation of supported activities after loan/credit closing) toward the achievement of Project Development Objectives (PDOs).
Borrower Performance	The extent to which the borrower (including the government and implementing agency) ensured quality of preparation and implementation and complied with covenants and agreements toward the achievement of PDOs.

of performance in the ICR. This may reflect some self-evaluation bias, and this pattern changes slightly with the IEG review of ICR ratings.

The performance of the FMIS ICT component was positively rated (satisfactory or above) for the majority of projects (71%, or 39 of 55 projects) in the final ISRs and in the ICRs.

Six projects were rated as HS and 33 projects were rated S. On the other hand, 16 projects were received ratings below satisfactory. The ICR rating for the achievement of the Project Development Objective (PDO) was also S or above for the majority of projects (76%, or 42 of 55) in ISRs/ICRs. The majority of these projects (40) were rated as S, while only two projects were rated as HS. Thirteen projects were rated below S. Implementation Performance was S and above for 76% (42 of 55) of projects, but only one of these projects was rated as HS in the ISRs/ICRs.

The project outcome rating, which measures the extent to which the project's objectives were achieved, or is expected to be achieved, efficiently, was S for 36 of 54 projects, or 67 %. Eighteen projects were rated below S in their outcome rating. See Figure 3.1 for a regional breakdown of the project outcome ratings. Both AFR and EAP received U ratings for a few projects. LCR had the largest number of projects (17) with S ratings.

The regional distribution of the Development Impact rating—defined as the extent to which a project improved an agency's or country's ability to make effective use of its human and financial resources—is presented in Figure 3.2 on a four-point scale (High (H), Significant (S), Moderate (M), and Negligible (N)). Ten projects were rated as H (16.7%), 20 projects as S (37.5%), and 24 were rated as M (45.8%). The AFR and LCR regions account for the majority of M ratings.

To assess sustainability, projects are rated on a four-point scale (Highly Likely (HL), Likely (L), Unlikely (UN), and Highly Unlikely (HUN)). The majority of the projects fell in the Likely (L) category (42 of 54 or 78 %). Five projects were rated HL, and seven projects received the rating U.

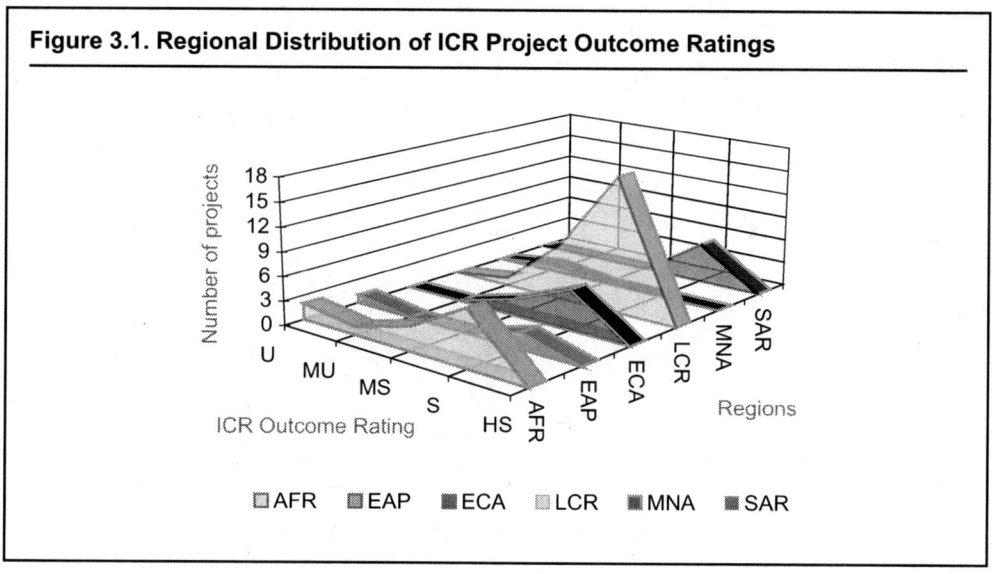

Figure 3.1. Regional Distribution of ICR Project Outcome Ratings

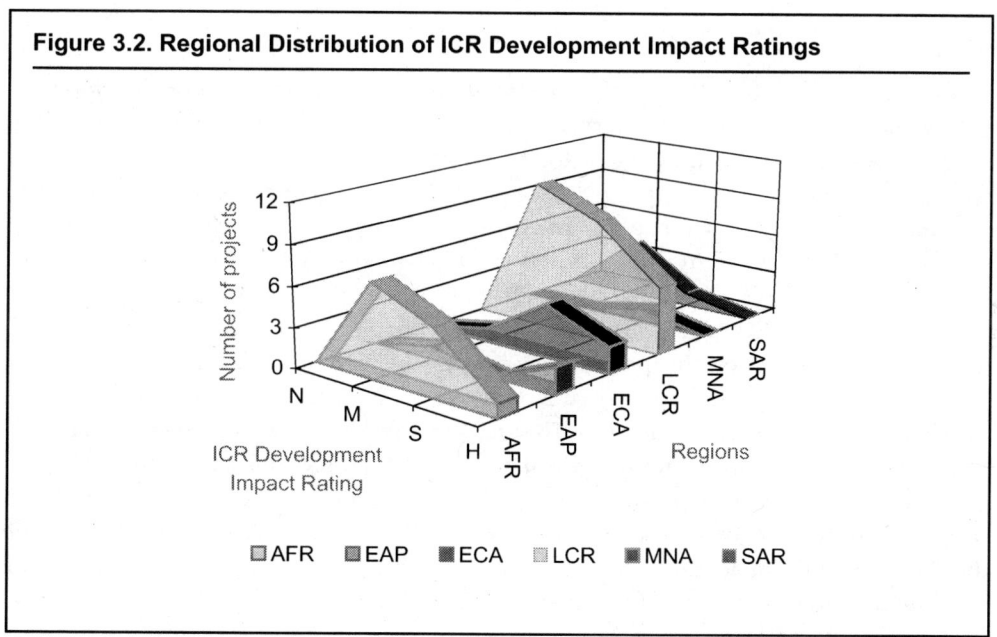

Figure 3.2. Regional Distribution of ICR Development Impact Ratings

Bank and borrower performance were very similar across all projects. In 61% of the projects, the Bank and borrower performance received satisfactory or above ratings. In 39 % of the projects, these ratings were moderately satisfactory or below. Fewer than five projects were rated HS in both Bank and borrower performance.

IEG Ratings

The IEG conducts an ex-post evaluation of ICRs and independently assesses ratings with a similar six-point scale (except "development impact" and "risk to development outcome" ratings) plus an additional scale: Not Rated (N/R). A comparison between

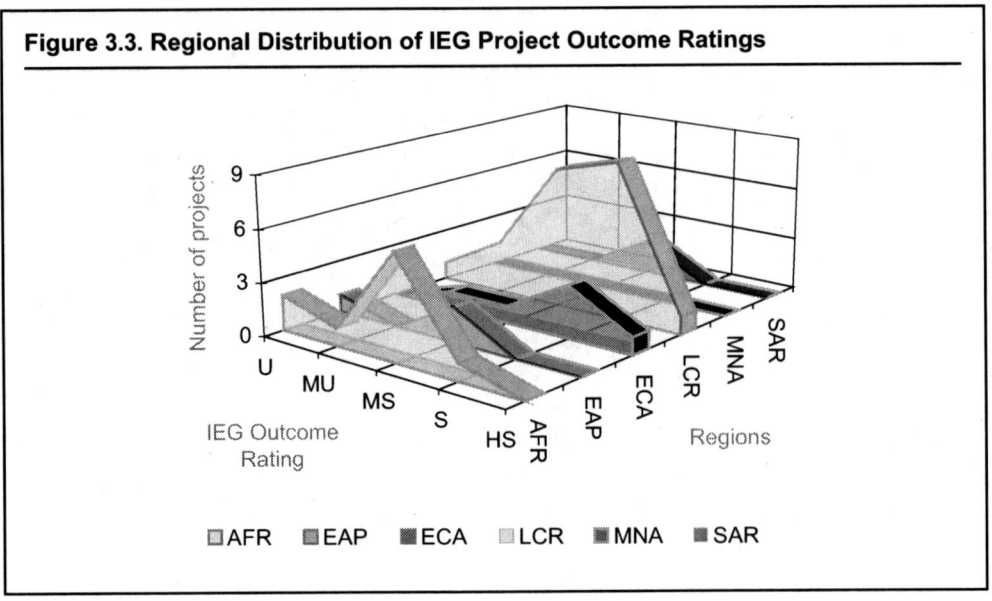

Figure 3.3. Regional Distribution of IEG Project Outcome Ratings

48 available ICR and 43 IEG ratings of project outcomes, sustainability, development impact, bank performance, and borrower performance reveals that just over half of the projects received a downgrading of their ratings after the IEG review. Three projects were upgraded across all ratings on the scale, four had mixed upgrading and downgrading among the ratings, seven saw no change, and 12 completed projects (7 ICRs pending) still need to be evaluated by an IEG. Given that ICRs are self-evaluations, it is logical to see differences when re-evaluated by an IEG.

An analysis of IEG ratings of project outcome, development impact, quality at entry, and sustainability reflects this pattern. The project outcome rating, as rated by IEG, gave 15 projects out of 43 (35%) a rating of S or above, which is significantly lower than the 76 % that received S or HS in the ICRs. The greatest shift by IEG was in moving 10 projects from S to MS. See Figure 3.3 for a regional distribution of IEG project outcome ratings.

The project sustainability rating by IEG is done on a six-point scale.[4] Of completed projects, 56% (24 of 43) were given a rating of L or HL—down from 78 % in the ICRs. For the Development Impact rating, the IEG uses the same four-point scal[5]. Eighteen out of 43 were rated as S (42 %), with two rated as H. Ten were rated as M and two as N. Eleven projects were Not Rated (Figure 3.4).

Bank and borrower performance were also slightly lower than ICRs ratings. Both received S or above ratings in 60.5% and 53.5% of projects, respectively. Fewer than three projects were rated HS in both Bank and borrower performance.

The IEG also assesses the quality at entry of projects. This measure captures the degree to which the project was designed in line with national strategies (e.g., the Country Assistance Strategy), the clarity of development objectives, and the incorporation of past lessons from similar work, among other criteria. Out of 43 projects, 22 were rated as S (51%), with one project rated HS. However, 2 were rated as MS, 6 were MU, and 12 were rated U.

In order to gain a richer understanding of FMIS project performance, this section considered various dimensions upon which to assess performance. Among ICRs, the

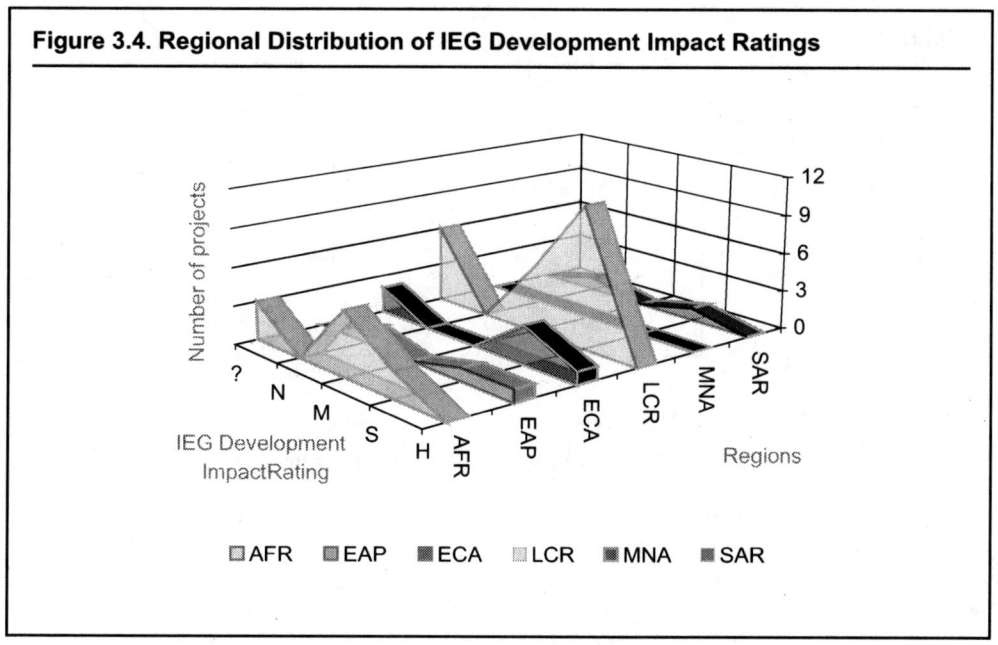

Figure 3.4. Regional Distribution of IEG Development Impact Ratings

majority of projects fall in the S range along most dimensions of performance. This pattern changes slightly with the IEG review. Nearly 64% of the projects reviewed by IEG (29 of 43) received a downgrading of ICR ratings from S to MS. On the other hand, among 55 completed projects, 49 T/F systems (89%) are operational, which suggests that from the perspective of obtaining results and sustainability, many of these projects achieved their technical and operational targets. Future analysis of the performance of these systems could usefully incorporate indicators such as those used in PEFA assessments to benchmark countries on the functionality and performance of the systems.

Operational Status

Another important success criterion tightly linked with project development outcomes is whether the financial management information system is operational or not at the end of the project (Appendix K).

Among 55 completed projects, 49 are currently fully or partially operational (89%). If we further break down the operational systems, 20 were Treasury systems and 29 were FMIS (Figure 3.5). Twenty-seven of these systems are supporting full-scale T/F operations; whereas 22 are pilot T/F systems, mainly supporting several central agencies. In LCR, subsequent projects expanded the scope of T/F systems and functionality over the years. Interestingly, six failed attempts (11%) were all FMIS projects: four in AFR, with one in both MNA and LCR.

Other basic criteria for measuring success include whether the project was delivered on time and on budget. As described in the previous chapter, the extension of FMIS projects is common in completed projects. Out of 55 projects, 44 projects (80%) were extended by 2.2 years on average. Short preparation periods, procurement delays, technical complications, and political instabilities are the main sources of such extensions. In terms of cost overruns, the sample reveals that the majority of projects were executed

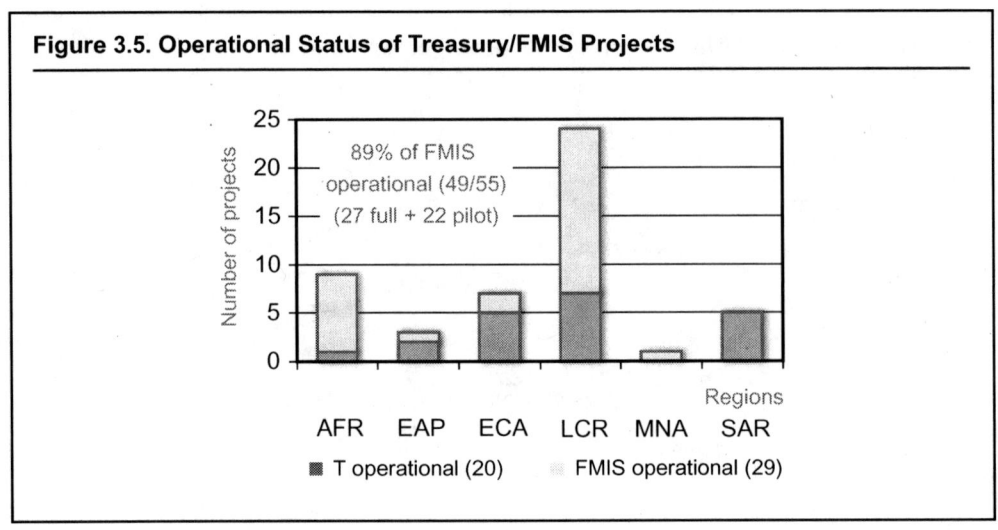

Figure 3.5. Operational Status of Treasury/FMIS Projects

on budget. A comparison of the actual versus the estimated cost of projects shows that the actual cost of 23 projects matched estimated costs with a 5% margin of error. Only 10 projects out of 55 exceeded their estimated costs, while 22 projects were under budget. In summary, around 82% of FMIS projects were completed within budget. The implementation status of all FMIS projects included in the FMIS database is summarized in Appendix L.

Preparation Approaches

The approach followed by the World Bank teams in the preparation of completed and active FMIS projects was also analyzed by checking the degree of attention to key preparation activities (details for each project can be found in the "T/F Eval" worksheet of the FMIS database). An initial assessment of PFM functions and capacity, development of a realistic FMIS design, focus on capacity building, availability of sufficiently detailed implementation plan for all activities, realistic cost estimates, linkages between designed activities and procurement/disbursement plan, use of country systems, and other important aspects were checked from the Project Appraisal Documents and Operations Portal. These aspects were selected in line with the recommendations on the design and implementation of FMIS projects, presented later in this study (see Chapter 5).

As shown in Table 3.2, nearly 60% (33 of 55) of the completed projects started with a proper PFM assessment during the preparation period in which existing capacities and practices were analyzed. However, there are other key aspects that might be desirable to at least begin during the preparation period, which were systematically not started until the project was under implementation. Over 91% of the projects did not design the PFM system or analyze or PFM related bidding documents (particularly for ICBs) during the preparation period. Moreover, country systems for project management, procurement, or financial management were rarely used throughout the lifecycle of the project. In the majority of completed projects, no PFM Reform Strategy or Conceptual Design was developed during preparation (in

Table 3.2. FMIS Project Preparation Approach in 55 Completed Projects

Key Aspects	Description	Approach #1	Freq	Approach #2	Freq	Approach #3	Freq
PFM Assessment	Assessment of existing capacity and practices during preparation	No PFM assessment	22	PEFA assessment was utilized during prep	0	FMIS Questionnaire / other assessment used during prep	33
PFM Strategy	Development of the PFM Reform Strategy during preparation	No PFM Strategy	41	PFM Strategy available	13	PFM Strategy developed + approved	1
Conceptual Design	Conceptual Design (func review, gap analysis, BPR, cap bldg needs, legal/inst changes, action plan)	Not available	47	Conceptual Design available	1	Conceptual Design developed during project preparation	7
Capacity Building	Capacity Building during preparation	No TA/training or capacity bldg effort during prep	18	TA/training for PFM cap bldg during preparation	37		
Unified CoA/BC	Presence of unified CoA aligned with BC	No unified CoA	14	Unified CoA is in use	12	Designed during prj prep/impl, operational with T/F system	29
TSA Established	Presence of TSA	No TSA	14	TSA is operational	14	Designed during project, operational with T/F system	27
Donor Coordination	Donor Coordination mechanism established during preparation	No donor coordination mechanism	29	Donor Coord unit in Implementing Agency	7	Donor Coordination meetings only	19
ICT Assessment	Assessment of existing ICT capacity	Not available	27	ICT capacity evaluated by task teams during preparation	28	ICT capacity reports (CoBIT, ITIL, etc)	0
ICT Strategy	Development of the ICT Modernization Strategy	No ICT Strategy	43	ICT Strategy available	11	Strategy developed+approved during prep	1
System Design	**System Design** (func & tech reqs, ICT architecture, impl plan, sequencing, cost-benefit analysis)	Not available	51	System Design was ready	1	System Design developed during project preparation	3
Detailed Cost Estimate	Preparation of detailed cost estimate linked with Procurement Plan (PP)	Not prepared during preparation	29	Detailed cost estimate (linked with PP) during prep	26		
Detailed Impl Schedule	Preparation of detailed implementation schedule for all component activities	Not prepared during preparation	30	Detailed activity schedule (linked w PP/disb plan) prep	25		
Bidding Documents	Preparation of PFM related bidding documents (ICBs)	Not prepared during preparation	52	ICB docs were ready	0	ICB docs developed during project preparation	3

(Continued)

Table 3.2. FMIS Project Preparation Approach in 55 Completed Projects (*Continued*)

Key Aspects	Description	Approach #1	Freq	Approach #2	Freq	Approach #3	Freq
Technical Coordination	Technical coordination mechanism established during prep	No technical coordination mechanism	4	Technical Coordination group in Implementing Agency	15	Technical coordination meetings only	36
Technical Cap Building	Technical capacity building activities during preparation	No technical capacity bldg activity	4	ICT dept/capacity exist. TA/ training provided.	22	Dedicated ICT team estd and staff trained during prep/impl	29
Prj Mgmt Capacity	Project Impl Unit (PIU) and capacity established during preparation	No PIU/capacity	1	PIU is available	9	Dedicated PIU established and staff trained during prep	45
Cnty Sys for Prj Mgmt	Using country systems for project mgmt	No country system for prj mgmt	53	Existing CS used for prj mgmt	2	CS was improved and used during prep/impl	0
Cnty Sys for Procurement	Using country systems for procurement	No country system for procurement	54	Existing CS used for procurement	1	CS was improved and used during prep/impl	0
Cnty Sys for Fin Mgmt	Using country systems for financial mgmt	No country system for financial mgmt	53	Existing CS was used for financial mgmt	2	CS was improved and used during prep/impl	0
Monitoring & Evaluation	Presence of monitoring and evaluation M&E mechanisms	No M&E mechanism	1	Existing M&E mechanism used	5	M&E mechanism developed during preparation	49

75% and 85% of completed projects, respectively). Finally, 78% of completed projects did not have an ICT modernization strategy in place from the start (43 of 55).

On the other hand, certain aspects were frequently developed during the preparation period and used during the implementation phase. In over 50% of completed projects, a unified CoA aligned with BC was designed or improved during project preparation or implementation and became operational with the T/F system. Technical coordination mechanisms were established throughout the project lifecycle to address implementation challenges. A dedicated ICT team was established and staff trained during the preparation and implementation periods. Most projects also had a PIU with trained staff. Finally, monitoring and evaluation mechanisms were established during preparation.

Similarly, Table 3.3 presents the FMIS project preparation approach observed in the 32 active/ongoing projects. The approach visible in the data from completed projects is quite similar to that of active projects. Two main differences are that in completed projects 53% of the projects had no donor coordination mechanism during preparation, but among active projects the number is significantly reduced, with only 16% of the projects lacking a donor coordination mechanism. This reflects a general consensus that donors need to better coordinate their strategies and interventions to improve the effectiveness and value-added of their assistance. The second difference is that among completed projects 75% had no PFM strategy, while among active projects only 48% had no PFM strategy.

In order to share the lessons learned from FMIS design and implementation, a checklist for task teams involved in FMIS project design and the simplified form of a FMIS questionnaire are presented in Appendix B as reference material.

Success Factors

Based on official evaluations, literature reviews, project documents, and interviews with task managers, a number of factors are commonly thought to be particularly relevant to the successful implementation of an FMIS project—these include political commitment and adequate IT systems, among others. The ICRs of 55 completed projects were reviewed to determine whether any similar factors of success were mentioned—while staying agnostic about whether the project or individual components were ultimately successful (or not). Table 3.4 presents an analysis of the frequency of factors mentioned in the ICRs and the regional distribution.

Among those success factors most frequently mentioned in the ICRs, the top four are:

1. proper attention to capacity building and training plans,
2. close World Bank supervision of the projects,
2. strong leadership and a conducive political environment, and
4. flexibility in the way the project was designed and managed.

With the exception of the ECA and LAC regions, most regions revealed a similar priority to the aforementioned factors. For the LAC region, the top factor was the political environment and committed leadership to the project, with close World Bank supervision second to it. On the other hand, for the ECA region, close World Bank supervision was the most frequently mentioned factor in ICRs.

Much of the literature on FMIS projects (see Appendix A) supports these findings, particularly with regard to the importance of strong leadership and long-term political

Table 3.3. FMIS Project Preparation Approach in 32 Active Projects

Key Aspects	Description	Approach #1	Freq	Approach #2	Freq	Approach #3	Freq
PFM Assessment	Assessment of existing capacity and practices during preparation	No PFM assessment	2	PEFA assessment was utilized during prep	7	FMIS Questionnaire/other assessment used during prep	23
PFM Strategy	Development of the PFM Reform Strategy during preparation	No PFM Strategy	15	PFM Strategy available	14	PFM Strategy developed + approved	3
Conceptual Design	Conceptual Design (func review, gap analysis, BPR, cap bldg needs, legal/inst changes, action plan)	Not available	25	Conceptual Design available	3	Conceptual Design developed during project preparation	4
Capacity Building	Capacity Building during preparation	No TA/training or capacity bldg effort during prep	7	TA/training for PFM cap bldg during preparation	25		
Unified CoA/BC	Presence of unified CoA aligned with BC	No unified CoA	1	Unified CoA is in use	13	Designed during prj prep/impl, operational with T/F system	18
TSA Established	Presence of TSA	No TSA	2	TSA is operational	14	Designed during project, operational with T/F system	16
Donor Coordination	Donor Coordination mechanism established during preparation	No donor coordination mechanism	5	Donor Coord unit in Implementing Agency	10	Donor Coordination meetings only	17
ICT Assessment	Assessment of existing ICT capacity	Not available	14	ICT capacity evaluated by task teams during preparation	18	ICT capacity reports (CoBIT, ITIL, etc)	0
ICT Strategy	Development of the ICT Modernization Strategy	No ICT Strategy	23	ICT Strategy available	1	Strategy developed+approved during prep	8
System Design	System Design (func & tech reqs, ICT architecture, impl plan, sequencing, cost-benefit analysis)	Not available	27	System Design was ready	1	System Design developed during project preparation	4
Detailed Cost Estimate	Preparation of detailed cost estimate linked with Procurement Plan (PP)	Not prepared during preparation	20	Detailed cost estimate (linked with PP) during prep	12		
Detailed Impl Schedule	Preparation of detailed implementation schedule for all component activities	Not prepared during preparation	22	Detailed activity schedule (linked w PP/disb plan) prep	10		
Bidding Documents	Preparation of PFM related bidding documents (ICBs)	Not prepared during preparation	29	ICB docs were ready	0	ICB docs developed during project preparation	3

(Continued)

Table 3.3. FMIS Project Preparation Approach in 32 Active Projects (*Continued*)

Category	Indicator	Option	n	Option	n	Option	n
Technical Coordination	Technical coordination mechanism established during prep	No technical coordination mechanism	1	Technical Coordination group in Implementing Agency	10	Technical coordination meetings only	21
Technical Cap Building	Technical capacity building activities during preparation	No technical capacity bldg activity	0	ICT dept/capacity exist. TA/training provided.	17	Dedicated ICT team estd and staff trained during prep/impl	15
Prj Mgmt Capacity	Project Impl Unit (PIU) and capacity established during preparation	No PIU/capacity	0	PIU is available	5	Dedicated PIU established and staff trained during prep	27
Cnty Sys for Prj Mgmt	Using country systems for project mgmt	No country system for prj mgmt	29	Existing CS used for prj mgmt	3	CS was improved and used during prep/impl	0
Cnty Sys for Procurement	Using country systems for procurement	No country system for procurement	31	Existing CS used for procurement	1	CS was improved and used during prep/impl	0
Cnty Sys for Fin Mgmt	Using country systems for financial mgmt	No country system for financial mgmt	30	Existing CS was used for financial mgmt	2	CS was improved and used during prep/impl	0
Monitoring & Evaluation	Presence of M&E mechanisms	No M&E mechanism	1	Existing M&E mechanism used	3	M&E mechanism developed during preparation	28

Table 3.4. Success Factors Observed in Completed FMIS Projects

Success Factors in Completed Projects	Prj	AFR	EAP	ECA	LCR	MNA	SAR
Focus on capacity building and training	33	6	3	5	15	1	3
Close Bank supervision	32	4	3	7	16		2
Suitable political environment & committed leadership	31	4	2	5	18		2
Flexible project management	28	4	2	3	15		4
Pre-existing enabling environment (ICT, HR, accounting)	15	1	2	3	8		1
Adequate preparation and clarity of design	13	4			8		1
Good project management and coordination	12	1	2	3	4		2
External environment (uncontrollable)	6			2	3		1
# of projects	**55**	**13**	**3**	**7**	**25**	**2**	**5**

commitment in reforming entrenched budget and treasury processes and systems. From the project design stage (often even at the project development stage) to the project implementation and maintenance stages, a lack of interest and commitment from top leadership is often cited as one of the most critical impediments for project success and long-term sustainability.

Failure Factors

On the flip side, the same 55 ICRs were reviewed to determine what factors contributed to failures, either of the system as a whole or of individual components. Mirroring those factors that most contributed to the success of the project, poor human resource capacity was mentioned in 33 of 55 projects (60%). Institutional and organization resistance was the second most common factor mentioned. The presence of strong leadership from senior management would have enabled projects to overcome some of this resistance. Finally, the complexity of project design and weak project preparation and planning were both mentioned in 22 of 55 projects (40%). In AFR, the primary factor leading to failure was poor human resources (HR), whereas in LCR both institutional resistance and complex project design contributed to failures. The frequency of failure factors and regional distribution observed in completed projects is presented in Table 3.5.

Patterns

It is difficult to develop meaningful correlations to clarify the relationship between the characteristics of FMIS solutions and expected results or performance of projects, due to a relatively limited set of rich but disparate data (from 55 completed and 32 active projects). However, general patterns of performance in successful and failed projects can be identified. Such patterns strengthen the arguments presented in the next section and also reinforce the lessons learned and suggested design and implementation approaches. The patterns presented in this section are a way of answering the question: what solution fits which problem in what situation. Pitfalls are also highlighted by answering: what are common deficiencies in design?

The pitfalls in the design of FMIS projects are highlighted in Figure 3.6. Most of the failed attempts were relatively ambitious FMIS projects in the Africa region (4 of 6 projects). The preparation period of these projects was short (less than 16 months in most cases), and

Table 3.5. Failure Factors Observed in Completed FMIS Projects

Failure Factors in Completed Projects	Prj	AFR	EAP	ECA	LCR	MNA	SAR
Inadequate capacity/training of project teams	30	10	2	5	8	1	4
Institutional/organizational resistance	23	4		5	12	1	1
Weak project preparation and planning	22	9	1	2	7	1	2
Complex project design/large # of procurement pkgs	22	9	1		12		
Organizational structure poorly suited for integration	20	7	2	2	5		4
Inadequate ICT infrastructure	18	7	1	1	4	1	4
Lack of leadership/commitment	17	4	2	2	6	1	2
Lack of proper skills in project team	17	8	2		6	1	
Inappropriate technology	13	4		2	6	1	
Ineffective project coordination	9	5		2	2		
External environment (political unrest, disasters)	8	2			2		4
Unclear delineation of authority to implement	6	3			1	1	1
# of projects	*55*	*13*	*3*	*7*	*25*	*2*	*5*

there was an inadequate focus on key project design steps, such as no concept document based on a PFM strategy, a lack of details on components and activities, no implementation plan with sequencing of activities, and an unrealistic procurement plan and disbursement estimates. The project activities related to the design and implementation of FMIS solutions were initiated after project effectiveness. Moreover, close to the anticipated completion date teams came to realization that either the allocated budget or time was not enough to achieve the desired objectives. As a result, it was only possible to complete the design of

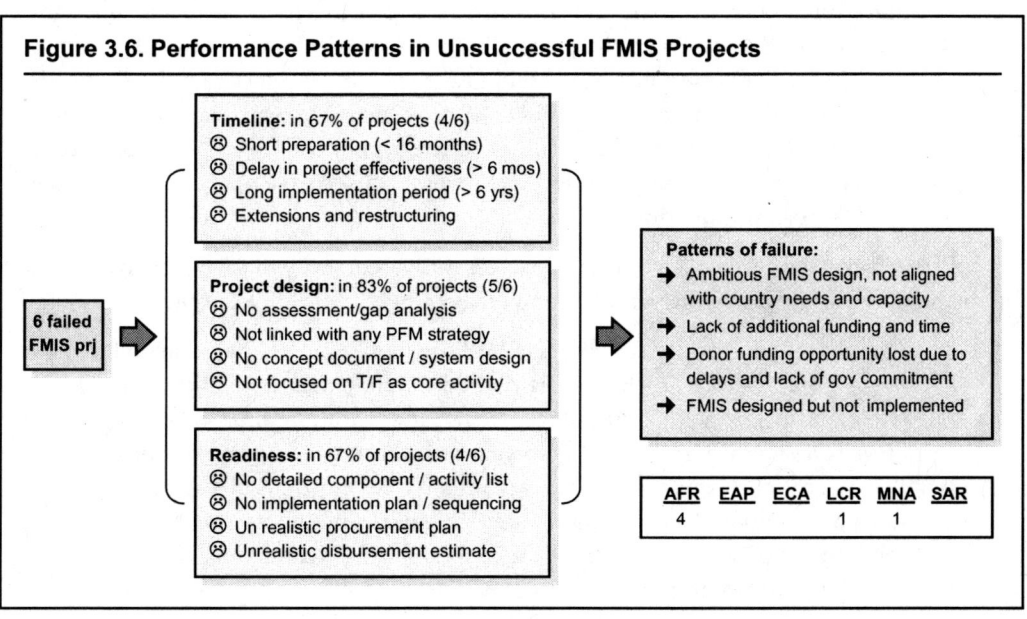

Figure 3.6. Performance Patterns in Unsuccessful FMIS Projects

FMIS solutions during project implementation (despite extensions and restructuring) and there was no funding or time left to actually implement any information system solution. The lack of government commitment was another key factor in poor project performance.

Based on the assessment of preparation stages in 55 completed projects, it seems that nearly 70% of these projects did not follow a consistent FMIS design approach (compared to the methodology described in chapter V, section 31) to properly define the problem for country specific PFM reform needs before the implementation of information system solutions. Most of the complications faced during project implementation could be avoided with a proper focus on certain key aspects in design. Examples include the alignment of FMIS design with PFM reform needs, the preparation of detailed implementation plans, focusing on capacity building to ensure sustainability of information systems, realistic procurement plan/disbursement estimates, and the preparation of bidding documents before project effectiveness.

Regarding those successfully completed or ongoing activities, several patterns appear, depending on the type of FMIS project. In analyzing the results and performance of these projects, Type 1 (designed and implemented as a new project to develop the first system or to replace an existing system) and Type 2 (expansion of the scope and/or functionality of an existing system) FMIS projects were considered. Types 3 and 4 (FMIS solutions developed or expanded during emergency technical assistance operations) were omitted to avoid the distortion of patterns, as these are exceptional cases.

Variations in the approaches to FMIS project design in six regions and differences in the level of readiness explain most of the delays and several cost overruns. Nevertheless, two performance patterns are visible in the 32 successfully completed Type 1 projects (comprehensive FMIS projects), and these are highlighted in Figure 3.7.

- First, most of the 17 fully functional FMIS solutions (10T + 7F) have similar characteristics. These include a proper assessment of PFM reform needs, a focus on FMIS as a core activity, supporting countrywide (C + L) operations, and detailed implementation plans. Nevertheless, these activities took longer than planned due to insufficient preparation and unrealistic procurement/disbursement plans.
- Second, an analysis of 15 pilot/partially functional FMIS solutions (4T + 11F) reveals longer preparation periods with less focus on alignment with PFM needs. Due to various technical and political reasons, these systems were implemented as pilot or partially functioning solutions to cover only a few critical PFM needs. Such projects are usually followed by several consecutive operations to expand FMIS scope and functionality.

Performance patterns observed in 13 successfully "completed" Type 2 projects (expansion of the scope and/or functionality of an existing system) reveal that:

- Most of the eight fully functional FMIS solutions (2T + 6F) appear to be better prepared and more quickly implemented due to existing institutional capacity in expanding proven solutions. However, the duration and cost of improving PFM performance is higher due to a number of consecutive operations.
- The second performance pattern is from the five pilot/partially functional FMIS solutions prepared and implemented in relatively shorter periods, again, as consecutive projects to expand the scope of FMIS solutions. Nevertheless, their impact on improving PFM practices is limited.

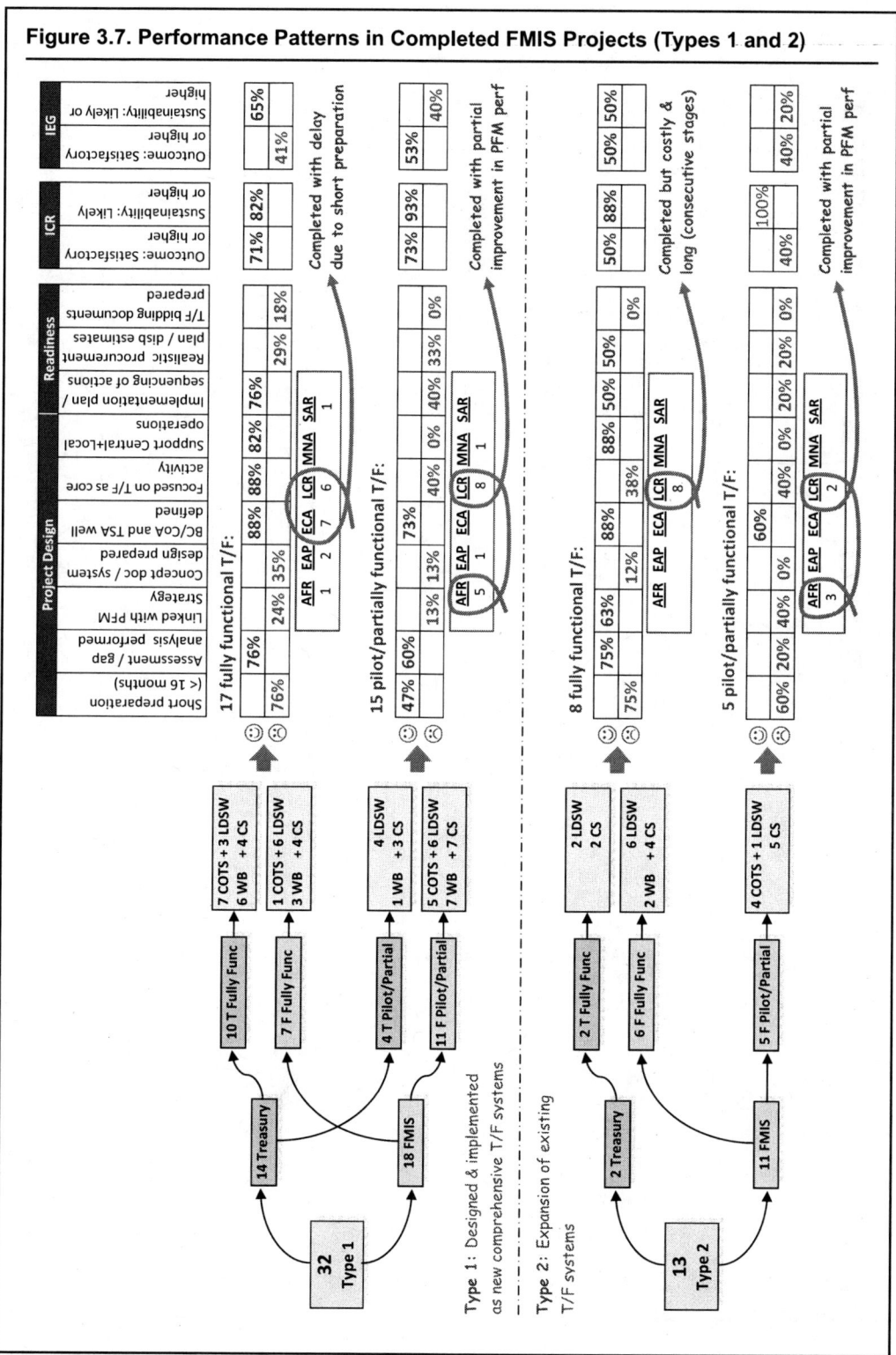

Figure 3.7. Performance Patterns in Completed FMIS Projects (Types 1 and 2)

Figure 3.8. Performance Patterns in Active FMIS Projects (Types 1 and 2)

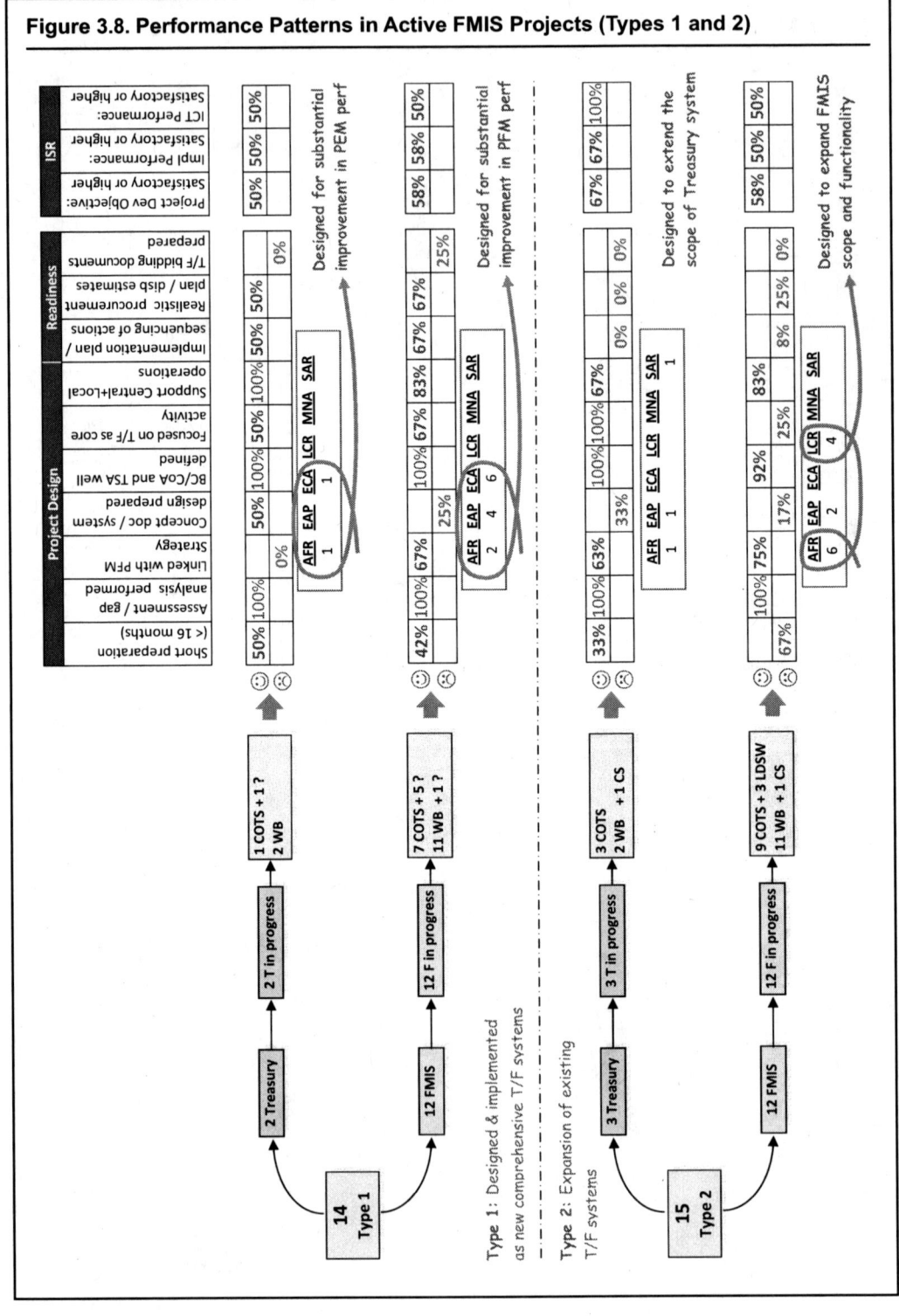

It seems that the technology architecture (Web-based versus client-server) and the selected type of application software (COTS versus LDSW) aligned with the advances in ICT solutions and did not have a major impact on the results and performance of Type 1 or Type 2 FMIS projects.

The 32 active FMIS projects appear to be better designed compared to completed activities. Based on accumulated experience, ongoing activities appear to be better designed and aligned with country needs and capacity, allocating sufficient time to define the problem during preparation (Figure 31).

- Most of the 14 ongoing Type 1 projects (2T + 12F) are much better designed (80% of these projects followed consistent FMIS design approach, especially in the ECA region), with proper focus on PFM reform needs and institutional capacity building. These activities will support countrywide (C + L) operations, benefiting from Web-based solutions and reduced cost and time of implementation. It is expected that these 14 ongoing FMIS projects will result in substantial improvements in PFM practices and policy decisions.

- There are 15 active Type 2 projects (3T + 12F) as a continuation of previously completed activities mainly in AFR and LCR. There seems to be more emphasis on alignment with PFM reforms in design, compared to previous operations. However, complications may appear during the implementation of ICT solutions. as some of these projects were prepared in a relatively short time without adequate detail on system design and cost estimates for the expansion of FMIS scope and functionality. Most of these projects will probably be restructured before the implementation of ICT solutions.

There seems to be a clear shift toward Web-based solutions based on COTS in 32 active FMIS projects. Overall, the performance patterns observed in completed and active projects are consistent with the success and failure factors already listed.

Comparisons to the Private Sector

As mentioned earlier, most of the COTS FMIS solutions used in public sector projects were originally designed to address similar needs in the private sector. Hence, an overview of the implementation of similar information systems in the private sector is presented below to highlight some of the common patterns of success and failure.

Information systems similar to FMIS are called Enterprise Resource Planning (ERP) systems in the private sector.

ERP solutions are designed to integrate all departments and functions across a company into a single computer system that can serve different departments' particular needs.[6] An ERP functional module generally includes Finance, HR, Manufacturing, and the Warehouse, in general. In general, private firms initiate ERP implementation by installing Finance and HR modules first, and expanding gradually to have the full package for domestic and international business needs.

As in public sector projects, commercial ERP packages require a substantial and costly change in the ways companies do business. In most cases, it takes several years to implement such changes. ERP vendors usually promise to implement the core modules in three to six months. This may be true for small firms, in which case the ERP system is nothing more than a very expensive accounting system. For a comprehensive ERP implementation, business processes need to be changed and staff must be trained in the new rules and procedures. Such complex transformational ERP projects usually run between one and three years, on average, despite high levels of ICT literacy in private firms and the large number of qualified consultants involved.

Transformations enabled by the Internet, such as cloud computing or software as a service (SaaS) may reduce the implementation time of ERP packages.[7] Nevertheless, changing business processes and company culture remain lengthy processes. Moreover, storage of confidential or business critical information in remotely hosted "trusted" servers should be handled carefully. Many companies are also benefiting from mobile services and advanced Web applications (Web 2.0) to improve the efficiency and reduce the cost of operations. The manifestation of these new trends in the public sector are not visible yet, due to the special arrangements needed to meet specific data storage and information security needs of PFM information systems, as well as the size of the problem (a relatively large number of concurrent users and connected nodes). Nevertheless, there are several Bank-funded projects initiated recently to explore the opportunities for such innovative solutions in ECA (eMoldova) and other regions mainly through e-Government projects.

One of the most often-cited studies of the total cost of ownership of ERP, completed by Meta Group in 2002 (acquired by Gartner in 2005) taking into consideration the hardware, software, professional services and internal staff costs, plus two year maintenance required, revealed that among the 63 companies surveyed — including small, medium and large companies in a range of industries — the average total cost of ownership was $15 million (the highest was $300 million and lowest was $400,000).[8]

Results from a 2007 Aberdeen Group survey of more than 1,680 manufacturing companies of all sizes found a correlation between the size (users and nodes) of an ERP deployment and the total costs. According to the report, "as a company grows, the number of users goes up, along with the total cost of software and services."[9] For example, large companies with more than $1 billion in revenues can expect to pay, on average, nearly $6 million in total ERP costs. This is comparable to implementation within the public sector.

Interestingly, internal resistance to change is often mentioned as one of the key factors for failure in private sector ERP projects. Another failure factor is the high level of customizations which make the ERP software more unstable and harder to maintain when it is finally activated. Not surprisingly, these are similar to the patterns of failure visible in the public sector as well.

Vendor lock-in and customization issues have led to the emergence of open-source ERP solutions within the last decade.[10] Open-source solutions that compete with commercial ERP packages are available today,[11] and there seems to be a growing interest in using integrated open ERP solutions in private sector, due to much better customization options and flexible support systems, as well as reduced costs. According to Gartner research, "open source has become a familiar presence in mainstream IT technology selections and in vendor technology innovation, but its transformational potential remains unrealized."[12] As cited by many market analysts, open source ERP is expected to become more rampant in coming years.

Notes

1. In August 2006, the ICRs rating system changed in two ways: (i) the outcome rating explicitly encompasses the project's institutional development impact, precluding the need for a separate institutional development rating; and (ii) the sustainability rating was replaced by a new rating of Risk to Development Outcome (on a four-point scale), which specifically assesses the uncertainties faced by the project's development outcome at the time of evaluation.

2. For detailed definitions of each level on the six point scale see pg. 40 in the ICR Guidelines.

3. The last completed project added to the database in July 2010 (P050706) does not have an ICR yet.

4. Sustainability ratings: Highly Likely (HL), Likely (L), Unlikely (UN), Highly Unlikely (HUN), Uncertain (U), and Not Rated (N/R) or Non-Evaluable (N/E).

5. Development Impact ratings: High (H), Significant (S), Moderate (M), and Negligible (N); plus Not Rated (N/R).

6. "ERP Definition and Solutions," CIO Magazine, updated in April 2008.

7. The software modules are hosted by a third party, and customers access the shared ERP applications via the Web.

8. "The Impact of OS/Platform Selection on the Cost of ERP Implementation, Use and Management," Meta Group, July 2002.

9. "The Total Cost of ERP Ownership in Mid-Size Companies," Aberdeen Group, July 2007.

10. "Is Open-Source the Answer to ERP?" CIO Magazine, February 2007.

11. List of Free/Libre Open-Source Software (Wikipedia).

12. Gartner-Predicts 2011: "Open-Source Software, the Power Behind the Throne," 23 November 2010.

## CHAPTER 4

Case Studies

Case study analysis is an ideal method to document and analyze qualitative information detailing the intricacies of FMIS design and implementation. Moreover, cases lend themselves to both generating and testing hypotheses and include an in-depth description of the endogenous and exogenous factors contributing to either the success or failure of a project. Finally, the presentation of case studies based on country experiences, rather than individual projects, provides a holistic perspective on the development of complex T/F systems. This complements the quantitative descriptive data analysis and analysis of performance presented earlier.

In selecting the case studies among FMIS projects, the following criteria were applied:

- Success/failure: Projects that were highly satisfactory or unsatisfactory in achieving its outcome and development impact, as well as in FMIS ICT component performance.
- Coverage: Projects that have been implemented beyond the central government (countrywide FMIS applications supporting daily operations and policy decisions).
- Diversity: Projects from different regions and implemented at different levels of GDP.
- Ownership: Projects that have been implemented by key PFM organizations rather than line agencies, with support from traditional PIUs.

An attempt was also made to identify cases not already documented in the literature. Based on these criteria, the following cases of Treasury/FMIS projects were selected for inclusion:

East Asia and Pacific
   ▓ Mongolia
Europe and Central Asia
   ▓ Turkey
   ▓ Albania
Latin America and Caribbean
   ▓ Guatemala
South Asia
   ▓ Pakistan

Each case study is explored from two perspectives: first, from a brief synopsis of the available data on the case project(s) contained in the FMIS Database, and second, from the perspective of individuals directly involved in the implementation of the projects in narrative form. The narrative section of each case study is organized according to the following format: (i) background (objectives, motivation); (ii) design (characteristics including scope, functionality, and technical dimensions); (iii) implementation (decision making, processes, cost, duration, number of users, operational status); (iv) impact (efficiency, fiscal outcomes, quality budgeting); and (v) influences (success/failure factors). Combined, these two perspectives provided a more nuanced understanding of what works and what doesn't during project implementation.

While the present analysis does not include any case studies from Africa, the broader literature on FMIS reforms includes references to a number of cases worth highlighting.[1] FMIS reforms in Africa started in the early 1990s, when countries with support from donors began to focus on the PFM improvements, in particular on budget and expenditure management reforms. A review of the literature on these reforms in Africa includes a number of references to various case studies on Tanzania, Ghana, Uganda, Malawi, Kenya, and Burkina Faso, among others. A case study by Diamond and Khemani on Ghana is particularly insightful. In 1996, the government of Ghana launched the Public Financial Management Reform Programme (PUFMARP), which included the development of an FMIS solution called the Budget and Public Expenditure Management System (BPEMS) alongside the introduction of an MTEF. The project suffered major delays and setbacks that resulted from the lack of a coherent strategy and ownership among the key stakeholders.

In addition to the case studies presented in this section, a timeline depicting the progressive development of FMIS solutions in Latin America is included in Appendix E, comparing the main characteristics of four consecutive projects from Guatemala and Nicaragua.

Mongolia

This section explores the case of FMIS implementation in Mongolia from two perspectives: first, from the data contained in the FMIS Database; and second, from the perspective of individuals directly involved in the implementation of the projects. Together, these two perspectives provide a more nuanced understanding of project implementation.

Based on a review of the information contained in the FMIS database, the World Bank has been involved in three FMIS related projects in Mongolia (P051855, P077778, P098426), with the first project approved in June 1998. Two of the projects are currently active; therefore, ICR and IEG ratings are not available. For the first project, which was closed in 2005, ICR ratings range from S to HS across the various dimensions of performance (Table 4.1). The IEG ratings are relatively consistent with the ICR ratings, with the exception of the outcome rating, which was downgraded to MS. The total costs of the

Table 4.1. ICR and IEG Ratings of the FMIS Project in Mongolia

P051855—Fiscal Accounting Technical Assistance Project (FMIS)		
Ratings	ICR	IEG
Outcome:	Satisfactory	Moderately Satisfactory
Sustainability:	Highly Likely	Highly Likely
Development Impact:	High	High
Bank Performance:	Satisfactory	Satisfactory
Borrower Performance:	Satisfactory	Satisfactory

three projects combined is around $27.2 million ($5.3M + $7.9M + $14M), and the total FMIS ICT costs is around $11.2 million ($4.1M + $5.3M + $1.8M) thus far.

Some of the main findings from a review of project documents reveal that (i) strong government ownership and a stable political environment contribute to implementation success; (ii) the preparation of a suitable country-specific action plan for capacity building and technical assistance needs during the preparation period is essential; (iii) an adequate level of supervision and monitoring by the task team is needed; and (iv) a focus on technical capacity building and assessment of ICT readiness in the early stages of project design is important.

Challenges identified in the completion reports include inadequate institutional capacity, deficiencies in organizational structure, and the lack of sufficient ICT skills in the task team. In addition to these challenges, short preparation time, delays in procurement phase, additional software customization needs identified during system development, and finally difficulties in transitioning from existing operations to a new system (capacity constraints, data migration, verification of data, and reports) are mentioned in the narrative below (Case 1).

Case 1. The Government Financial Management Information System in Mongolia

I. Background (objectives, motivation)

The PFM reform in Mongolia began in 1993. The main objectives of reform were to maintain aggregate fiscal discipline, allocate public resources in accordance with strategic priorities, promote the efficient provision of services, and strengthen financial transparency and accountability. Within this context, the government sought to institute a MTBF, linking policy priorities with budget resources, improve budget comprehensiveness, rationalize the system of norms and procedures, introduce a TSA system, and improve reporting. The government intended to align fiscal and tax policies to achieve macroeconomic stabilization, financial sustainability, improved fiscal balance, improved access to social services, and increased pro-poor orientation of public spending. These reforms were grounded in the technical assistance provided by the World Bank and other donors. The World Bank supported these PFM reforms through three consecutive projects: the Fiscal Accounting Technical Assistance Project (P051855: 1998–2005), the Economic Capacity Building Technical Assistance Credit (ECTAC) (P077778: 2003–2011), and the Governance Assistance Project (P098426: 2006–2012). The first project was completed successfully. The last two projects are still active.

II. Design (characteristics including scope, functionality, and technical dimensions)

To address the inadequacies in public sector management, the government proposed the Public Sector Financial Management Law in 1997 as a major instrument for reasserting budget discipline. Although it was acknowledged that the scope and demands of the Law exceeded the existing capacity and infrastructure of Mongolia, the willingness of the government to implement this agenda was strong. After a long debate, the revised Law was approved by the Parliament in June 2002. Acknowledging the capacity deficiencies in implementing the new Law, the World Bank worked with the government to improve practices and institutional capacity. The Law became the centerpiece for all donors to engage with the government and consequently played an important role in harmonizing donor interventions around a coherent framework. Overall assistance to PFM reforms was based on the findings of a 2002 Public Expenditure and Financial Management Review by the Bank in collaboration with other donors. A sequenced action plan based on the findings of this review and the analysis of gaps in PFM capacity was agreed on with the government.

The first project was designed to provide advisory support and training in the areas of government accounting, treasury, debt and cash management, auditing, management skills and related disciplines, as well as the implementation of a government financial management information system (GFMIS). GFMIS was initially designed as a core Treasury System supporting budget execution, TSA operations, cash and debt management, financial commitment controls, accounting and reporting needs, as well as the MoF internal controls and external audit. Subsequent projects were designed to expand the core treasury system towards a core FMIS solution by adding a budget preparation module (with MTBF support), procurement and performance monitoring functions, and a HRMIS.

III. Implementation (decision making, processes, cost, duration, number of users, operational status)

The GFMIS deployment included the following steps: (i) establishment of the TSA; (ii) development of a unified chart of accounts; (iii) adoption of software to the Mongolian environment in budget controls, language, and financial management setup; (iv) training of staff; and (v) assistance with change management. The first project achieved its original objectives, despite the tremendous challenges and the odds facing the government, with a total cost of $5.3 million. The GFMIS implementation was completed with $5.2million ($3.6M from Fiscal TA and $1.6M from ECTAC). The debt management system (DMFAS) was implemented for $0.537 million. The GFMIS component of the first project went through three procurement processes spanning a period of two years. This caused major delays and led to substantial government apathy. The lesson learned was that familiarity with procurement guidelines and systems is crucial to ensure the timely and successful completion of ICT procurement.

The government of Mongolia opted for Free Balance as its GFMIS application software (running on Oracle RDBMS). As with all COTS software solutions, a degree of customization was needed to fit the local functional and reporting requirements. There were two options: (a) fit the COTS solution to the organization's improved processes or (b) fit the organization's practices to the COTS solution. Mongolia chose a middle ground by customizing the software slightly and by altering certain organizational practices. The lesson here is that the extremes on either side are not possible. A well-thought-out mix allows for effective software deployment without completely changing well established or improved organizational practices.

The 2002 reorganization established treasury offices in all 329 of the lowest level administrative centers (soums) in Mongolia, 21 provincial centers (aimags) and Ulaanbaatar city and its nine subdivisions (districts). Currently, 294 soums, all aimags and Ulaanbaatar city and all its districts have access to GFMIS. The main impediment to GFMIS access now is lack of reliable electricity supply in some soums. Around 5,000 budget entities, such as schools and clinics, in both central and local governments use the Treasury system. Total number of licensed system users is 750, and external access is provided through interfaces with locally developed systems.

The subsequent projects are focused on expanding this core treasury system and linking with other PFM information systems to cover FMIS needs. New budget preparation information system (BPIS) will be used as a pilot application in 2010, and full roll-out is planned for next year. Locally developed applications on procurement, donor information system, HRMIS, and wage module are expected to be integrated with GFMIS in 2011.

IV. Impact (efficiency, fiscal outcomes, quality budgeting)

The GFMIS became operational in January 2005 with success, after a long and hard implementation period of nearly six years (four extensions). The government signed the acceptance certificate on April 15, 2005. The GFMIS improved the budget execution and accountability, enabled accurate and timely reporting, strengthened budget oversight and monitoring, and improved budget accounting and internal auditing capacity at the central and regional levels. Vendor payments are made reliably and promptly, there has been no proliferation of bank accounts, and aggregate cash balances and flows are more accurately reported and controlled.

The system capabilities are being enhanced to improve the management of public resources, enhance budgetary controls and strengthen fiscal discipline. Due to inconsistencies between budget classification and the GFMIS chart of accounts, and lack of adequate data for budget entities in soums, the GFMIS is not used for all accounting needs and is not the only reporting tool yet. The World Bank is also providing TA to improve the fiscal policy statement and the MTBF, as well as the internal audit framework. Ongoing activities are expected to strengthen debt management and public investment program, support decentralization of budget execution, improve the efficiency of civil service spending, and consolidate public sector accounting reform.

V. Influences (success/failure factors)

While implementing GFMIS in Mongolia, some problems were identified: (a) lack of information technology capacity in the government to develop technical requirements and manage system implementation; (b) lack of capacity to manage and sustain complex system implementation; and (c) difficulties in changing business processes and aligning these with international practices introduced by integrated systems. These capacity gaps were filled through the use of consultants who conducted requirements analysis, developed specifications and assisted in procurement. Additional advisory support was provided to manage the implementation and provide technical training to specialists. The government also agreed to adequately allocate resources and staff the ICT function in the Ministry of Finance and Economy.

As highlighted in the ICR, strong ownership and stable political environment are listed as the key factors influencing project performance. Preparation of a suitable country-specific action plan for capacity building and technical assistance needs during preparation is also important. An adequate level of supervision and monitoring from the Bank staff was mentioned as another critical aspect in such a challenging environment. Focusing on technical capacity building and assessment of ICT readiness at early stages of project design are also crucial for a realistic project design. Finally, in comprehensive FMIS projects there is a high risk in the implementation of ICT solutions. This is because the system's functional and technical requirements and customization needs should be well understood by all parties before system development and the transition from existing operations to new system should be planned carefully to avoid premature arrival of a complex system without adequate capacity and verification of data and reports. The subsequent projects (ECTAC and GAP) supporting the public sector reforms in Mongolia incorporates these lessons to improve the PFM practices.

Source: Shabih Ali Mohib ("Mongolia: Capacity Development in PFM," prepared by the World Bank EAP PREM and FM Anchor, December 2004), and David T. Gentry [resident IMF budget and treasury advisor].

Turkey

This section first begins with a review of the data contained in the FMIS Database on the development of a Treasury system in Turkey and then turns to a narrative analysis of the project from the perspective of individuals directly involved in the implementation of the project.

Turkey has had only one World Bank funded project in PFM domain (P035759), approved in 1995 and closed in 2002. The entire cost of the project was $78.5 million. After several years of implementation, the MoF and the Bank agreed to restructure the project in 1999, and the MoF initiated the implementation of Public Expenditure Management (PEM) component to implement a modern Treasury system as a separate activity funded from the MoF budget. Project funds were used to develop a customs information system and improvement of debt management system, together with related advisory support. The Treasury system (say2000i) was implemented as a government led activity in parallel to the project, and Treasury ICT cost was around $15.7 million.

The ICR ratings for the outcome, bank performance and borrower performance were satisfactory and the sustainability rating was likely while the development impact rating was substantial (Table 4.2). On the other hand, the outcome rating was downgraded to moderately satisfactory, the development impact rating was upgraded to high and the borrower performance was downgraded to unsatisfactory.

Based on project documents, the main findings include (i) adequate preparation and realistic system design, (ii) a focus on technical capacity building and assessment of ICT

Table 4.2. ICR and IEG Ratings of the PFMP Project in Turkey

P035759—Public Finance Management Project (Treasury System)		
Ratings	ICR	IEG
Outcome:	Satisfactory	Moderately Satisfactory
Sustainability:	Likely	Likely
Development Impact:	Substantial	High
Bank Performance:	Satisfactory	Satisfactory
Borrower Performance:	Satisfactory	Unsatisfactory

readiness at early stages of project design, (iii) an adequate level of supervision and monitoring of the task team, and (iv) pre-existing ICT infrastructure. Using country systems for procurement of FMIS ICT solutions to shorten the development period is mentioned as another key aspect in project implementation according to the case study below (Case 2).

Case 2. An Overview of Developments in Turkish Financial Management Information Systems

I. Background (objectives, motivation)

Within the last decade, the Turkish MoF General Directorate of Public Accounts (GDPA) modernized and fully automated most of the critical PFM processes benefiting from the advances in ICT. The roots of the MoF's modern FMIS solutions can be found in the World Bank–funded PFMP initiated in 1995. After several years of implementation, the MoF and the Bank agreed to restructure the project in 1999, and the MoF GDPA initiated the implementation of PEM component as a separate activity funded from the MoF budget. This decision was taken mainly due to time and budget constraints of the coalition government, committed to implement urgent PFM reforms to recover from high inflation and fiscal instability in early 2000. The main objective was to improve decision support mechanisms, transparency, and accountability in PFM practices through an integrated and cost effective system that could be used as the foundation for future process improvements.

II. Design (characteristics including scope, functionality, and technical dimensions)

The MoF initiated the design of say2000i—a Web-based public accounting system—in March 1999 to provide short-term solutions for urgent PEM reform needs. In early 1999, most of the operations were manual, with a lengthy centralized consolidation process on a relatively old ICT platform. The say2000i prototype was developed rapidly (within 6 months) since it was initially aimed at automating existing processes. After a successful pilot test in Ankara, the decision to implement a countrywide solution with improved processes was taken in early 2000. Preparation of the functional and technical requirements and bidding documents, further pilot testing, revision of the chart of accounts, and improvements in TSA operations and reporting were performed in 2000, in parallel to substantial capacity building and training activities.

The say2000i system was designed as a centralized Web-based application accessible through a secure countrywide virtual private network (VPN) established for the whole MoF units. The system would be ready for the execution of the 2002 budget and the MoF funds available for the development all ICT solutions was around $15M. Application software was locally developed with support from local Oracle consultants. A training program was developed to train all MoF GDPA staff (around 15,000 with 15% IT literacy) through a group of 360 trainers and using a renovated training center (3 computerized classes, each with 20 seats). A core team of ICT specialists (about 40) were recruited with proper incentives and trained to take over system development, management and support roles during the preparation stage. Almost 2 years were spent to complete the system design, develop, and pilot test a prototype and strengthen the institutional capacity before the development of ICT solutions.

III. Implementation (decision making, processes, cost, duration, number of users, operational status)

A high level of commitment from the Minister and GDPA General Director played an important role in successful implementation of the say2000i project. The procurement phase was completed within 6 months, after one year of preparation (four bidding documents were published on the Web in 1999, and revised 17 times until mid 2000) following the country public procurement rules. The total cost of four separate contracts signed for all ICT solutions was around $15.7M in 2000. Additionally, the MoF decided to spend another $5M to renovate the accounting offices and change the image of public employees. The say2000i project was operational in January 2002, for PEM, accounting and reporting needs (initially serving 6,000 concurrent users in 1,456 Accounting Offices (AOs) located in 81 cities and 850 towns).

The functionality, scope, and technical infrastructure of the say2000i system was substantially extended (with a personnel database and payroll calculations; health expenditures) from 2002–06 (in order to serve 12,000 concurrent users in 1,464 AOs). This resulted in significant improvements in the transparency and comprehensiveness of the PFM systems. This process also paved the way for the implementation of remaining PFM reforms. The GDPA IT Department capabilities have also been gradually expanded since 2002, to focus more on modern Web-based, in-house developed applications and open-source solutions to provide secure online access to a broader group of authorized budget users and auditors over the years. In the meantime, IT literacy of the GDPA staff (nearly 15,000) went up from 15% to 65%, based on site visits and surveys performed in 2001.

Starting in 2006, the Public Expenditure and Accounting Information System (KBS) was introduced as the expanded version of say2000i for nearly 46,000 spending units (SUs). Currently, KBS supports more than 110,000 users across the country. In 2006, a centralized calculation of public employee salaries (nearly 1.8 million employees) has been initiated. In 2007, an open source salary calculation module has been accessible to all SUs via the Internet. In 2008, the KEOS (Public Electronic Payment System, implemented by GDPA, Undersecretariat of Treasury and Central Bank) was launched for direct daily payments of all central accounting units. Furthermore, the Gumkart application (GDPA, Undersecretariat of Customs & Vakıfbank) was initiated to centralize payment of customs duties. The KBS-General Government Financial Statistics Application is used for collection of accounting reports from all Local Governments. The KBS Budget Execution Reports module provides online information about the performance of budget execution to all central and local budget users since 2006. Financial statistics have been produced according to international standards via say2000i/KBS and submitted to international institutions (IMF, WB and, Eurostat) since 2006. Web publishing of all budget reports are linked to centralized databases to ensure monthly automatic updates from reliable FMIS databases. Development of new KBS modules (SU Payment Orders, Movable Assets Management, etc.) designed for full integration of SUs with AOs has been initiated in 2009.

As a part of PFM modernization efforts, the MoF General Directorate of Budget and Fiscal Control (GDBFC) developed the e-Budget (e-Bütçe) as a centralized Web-based budget preparation and monitoring system for all line ministries and central government agencies in 2006. The e-Budget system includes a large number of modules to cover key requirements of new regulations in the Public Financial Management and Control (PFMC) Law. The interface between KBS and e-Budget substantially improved the daily information exchange on budget allocations, payment orders and execution results. In 2008, the MoF Strategy Development Unit (SDU) introduced SDU.net (SGB.net) as a distributed Web-based application supporting the PFM needs of line ministries and central agencies.

IV. Impact (efficiency, fiscal outcomes, quality budgeting)

The successful implementation and gradual expansion of several key FMIS components contributed considerably in improving the efficiency of public resource allocation and use. The integration of core budget preparation, execution, accounting and reporting functions and linkages with other PFM systems (Tax, Customs, Procurement, Payroll, Debt and Asset Management) have created a reliable FMIS solution to support daily countrywide operations effectively, and provide valuable feedback for performance monitoring and economic policy formulation. The recently completed

PEFA assessment (December 2009) underlines most of these achievements, together with possible improvements for a more comprehensive PFM system.

V. Influences (success/failure factors)

Since the early 1960s, most of the MoF Directorates decided to create strong in-house software development, system management, and help-desk capabilities to ensure effective technical support for PFM processes (the TSA operation with the Central Bank was initiated in 1972). The GDPA has managed to sustain all information systems with a competent team of specialists (currently 77) working under the GDPA Information Technology Department (ITD) and benefiting from the technical support of various ICT suppliers under the warranty agreements. Thus, strong commitment, innovative solutions and key technical capabilities embedded in the critical MoF units were crucial to ensure successful implementation and sustainability of FMIS solutions.

Enhanced capabilities of say2000i/KBS, e-Budget and SDU.net and linkages with external PFM systems cover most of the core FMIS requirements. The MoF is in the process developing several additional modules (e.g., SU payment orders, recoding all invoices, moveable assets, electronic payments, commitment management) to improve PFM practices and develop a fully integrated FMIS until 2012. It is also important to note that most of the PFM reforms and implementation of information systems were funded from the MoF budget so far. The MoF officials are also committed to the development of proper ICT standards and governance model in line with the international good practices and coordinate their efforts with ongoing e-Government (e-Türkiye) program.

Source: Cem Dener (based on the findings of the rapid assessment of PFM systems completed as a part of the Second Programmatic Public Expenditure Review (P117633) activities in May 2010)

Some of the challenges identified in the completion report highlight the short preparation time, low level of IT literacy at the start of project and institutional resistance. The case study indicates the changes in government ownership and PFM reform priorities, as well as the complex initial project design as other challenges.

Albania

The first PFM project in Albania lasted from 2000–06 for a total cost of $8.8 million, of which $5.2 million was spent on the development of a Treasury ICT system. The initial project design included a pilot Treasury system implementation. However, the government decided to expand the scope and implement a countrywide Treasury system later on. The Treasury ICT solutions were completed in December 2006, but the new Treasury system was not fully utilized until 2009, due to a number of technical and operational difficulties as well as inadequate government commitment to use the system.

In general, the ICR and IEG ratings suggest that this project was not successful (Table 4.3). The ICR outcome rating was moderately satisfactory, which was subsequently downgraded to moderately unsatisfactory by the IEG. The ICR sustainability rating was unlikely.

Table 4.3. ICR and IEG Ratings of the Treasury Project in Albania

P069939: Public Administration Reform Project (Treasury System)		
Ratings	ICR	IEG
Outcome:	Moderately Satisfactory	Moderately Unsatisfactory
Sustainability:	Unlikely	n/a
Development Impact:	High	n/a
Bank Performance:	Moderately Satisfactory	Moderately Satisfactory
Borrower Performance:	Moderately Satisfactory	Moderately Satisfactory

Some of the principle findings from the ICR include the need for committed leadership and close supervision and monitoring of the task team. A focus on improving ICT capacity was another important aspect of implementation at later stages of project implementation.

The challenges, as mentioned in project documents, reflect some of these findings:

- Inadequate preparation, technical difficulties, and capacity issues.
- Long procurement phase.
- Changes in priorities after the elections in 2005.
- Frequent changes in the task team.

Case 3. The Albanian Ministry of Finance Treasury System

I. Background (objectives, motivation)

The Albanian Ministry of Finance Treasury System (AMoFTS) implemented under the Public Administration Reform Project (PARP) was initiated in mid-1999 to support an ambitious reform agenda of the Government of Albania (GoA) including the development of a human resource management system, policy formulation and coordination as well as PEM. The project was approved in March 2000 (with $8.5M IDA Credit + $0.47M GoA funding) and completed in December 2006, after an extension period of two years. It was complemented by a series of policy-based adjustment operations and extensive economic and sector-related work and PFM reform activities funded by other development partners. The development of a treasury system was briefly mentioned within component activities, but it was not the main focus of this project at the start.

II. Design (characteristics including scope, functionality, and technical dimensions)

The project included three main components: (i) public expenditure management, (ii) human resource management, and (iii) policy formulation and coordination. Improvements in PEM practices and development of a pilot treasury system to be tested in the Central Treasury Office (CTO) and Tirana Treasury District Office (TTDO) were included as key activities to be completed in four years with a modest budget ($2M). Other PEM-related support focused on macro-economic forecasting, MTEF, accounting reforms, procurement and the MoF organizational restructuring ($3.2M). The second component included the development of a HRMIS and payroll module, as another major ICT activity.

The treasury modernization activities were grouped in two parts under the first component:

Part 1: Implementation of short-term improvements for Treasury ("quick wins"): The development of a new budget classification, capacity building for MoF/CTO and TTDO staff, and establishment of network connection between the CTO and TTDO were included in the first phase of treasury modernization.

Part 2: Enhancement of Treasury ICT systems and development of a new Treasury System: The development of a blueprint and modernization plan for the treasury and overall public finance system, functional and technical design of the new Treasury system, establishment of ICT infrastructure and development of application software were included as the next phase.

III. Implementation (decision making, processes, cost, duration, number of users, operational status)

Originally, the project would be completed in December 2004. However, only the implementation of Part 1 activities for treasury modernization was completed in 2004, due to delays in the completion of "quick-wins." There was also a change in task team composition (new TTL and ICT specialists arrived) by the end of 2004. There was no restructuring, but the new team and the MoF mutually agreed on the revision of several activities and reallocation of budget, as the funds reserved for Part 2 were inadequate. The project gained speed after these adjustments and two ICT contracts were signed (around $5M in total) after competitive bidding processes in late 2005 (Web-based application software based on COTS; Oracle Financials; and all related central servers, data storage units, and network equipment).

The HRMIS and Payroll solutions were designed and developed by the DoPA IT Department, as LDSW with help from local firms. DoPA has already implemented a personnel database as a result of the EU grant activities in 2000. The project funds assisted in extension of the capabilities of this existing personnel database in a web-based environment and inter-connecting all line ministries in Tirana through a secure high-speed network (GovNet). The HRMIS and Payroll calculations were pilot tested in 2006 and were ready for full deployment in January 2007.

Despite difficulties experienced during implementation, the MoF officials managed to complete the development of the AMoFTS by the end of 2006, and the system was operational in 35 treasury district offices (for nearly 300 concurrent users) in January 2007. The AMoFTS was also connected to the new HRMIS, which was not fully activated despite several attempts due to changes in government priorities. Only 1,600 out of 83,000 personnel records were entered into the HRMIS in early 2007, without payroll calculation (only tested for the MoF).

IV. Impact (efficiency, fiscal outcomes, quality budgeting)

While a fully functional Treasury System was installed against significant challenges (inadequate preparation, a longer than expected procurement phase, changes in priorities after the elections in 2005, technical difficulties and capacity issues), its full impact on budget execution is yet to materialize. The new system (AMoFTS) was only partially used in 2007, mainly due to technical difficulties (frequent power outages, network connection issues, poor service quality of system developers and suppliers). The MoF developed an action plan to overcome these technical difficulties, and this plan was largely successful in correcting the technical issues by the end of 2007. However, the AMoFTS was not utilized during the execution of 2008 budget due to operational difficulties that stem from inactive banking system (TSA) interface and other organizational and functional deficiencies.

In the meantime, the MoF initiated the Integrated Planning System (IPS) project in April 2008, to design a monitoring and reporting system that meets the GoA needs (and EU integration requirements), and help the Ministries deliver their periodic reports in due time. The IPS project includes the development of an Albanian FMIS solution to be built on AMoFTS, by introducing new modules for MTBF and Public Investment Management, as well as the IPS Information System (IPSIS) and the External Assistance Management Information System (EAMIS) for the Department for Strategy & Donor Coordination (DSDC) needs until September 2011.

In 2009, another attempt was made for the resolution of remaining AMoFTS functional and operational issues, and it was largely successful. In April 2010, all treasury offices started to work with the AMoFTS only, in fully automated mode. It is expected that the AMoFTS capabilities will be fully utilized by the end of 2010, and the expansion to AFMIS will be completed by the end of 2011 to assist in overcoming the existing deficiencies in budget formulation and execution processes and improve the PEM practices.

V. Influences (success/failure factors)

In general, the design of the treasury modernization component was in line with the FMIS design methodology followed in ECA. However, the preparation period was too short and the project activities proposed for treasury modernization were not detailed enough to produce a realistic budget estimate and time frame for implementation. Similarly, design and implementation of HRMIS and Payroll calculation modules were not initially foreseen due to their inclusion in other donor activities.

During mid-term review in May–June 2003, it was realized that the implementation of the Treasury System would require more resources than originally allocated. To ensure adequate support for strengthened budget execution, the GoA and the Bank agreed to reconfigure the resource allocations in August 2004 by nearly doubling the amount allocated for Treasury system. These corrective actions were complemented by changes in the task team, close supervision and high quality technical advice, and resulted in completion of a countrywide treasury system implementation within 20 months (March 2005–December 2006). The task team spent considerable time on capacity building and raising the awareness of the MoF management on the value of AMoFTS not as an operational platform, but also as a key decision support mechanism and a tool to produce reliable and realistic budget estimates and execution results to meet line ministry and public expectations. The first financial statement of the government was produced from AMoFTS in 2010.

Source: Cem Dener (based on the rapid assessment of Treasury system operations in February 2010, as well as the ongoing supervision of Integrated Planning System (P105143) activities since April 2008)

Table 4.4. ICR and IEG Ratings of the FMIS Projects in Guatemala

P007213: Integrated Financial Management Project (FMIS)		
Ratings	ICR	IEG
Outcome:	Satisfactory	Satisfactory
Sustainability:	Likely	Likely
Development Impact:	Substantial	Substantial
Bank Performance:	Satisfactory	Satisfactory
Borrower Performance:	Highly Satisfactory	Highly Satisfactory

P048657: Integrated Financial Management Project II (FMIS)		
Ratings	ICR	IEG
Outcome:	Satisfactory	Satisfactory
Sustainability:	Highly Likely	Likely
Development Impact:	Substantial	Substantial
Bank Performance:	Satisfactory	Satisfactory
Borrower Performance:	Satisfactory	Satisfactory

Guatemala

Guatemala has had four World Bank projects since 1995, two of which are still active. The first two projects received generally positive ratings of satisfactory. The ratings across both projects were consistent between ICR and IEG ratings (see Table 4.4 for further details). The first project (P007213) cost $10.3 million, of which $5.6 million was spent on the ICT system. The second project (P048657) cost $17.5 million, of which $7.6 million was spent on FMIS ICT solutions.

Based on a review of the ICRs, the main findings from the two completed projects are first, a suitable political environment and committed leadership, and second, close Bank supervision and flexible project management.

The main challenges indentified include the following:

- Inadequate focus on capacity building for FMIS ICT solutions.
- Changes in priorities and revision of activities during implementation.
- Extensive use of consultants to perform project activities and FMIS development.

Case 4. Guatemala PFM Modernization Projects 1997–2010

I. Background (objectives, motivation)

The Bank started supporting Public Finance Management (PFM) reforms in Guatemala in 1997 when the first PFM modernization project, named the Sistema Integrado de Administracion Financiera (SIAF I), kicked off. Since then two operations, named SIAF II and SIAF III followed, incorporating new modules and capabilities. The main objective was to make the budget cycle more efficient, transparent, and accountable, and to aggregate key information automatically at various levels of government. The main principle of the system centered on the control of public finances by the MoF and a decentralized operation of the system by line agencies. In addition to core budget and treasury functions, the MoF developed and implemented a management module named SIGES to support entities in carrying out administrative processes such as the procurement of goods and services, registry of inventory movements, human resources management, and debt management, among others. A distinctive feature of the PFM modernization projects in Guatemala is that it was developed and implemented through an in-house strategy with a combination of local capabilities and international expertise, particularly at the start. This approach is visible in many other Latin American countries.

II. Design and Implementation (characteristics including scope and technical dimensions)

Since overcoming a number of initial challenges, the PFM modernization efforts in Guatemala have progressed relatively well. The implementation strategy was based on adding different functionalities to a core Sistema de Contabilidad Integrada (SICOIN) system. The SIAF II operation replaced the original application with a new system called SICOIN still framed by client-server architecture, but incorporating the overall central government entities and new entities such as the decentralized and autonomous ones. In addition, the creation and consolidation of the Superintendent of Tax Administration (SAT) in 1998 enabled the Treasury office to implement the Single Treasury Account (STA) based on the consolidation of the taxes and duties collected and the cleanup and closure of the commercial accounts of the central government entities. With this consolidation, the Treasury office started to implement electronic payments transfer to the state vendors and to public employees. As a result, the quality of information on the liquidity resources improved and enabled central government entities to prioritize payments accordingly.

In the third phase (SIAF III), the PFM modernization efforts made significant progress by upgrading the IT architecture to a Web-based platform to connect the central government with decentralized, autonomous entities, municipal governments through a municipal version of the SIAF (based on a client-server application), and state enterprises. Finally, the MoF decided to roll-out an improved Web application called SICOINGL to support municipal financial management, adopted by municipalities with reliable telecommunication services.

In the case of Guatemala, the first attempt to modernize the PFM systems confronted a number of challenges: functionality of the system (with dual systems implemented for the MoF and line ministries) and IT limitations. Guatemala adopted an in-house application developed by an international firm which used an Argentinean application offered to Guatemala free of charge. However, the IT architecture was based on a client-server which used two separate applications to consolidate information, one for the MoF (SICOIN) and another system for the ministries and secretaries of the central government (called the SIAFITO).[2] Eventually this problem was overcome. Another key challenge in getting this approach to work was over the difference between public sector salary scales and project consultant fees.

III. Impact (efficiency, fiscal outcomes, quality budgeting)

The integration of diverse applications into the central SICOIN system and the coverage of system was a priority. In this sense, the budget, accounting, and treasury systems, as well as the administrative systems that are integrated somewhat into the central SICOIN have been consolidated progressively. The modernized version of the SICOIN based on a fully Web-based platform allows line agencies to interact with the system online. This enables agencies to formulate, modify, and execute their budgets in a decentralized manner, facilitating service delivery. The decentralized approach also provides the Treasury with information about the cash demands of the line agencies, demands that are met according a cash plan and the availability of the earmarked taxes. At the same time, the MoF centrally consolidates the financial information and controls the use of resources.

Conceptually the PFM systems were designed to preserve macro stability and facilitate the delivery of services and the SIAF plays a critical role in achieving both objectives. The key outcomes already accomplished include:

a)   Increased effectiveness, efficiency and transparency of public sector financial management and control, as evidenced by progress towards meeting the main outcome indicators: (i) the national budget now includes improved performance indicators consistent with the medium-term expenditure framework; (ii) the SIAF has been extended to all central government budget executing agencies; (iii) the budget, accounting and treasury functions are more efficient; and (iv) budget execution, debt service, transfers and procurement information is accessible to the public through the internet.

b)   The SIAF system operates within a modern platform. The system was upgraded to a Web-based application and is now fully operational in all central government agencies and most of the decentralized entities, and furthermore covers approximately 300 executing-level units. It includes most PFM functions.

c) New financial management procedures and systems were successfully implemented in all municipalities.

d) An automatic and fully integrated payroll system is being implemented throughout all central government agencies, including the health and education sectors.

e) An automated workflow system to support the Comptroller General's Office's audit processes has been developed and is under implementation.

f) The e-procurement application is now operating and registering all central government agencies transactions and is gradually being expanded to decentralized entities and municipalities.[3]

Indeed, Guatemala macroeconomic stability reflects a long tradition of prudent fiscal and monetary policies. In the last 10 years, the inflation rate on average has been 3.2% and the debt burden in GDP terms has been 20%; the lowest in Central America.

IV. Continuing Challenges

Although the SIAF system helps manage the country's PFM processes, some practices have been lessening the credibility of the system. These practices are related to the creation of trust funds and other mechanisms to execute budgeted resources outside the budget. The main reason for the creation of such mechanisms is the cumbersome procurement legislation that makes it difficult to execute the budget within a fiscal year, especially for multiyear contracts. The pressure for government officials and politicians to show results has also influenced the creation of these mechanisms, further undermining the credibility of the PFM systems. In general, such mechanisms are not transparent because most of them are regulated by private legislation. As a result, sectors execute their budgets outside the SIAF system, which only registers a budget transfer affecting the quality of information. The legal aspects around these complaints are of significant importance for the credibility of the budget, although it is true that the current legislation prohibits and penalizes the generation of accruals without budget availability, the practice of generating accruals outside the budget has been frequent. These cases have been named "floating debt." The main reason is that no effective sanctions have been applied to punish and deter this kind of practice; therefore, sectors continue to use these mechanisms. Partial solutions to tackle these issues have been incorporated to the SIAF functionalities through the contracts module that registers the relevant information about multiyear contracts.

Source: World Bank experts: Jose Eduardo Gutierrez Ossio, Alberto Leyton (TTL), Antonio Blasco; Guatemala MoF

Pakistan

The World Bank has been involved in one completed and one active project with major FMIS components in Pakistan. The completed project was perceived as generally satisfactory in the ICR, but this was downgraded in the IEG ratings (see Table 4.5). The completed project cost $34 million, of which $18.4 million was for the FMIS ICT component. The active project also has a similar figure for the FMIS ICT cost ($18.7 million), but the overall project cost is $93 million.

The main findings from the ICR highlight the need for commitment and support of the government and a project design focused on core accounting system improvements (instead of PEM).

Some of the challenges noted in the ICR include the following:

■ Political economy issues (resistance to changes from provincial governments);

■ Weak project management and technical capacity for Treasury system implementation; and

■ Resistance to the separation of Audit and Accounts; lack of career prospects for IT staff.

Table 4.5. ICR and IEG Ratings of the Treasury Project in Pakistan

P069939: Public Administration Reform Project (Treasury System)		
Ratings	ICR	IEG
Outcome:	Satisfactory	Moderately Unsatisfactory
Sustainability:	Likely	Likely
Development Impact:	Substantial	Substantial
Bank Performance:	Satisfactory	Unsatisfactory
Borrower Performance:	Satisfactory	Unsatisfactory

Case 5. Improvements to Financial Reporting and Auditing in Pakistan (PIFRA)

I. Background (objectives, motivation)

The process of improving fiscal and financial reporting in Pakistan was initiated in the early 1990s after observations by both the World Bank and the IMF and a diagnostic study undertaken by the Auditor General of Pakistan (AGP) indicated that the (then manual) accounting and reporting system did not meet adequate standards for financial reporting. Notably, both accounting and auditing were directed by the AGP (an anomaly from pre-1947) and budget reports by the MoF were not fully reconciled with accounting reports by the AGP and provincial AGs. The CoA was not compliant with IMF Government Finance Statistics (GFS) standards for fiscal reporting, and neither financial nor fiscal reports were timely or reliable. To meet these challenges, the Pakistan Audit Department (PAD) launched the Pakistan Improvement to Financial Reporting and Auditing (PIFRA) Program in 1995 with IDA support. Under this program two projects have been executed, PIFRA I and PIFRA II. PIFRA I was completed in 2005, and PIFRA II, launched in 2005, is currently ongoing and scheduled to close on December 31, 2010.

The PIFRA program aims to (a) modernize the institutional framework for budgeting and accounting, strengthening financial management practices, tightening internal controls to minimize occurrence of errors and irregularities in processing of payments and receipts; (b) introduce modern automated systems to support budgeting and accounting processes; (c) establish a capacity to generate complete, reliable and timely financial information to fulfill statutory reporting requirements and facilitate informed government decision making; and (d) modernize government audit systems, procedures and adopting internationally accepted auditing standards.

II. Design (characteristics including scope, functionality, and technical dimensions)

As the core component of the project, a major mission critical country-wide integrated Government FMIS (GFMIS) is being implemented to spearhead the reforms and assist the government in the functional processes associated with financial accounting and budgeting at the Federal, Provincial and District levels. The GFMIS has been implemented using an internationally well known off-the-shelf application software package (SAP) that was acquired after international competitive bidding. The functional requirements of the system were developed by an international consulting firm. The direct costs related to systems implementation have been about US$40 million, and are comparable with costs for similar projects in other countries. The system has been implemented in a partially distributed architecture: (a) Federal Government Budgeting and Accounting transactions are carried out on a central server located in Islamabad; (b) Provincial Government Budgeting and Accounting transactions are carried out on servers located in each of the provincial capitals, Lahore-Punjab, Karachi-Sindh, Peshawar-NWFP and Quetta-Baluchistan; (c) District government budgeting and accounting transactions are carried out on the respective provincial servers.

III. Implementation (decision making, processes, cost, duration, # of users, operational status)

The project is managed by a PIFRA Directorate in the office of the AGP. Policy guidance is provided by a steering committee with representatives from all principal stakeholders including the MoF, the provincial Finance Departments, and the Controller General of Accounts. The Financial Accounting and Budgeting System (FABS, name given to implemented GFMIS solution) is now used by the Federal, Provincial and District governments to:

i) prepare and compile the Annual Budget Estimates and fulfill associated reporting requirements;

ii) exercise ex-ante budgetary control on and enable processing of all government expenditures and receipts;

iii) implement commitment controls on contract amounts exceeding PKR 0.5 million;

iv) make payments (currently by check) against Bank accounts where government funds are held;

v) prepare the payroll for some 1.9 million government employees across all levels of Government;

vi) make pension calculations for all Government pensioners;

vii) maintain the GPF accounting for all Government employees; and

viii) prepare periodic budget execution and fiscal reports for all stake holders including the MoF/Provincial Finance Departments/Line Ministries and Departments.

A large number of government staff, approximately 35,000 state functionaries (including executives, financial managers, and accounting and auditing professionals), working on assignments related with accounting, auditing and finance at all tiers of the government (federal, provincial, district, and tehsil or local government), have been given training to perform their day to day operations using the new systems.

Training interventions coupled with change management initiatives have been used to facilitate acceptance of new policies, business processes, procedures and systems at all levels of management. In addition, with the implementation of the FABS, a repository of all Government expenditure and receipt transactions is now available to the Government Audit organization to perform their audit functions. The audit organization has deployed a number of automated tools to perform their work, including ACL and other software. This has made the national external audit system both timely and more effective as a result of the application of computer aided audit techniques and modern performance and systems-based audit.

IV. Impact (efficiency, fiscal outcomes, quality budgeting)

PIFRA I and II introduced major changes to government budgeting, accounting, and financial reporting, as well as auditing. The PIFRA I program effectively addressed all of the key issues identified in the diagnostic study and the World Bank/IMF reviews. The first project accomplished the policy goals of (a) modernizing the institutional framework for budgeting and accounting processes and separating accounts and audit (and placing the former as an attached department of the MoF), (b) designing a New Accounting Model and introducing a budget classification structure and CoA that was compliant with international accounting and GFS standards, and (c) designing and implementing an automated information system to support budgeting and accounting.

PIFRA II has built on this base and introduced modern accounting, reporting, and audit methodologies that cover core government. As a result, financial reporting of accounts has become timely and reliable. Audit reports and financial statement certifications that hitherto were completed and submitted to the legislature in 18–21 months are now completed and submitted within 8 months of the end of a fiscal year. Transparency has improved due to the strengthening of internal controls and access of stakeholders to financial information. Accounting and Payment processes have now been fully automated and the objectives of accuracy, completeness, reliability, and timeliness of accounts have been substantially achieved. Specifically, PIFRA has enabled the:

a) preparation of IPSAS-compliant cash basis financial statements for audit within 2 months of year end;

b) presentation of audit reports to the President and Governors (for provincial assemblies), based on international standards, for onward submission to the respective legislatures within 8 months of year end;

c) establishment of system-generated monthly and quarterly fiscal reports for macro-economic review and analysis by the MoF and international community; and

d) timeliness of audit reports has increased effectiveness of parliamentary oversight.

V. Influences (success/failure factors)

The main problems faced in PIFRA program relate to (i) political economy issues, specifically resistance from provincial governments over federal control of the payment function for provincial expenditures; (ii) the dearth of project management capacity and technical capacity within government for implementing modern computer based automated systems; (iii) resistance to the separation of Audit and Accounts and the feeling of loss of career prospects for audit and accounting cadre officers; and (iv) the lack of career prospects for technical IT staff within government.

Some of the key lessons learned include the (i) commitment and support of the MoF—such projects should be framed as PEM system reform initiatives, rather than just accounting systems reform (senior level policy makers in MoF and donor organizations relate to this better); (ii) linkages can then be established between project and requirements under policy based lending; (iii) the project manager should be a senior official from a functional unit with stature within the bureaucracy, and with adequate financial and administrative powers; and (iv) a core team of officials from the core functions should be involved in design, who can subsequently act as change agents. Institutional and political economy issues are more difficult to resolve and take more time for resolution than technical issues. Finally, the reform of underlying fiscal management processes should be the basis for the design of the system.

Source: Ali Hasim (based on the supervision of PIFRA I and II implementation (P036015 and P076872) so far)

Notes

1. For further details see (i) Jack Diamond and Pokar Khemani, "Introducing Financial Management Information Systems in Developing Countries," IMF Working Paper, October 2005, and (ii) Africa Region Working Paper Series No. 25, "Design and Implementation of Financial Management Systems: An African Perspective," January 2002.

2. The SICOIN system (i.e., the accounting system), implemented by the MoF, registers and consolidates multiple financial transactions to produce financial information and statements to reflect the financial and fiscal situation of the central government. The SICOIN system forms part of the IFMS named SIAF. The other system was the SIAFITO (the small "SIAF") for the ministries and secretaries of the central government.

3. Although the application has yet to support online transactions (e.g., electronic bidding or purchasing), this system has successfully promoted higher degrees of transparency in the public procurement practices evidenced by improvements in user perceptions and a recent award granted by the private sector association in Guatemala.

## CHAPTER 5

Conclusions

What Have We Learned That Could Be Useful for Future Projects?

Based on a review of the completed and active FMIS projects, a number of "lessons learned" by task managers and the management emerge; they deserve special attention while implementing FMIS reforms. These are summarized below, together with FMIS prerequisites, recommendations and concluding remarks.

Findings

FMIS solutions can be considered "complex systems."[1] Such information systems exhibit "organized complexity," and the main challenge is to integrate a limited number of interlinked PFM functions through a centralized system that supports countrywide decentralized operations. As highlighted in a special edition of *Science Magazine* about complex systems: "complex systems are systems in process that constantly evolve and unfold over time" (W. Brian Arthur) and "a complex system is one that by design or function or both is difficult to understand and verify" (Weng, Bhalla, & Iyengar).[2] Hence, the design and implementation of effective FMIS solutions is a challenging reform process and requires the development of country specific solutions to meet a number of functional and technical requirements related to the PFM agenda.

Based on the available data set, which is relatively small (94 projects), the observed properties of FMIS solutions does not lend itself well to correlations or statements of causations. Nevertheless, a number of useful conclusions can be drawn based on the experiences gained in the design and implementation of FMIS solutions since 1984. These are presented below.

1. **The political commitment and ownership of the borrower matter**
   The World Bank needs to ensure that top leaders in government communicate their strong interest and commitment to the FMIS reform along with the readiness to make any sacrifices, if necessary. Moreover, an explicit target FMIS completion date should be announced early in project implementation and monitored closely at the highest level.

   Another important aspect of leadership is consistency. Initial excitement and commitment of leaders in FMIS projects has often been abated or lost once projects are underway. Such bureaucratic challenges require not only that implementation champions remain in their positions throughout the project, but also that the right set of incentives exists to make newly implemented reforms live beyond the champion's period. The danger of relying on personal commitment and dedication of a few people becomes much higher in FMIS projects. Proactive ownership and involvement in defining needs by the client is imperative.

Comprehensive FMIS projects take a minimum of six to seven years to complete, and there is often at least one election cycle during this period. Elections may have a significant impact on such PFM reform projects due to changes in key management positions and priorities of new governments. Therefore, continuity of the initial commitment of leaders is crucial to ensure the introduction of necessary changes in business processes and culture of PFM organizations within the project timeframe. Frequent changes in World Bank teams should also be avoided to ensure the consistency and continuity in advisory support and progress monitoring during project implementation.

2. **Success depends on adequate preparation**
   The longer the time available to design FMIS projects during the preparation stage, the greater likelihood that all components will be thoroughly assessed — and, potentially, the shorter the implementation period. The development of realistic functional and technical requirements, cost/time estimates, and procurement/disbursement plans (as well as draft bidding documents) should be completed prior to Board approval.

3. **FMIS priorities and sequencing should be addressed carefully**
   There is no prescription for FMIS project reform sequencing and prioritization ex-ante, but there are some useful guiding principles. FMIS projects in which the preconditions for PFM reforms were properly assessed and a time-bound action plan was developed with sequencing of reform activities tend to produce more effective solutions in a shorter time. A rapid assessment of key PFM functions (e.g., FMIS questionnaire) or a more comprehensive diagnostic study (e.g., PEFA assessment) completed during or before the preparation phase helps considerably in identifying the priorities and sequencing of key actions based on country-specific conditions to improve the performance of FMIS projects. As critical aspects of sound financial management, an accounting architecture based on good standards needs to be in place or designed, and adequate FMIS auditing capability should be available within the government. In general, a layered approach, wherein a basic transaction processing and accounting system is first implemented (to automate budget execution and reporting) and followed by enhancements in other areas, is advisable.

4. **A focus on developing internal client capacity early in the process is crucial**
   Strengthening the capacity of government officials is usually one of the key factors influencing the development of successful FMIS solutions in line with the reform objectives. However, improving capacity is also a complex problem, in part because of the peculiarities of public sector pay and incentive structures present within a given country. The excessive use of external consultants to perform the tasks of government officials should be avoided (especially in low capacity environments), and key PFM organizations should have a capacity building plan, starting from the preparation phase of FMIS projects, to be able to assume the responsibility of running all daily operations through information systems.

5. **FMIS implementation is complex enough to deserve a dedicated project**
   Projects which focus exclusively on the difficult task of implementing FMIS solutions, rather than on a broader set of public sector reforms with a large number of unrelated components, often have better outcomes. FMIS implementation is complex enough to deserve a dedicated project, team, and counterparts all focused on key PFM reform objectives. Embedding a large FMIS

component into a broader public sector reform project (or ambitious integrated PFM activities) should be avoided.

6. **The scale of the FMIS solution influences implementation**
   Comprehensive FMIS projects (Type 1), which are designed and implemented mainly through the WB funds, constitute the majority of completed projects (32 out of 55). Half of these projects (16) are countrywide ICT solutions with comprehensive coverage. The remaining half resulted in centralized systems, which have been expanded through consecutive projects later on. These different approaches are mainly due to regional characteristics, as explained before. However, in general, the comprehensive FMIS projects have been more successful than other types.

7. **The presence of an ICT expert in the World Bank Team is important**
   Having a Bank staff with ICT expertise within the task team may help in the design, procurement, and implementation phases of FMIS projects and contribute to accumulation of institutional memory for consistent good quality advice and better performing projects. The task teams are expected to supervise the design and implementation of all FMIS ICT solutions closely to ensure timely development of desired functionally and technology infrastructure and to minimize the corruption risks. In this regard, both ICT and public sector specialists must work very closely together starting from the inception phase, in coordination with the procurement and financial management specialists.

8. **The number and complexity of procurement packages influence project duration**
   All FMIS ICT solutions can be implemented through one or two International Competitive Bidding (ICB) packages if carefully designed. Single- and two-stage ICB procedures may take at least 12 to 18 months, respectively. Hence, a smaller number of procurement packages results in shorter project completion periods in FMIS projects. Moreover, the development of the draft ICB documents during the project preparation phase may substantially reduce the overall duration of procurement phase during project implementation. Several procurement options frequently used in the implementation of FMIS ICT solutions are summarized in Appendix D, together with suggestions to improve the design of procurement packages.

9. **FMIS projects disburse late due to large ICT contracts, signed at later stages**
   In comprehensive FMIS projects, low disbursement rates (less than 10%) are normal during the initial stages of implementation. Relatively high disbursement rates at early stages are only visible in emergency support operations where the FMIS ICT solutions are implemented through limited international bidding or direct contracting. Disbursements in comprehensive FMIS projects tend to rise after the contract signature and the bulk of payments are made during rollout and operational acceptance stages, usually within the last year of projects.

10. **ICT-related risks need to be clearly identified during project preparation**
    In general, it is accepted that the use of proper IT and ICT solutions in public sector operations and decision making process improves governance. It should be noted that, although ICT can be used effectively to detect and reduce corruption and other risks, it can also provide opportunities for new types of corrupt practices.

The implementation of large-scale (and expensive) FMIS ICT solutions in an environment with inadequate internal or external control mechanisms and weak accountability may increase the probability of corruption. Procurement of ICT systems in a high-risk environment requires close monitoring and proper control mechanisms. Even if all information security and system management concerns are addressed, the reliability of operational information systems and databases needs to be ensured by an independent oversight agency and competent ICT teams.

The estimation of the cost of FMIS ICT solutions needs to be performed carefully during project preparation based on a detailed assessment of key "design parameters" (total number of concurrent users or Web-based system users, offices, or nodes to be connected; server performance benchmarks; adequate network connection bandwidth; etc.) and basic "system requirements" (functionality of FMIS application software, workload estimates, data storage and transaction processing requirements, etc.). In the absence of such design parameters and system requirements, a realistic cost estimate during project preparation is not likely. This may lead to the acceptance of relatively large margins of error (or contingency) for FMIS ICT solutions, resulting in ICT costs much higher than market rates due to this initial uncertainty. Therefore, initial cost estimates should be verified based on the actual cost of similar solutions in other projects using the FMIS database and other sources to reduce the risk of cost overruns or corruption. The project and task team members should also be careful in their interactions with the bidders/suppliers, especially during the procurement phase and execution of contracts, to ensure fair competition. Some of these key aspects can be addressed during the preparation of a project operations manual while defining the roles and responsibilities of all project team members and clarifying the expectations from the evaluation committees and project implementation unit. The composition of the evaluation committees and competencies of designated officials should be reviewed by the task teams to ensure that subject experts are involved in the evaluation of technical proposals and key project team members and managers provide written comments on all proposed solutions.

Prerequisites

In most of the relatively successful completed FMIS projects, an adequate focus on preparing the foundations for successful implementation of ICT solutions is visible. Core elements of this enabling environment can be referred to as "FMIS prerequisites," which are expected to be substantially completed before the contract signature with FMIS solution provider(s) to reduce potential complications during system development and roll-out stages. These prerequisites are also highlighted in a number of technical guidance notes and working papers related to the design and implementation of FMIS solutions (Appendix A). Of course, country context will influence the degree to which prerequisites should be met ex-ante, and thus there will also be a degree of subjectivity to any assessment. Some of the key FMIS prerequisites (also included in the checklist and FMIS questionnaire presented in Appendix B) visible in completed/ongoing projects are listed below in three groups (functional, technical, and HR):

Functional Aspects

1. **Improvement of BC**
   In most of the FMIS projects, a substantial amount of time may be needed to improve various segments of the BC (e.g., economic, functional, program/

activity, administrative) to support standard annual budget process, as well as the transition to MTBF/MTEF, program-based budgeting and public investment management. Such improvements need to be substantially completed before the FMIS software development efforts (ideally before contract signature with the FMIS developers).

2. **Development of a unified CoA, integrated with BC**
    Presence of a unified CoA, harmonized/integrated with the BC is essential before any FMIS development effort, to benefit from the full potential of application software in recording and reporting all transactions with minimum effort and maximum flexibility. Usually, the CoA is implemented as a subset of economic segment of the BC. Moreover, a unified CoA can be designed to support different accounting needs (cash-based at central level and accrual-based for spending units).

3. **Improvement of TSA operations**
    There are a number of ways to implement a TSA, depending on country specific conditions (regulations and electronic payment system arrangements, etc.). In many countries, centralized TSA operation is preferred to monitor daily collections and improve effectiveness of cash management during budget execution. A reliable TSA infrastructure needs to be established before the implementation of FMIS solutions, since the core modules of the information system will rely on direct secure linkages with the banking system and established EPS operations to improve the operational efficiency and cash forecasting and resource management practices.

4. **Development of commitment control and monitoring mechanisms**
    Properly designed FMIS solutions can provide extremely useful tools to register all commitments (e.g., current expenditures, recurrent costs (RC), and contractual commitments), monitor obligations and provide useful feedback for cash management. Hence, the presence of proper commitment control and monitoring mechanisms in FMIS design and establishment of necessary linkages with relevant information systems (procurement, asset management, HRMIS/payroll) are very important before the development of FMIS software to ensure the development of necessary capabilities during FMIS implementation.

5. **Establishment of cash management functions**
    The development of an effective cash management module within the FMIS solutions depends on several critical factors (legal/institutional framework, existence of trained cash management unit, linkages with relevant PFM information systems, reliable TSA infrastructure, etc.), which need to exist before the development of application software.

Technical Aspects

6. **Establishment of a secure countrywide communication network**
    As most contemporary FMIS solutions are Web-based applications, the most important technical precondition before any FMIS implementation is the existence of a reliable countrywide network. Usually, the internal users of FMIS modules (line ministries, regional/district offices, auditors, parliament, etc.) are connected to centralized Web-based applications through a secure virtual private network (VPN), which can be established on any public network infrastructure. For external users of FMIS (spending units of line ministries, local

governments, municipalities) and interest groups (citizens, businesses, civil society organizations, international organizations), a Web portal is developed to provide authorized access to FMIS resources/capabilities. The World Bank usually supports the supply and installation of network equipment to establish necessary network connectivity. However, the government is expected to contribute to the establishment of physical network connections on available countrywide network infrastructure before signing the ICB contracts with the FMIS solutions provider(s).

7. **Preparation of system/data centers**
   The rehabilitation or construction of the Main System Center (MSC) and the business continuity center (or Disaster Recovery Center (DRC), as a replica of the MSC) premises should be substantially completed before signing the ICT contracts for FMIS implementation. Related government ICT specialists should be actively involved in such activities to develop critical system management and support capabilities.

Human Resources

8. **Presence of a core team of ICT specialists within PFM organizations**
   In most countries, the total number (and skill levels) of ICT specialists working in IT departments of PFM organizations are inadequate. Public entities tend to rely on outsourcing for ICT needs. Outsourcing is necessary to establish and maintain the ICT infrastructure. However, system administration and information security tasks, as well as securing the reliability of central databases and controlling user access, are the responsibilities of the implementing agency. Hence, a core team of dedicated ICT specialists needs to be recruited within the implementing agency at early stages, and their training on core ICT skills should be completed before any engagement with selected FMIS solution provider(s). These technical specialists usually work either under the IT Department or within a state-owned enterprise established by the beneficiary, ensuring the sustainability of skilled and experienced technical staff by providing necessary incentives.

Recommendations

The PREM and FM units of the World Bank have extensive experience in the modernization of PFM systems and, in particular, defining the functional requirements and technology architecture for integrated FMIS solutions. Based on the lessons learned from FMIS projects, particularly in the ECA region of the Bank, there has been an attempt to define the basic steps in design and implementation of FMIS projects and apply this approach consistently in a number of new projects initiated since 2005. A checklist for task teams involved in FMIS project design and the simplified FMIS Questionnaire used in the design of several Bank-funded projects are presented in Appendix B.

This section covers recommendations on FMIS (i) design and implementation, (ii) performance indicators, and (iii) quality and reliability.

Recommendations on the Design and Implementation of FMIS Projects

1. **Identify the PFM reform needs of the Government (What? Why?)**
   - Assess existing capacity and practices (e.g., PEFA, FMIS Questionnaire) to identify strengths and possible improvements.
   - Assist in the development of a PFM Reform Strategy (if not available), setting government priorities and operational needs, together with the Government.

■ Identify Priorities and Sequencing of PFM reform actions.
■ Develop the Conceptual Design covering the functional review of PFM organizations, the recommendations for improving the institutional capacity, and the definition of FMIS functional modules (business processes and information flows), together with necessary procedural and organizational changes needed.
■ Provide advisory support and training on specific PFM reform needs, if needed.

2. **Develop customized solutions (How? Where? When?)**
■ Assess existing ICT capacity (using a methodology like COBIT[3] or ITIL[4]).
■ Develop an ICT Modernization or e-Government Strategy (if not available).
■ Develop the System Design to define FMIS functional requirements, technology architecture (network infrastructure, application software, central servers and data storage, field hardware, engineering systems, security, system/network management and support) and implementation method, in line with the conceptual design.
■ Prepare realistic cost/time estimates, as well procurement/disbursement plans.
■ Identify the FMIS prerequisites to be completed before the signature of contracts with FMIS ICT system developer(s).
■ Develop the detailed Technical Specifications for all ICT systems in line with the system design, and related procurement packages (one-stage or two-stage ICBs).
■ Coordinate with e-Government initiatives and other large scale public ICT projects to ensure compliance with interoperability standards and share common resources.

3. **Strengthen institutional capacity to manage project activities effectively (Who?)**
■ Form a PMG composed of key managers from all stakeholder groups. Establish a PIU within the client's organizational structure for building/strengthening institutional capacity for project preparation and implementation (based on existing country systems, if possible). The PIU is expected to provide administrative and procurement support to the PMG.
■ Promote the use of country systems for (a) coordination and administration of large-scale investment projects; (b) financial management, accounting, reporting, and auditing; and (c) procurement (if country standards are in line with Bank guidelines).
■ Prepare draft Terms of References (selection of consultants) and ICB documents (technical requirements for supply and installation of FMIS ICT solutions) before the Board approval, if possible.
■ Establish mechanisms for M&E of project implementation, procurement and financial management activities (surveys, maturity framework, etc.). Clearly define the measures of success for the project.
■ Design key activities for capacity building and change management.

A graphic presentation of above steps, highlighting typical priorities and sequencing of actions, together with expected duration of each step, can be found in Figure 5.1. These stages are expected to be mostly completed during the preparation of FMIS projects, ideally within 18–24 months. Including the project approval and effectiveness

Figure 5.1. FMIS Design and Implementation Approach

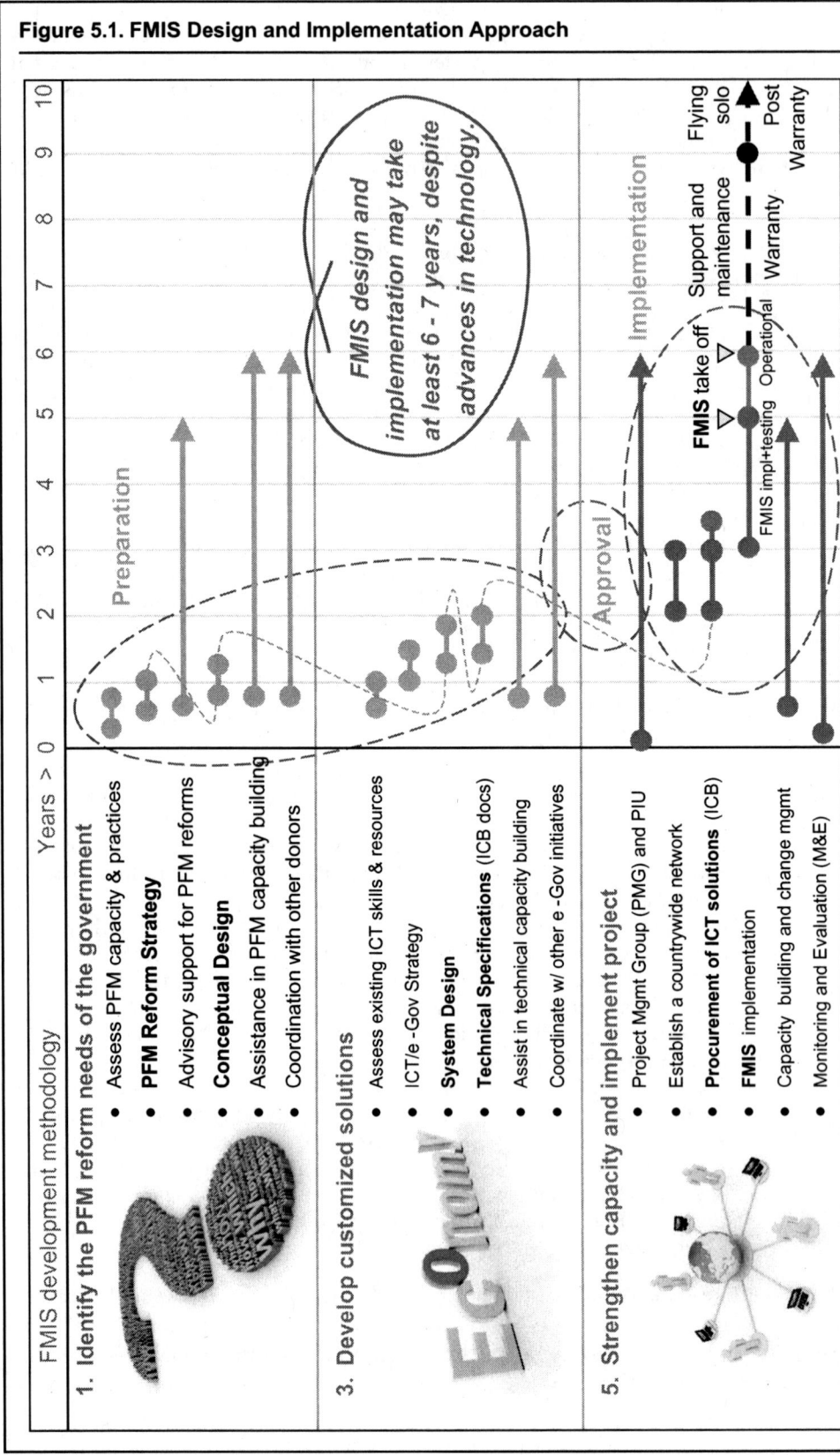

Images: jscreationzs / FreeDigitalPhotos.net

periods, the total duration before the initiation of the procurement phase of the FMIS solutions may be around 2–3 years minimum. However, it is extremely important to develop a realistic project design and initiate capacity building and advisory support activities at early stages to minimize implementation risks. Many FMIS projects benefit from the PPA or donor grants for funding the preparation activities until project effectiveness.

A summary of completed/active ECA FMIS projects is presented in Appendix J. The FMIS design and implementation approach described in this section was followed in several ECA projects (e.g., Ukraine, Georgia, Moldova), as well as the verification of design methodology in ongoing activities (e.g., Kyrgyz Republic, Tajikistan) since 2005. The bottom part presents the advances in information technology (milestones in introduction of Web innovations) together with the general trend in e-Government initiatives, highlighting the evolution of the eEurope program, as these are relevant to most of the T/F information systems implemented in ECA.

Key design documents expected to be prepared during the preparation of FMIS projects are shown in Figure 5.2. The linkage between procurement plan (PP) and component activities needs to be established clearly in the PAD (see Figure 5.3). In order to simplify the FMIS design and minimize the workload during implementation, it is always advisable to combine similar activities under one component. For example, advisory support, capacity building, and training can be grouped under one component, and FMIS implementation can be grouped in another. Furthermore, each activity can be designed to cover similar technical assistance or training needs (highly fragmented activities are difficult to monitor and link with the PP). Each procurement package is expected to cover one or more of these activities. Linking each activity with one procurement package is a good idea to simplify the project design. This also helps in the simplification of calculations on cost estimates, funding needs, and the disbursement plan. When a procurement package is related with more than one activity, management of project resources and monitoring of results/outputs tend to be more difficult due to increased complexity.

Figure 5.2. Typical FMIS Design Documents Developed During Project Preparation

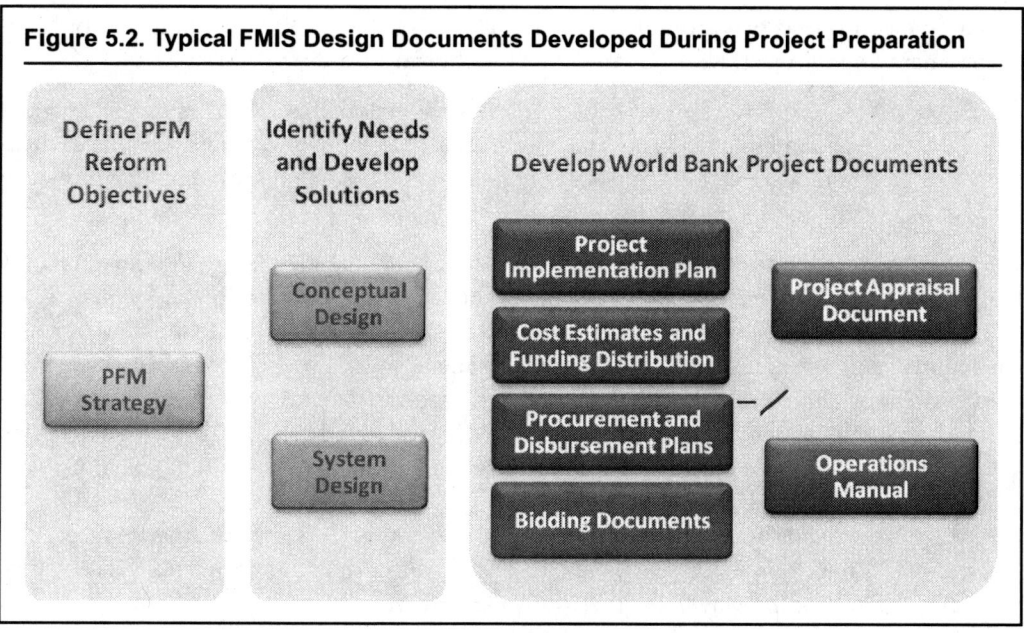

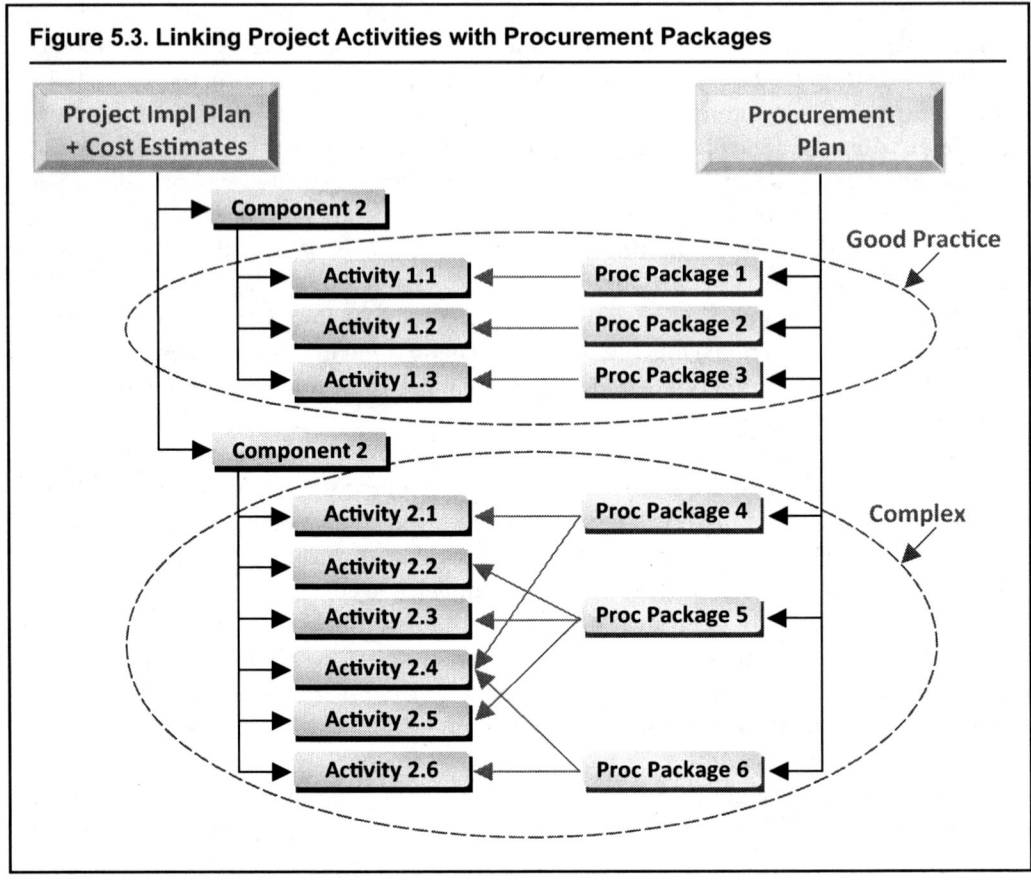

Figure 5.3. Linking Project Activities with Procurement Packages

Recommendations Related to Performance Indicators

The average number of indicators included in the results monitoring framework of the completed projects was around 3, with a broad range from 1 (Brazil's Public Sector Management Loan Project) to 19 (Ghana's PFM Technical Assistance Project).

■ A review of the quantity and quality of indicators in the PADs suggests that the development of more meaningful indicators is necessary in order to better measure progress and the impact of Treasury and FMIS projects on a government's ability to manage its finances.

Most of the indicators included in PADs and ICRs do not actually measure achievement in any meaningful way (partly due to the fact that the actual impact of FMIS solutions on PFM takes several budget cycles to measure). Instead, these indicators reflect activity commitments (e.g., computerize financial management) or output measures. Very few provide outcome indicators or even baseline data. Many projects included indicators in PADs that were later dropped or redefined during restructuring or extension. Such findings are not inconsistent with many IEG or quality assessment group reports, which have also raised such concerns.[5]

One particularly promising direction for developing robust performance indicators for FMIS projects is to draw on performance indicators included in the PEFA assessments. Launched in May 2006, the PEFA Performance Measurement Framework is an indicator-based assessment tool developed by the PEFA initiative. The PEFA framework has been applied in a number of countries and reports provide detailed accounts of the performance of PFM systems along various dimensions (see Appendix H, Table H.1 for a list of the PEFA indicators used in 7 out of 32 active FMIS projects).

■ Consider PEFA as a vehicle through which to assess the enabling environ-
    ment and perhaps, in the future, the operational status of PFM information
    systems.

In addition to indicators, a comprehensive results framework with clear linkages between objectives, intermediate results, and corresponding indicators provides a use-ful guidepost in measuring progress, and ultimately impact. Appendix H, Table H.2, provides a sample project development objective (PDO) with corresponding intermedi-ate results linked to three components: improvement of PFM functions, the design and development of an FMIS, and capacity building. Sample results indicators are included at each level of the framework.

Recommendations to Improve the Quality and Reliability of FMIS ICT Solutions

Benefiting from the advances in technology, new FMIS projects are designed with better focus on the quality and security of information to minimize the risk of corruption and improve the reliability of systems. Widespread use of centralized Web-based ICT solu-tions available on high-speed countrywide networks has contributed substantially to the performance of T/F systems since the early 2000s. FMIS projects also benefited from the alignment of available commercial software packages to public sector needs (after customization), wider use of open-source software in the public sector, and faster hard-ware performance. In addition to these factors, simplification of the PFM procedures and stable legislative framework are key factors to benefit from advances in technology effectively.

Some of the instruments that can be in FMIS projects to improve the reliability, cost effectiveness, and accountability of information systems are listed below.

1. **Using EPS for all government payments**
    Movement towards web-based T/F systems fully integrated with the EPS to
    channel all government payments directly to the beneficiary bank accounts
    through countrywide banking systems is being observed as a common good
    practice in many developing countries within the last decade.

2. **Benefiting from digital/electronic signature for all financial transactions**
    Using digital (DS)/electronic signature (ES) for all financial transactions and
    interagency processes, and elimination of checks processing and cash handling
    within treasury/accounting offices are other standard practices observed in
    many modern T/F systems (see Appendix C for a survey on using EPS and DS
    in the PFM practices of selected ECA countries).

3. **Electronic records management**
    There seems to be an interest in using proper electronic records management
    tools as a part of FMIS solutions. A number of guidance notes have been
    developed in recent years (EU, International Records Management Trust) and
    new FMIS projects include necessary requirements for records management, in
    addition to audit trails and other database integrity checks.

4. **Publishing the budget execution results and performance monthly on the Web**

The development of Web sites/portals to publish budget execution results and performance regularly (monthly) with dynamic links to a reliable PFM database for timely updates is becoming a key indicator for transparency and availability of modern T/F systems. The Chilean and Turkish FMIS solutions include such dynamic Web publishing capabilities to present the current and past performance of budget execution, and similar capabilities are included in the design of new FMIS projects in many countries.

5. **Interoperability and reusability of the information systems**

Most of the FMIS ICT solutions developed within the last decade have been designed as a part of e-Government initiatives in many countries. Proper focus on interoperability and reusability/expandability of application software and infrastructure elements play an important role in the development of effective data exchange mechanisms and ensuring sustainability for integrated PFM information systems.

6. **FMIS development and project management based on industry standards**

Most of the modern FMIS projects are designed around a number of industry standards to ensure compliance with the International Standards Organization (ISO)/International Electrotechnical Commission standards. In general, the ISO 9001–2001 standard is used in implementing the quality assurance systems of PFM organizations and is usually included as one of the qualification requirements of FMIS suppliers. The FMIS design documents include application software development, information security, and other technical requirements to ensure compliance with selected standards during the design and implementation of ICT solutions (e.g., ISO 15022/20022 for financial services messaging; ISO 12207 for software lifecycle processes; ISO 15504, also known as Software Process Improvement and Capability Determination (SPICE), as a framework for the assessment of processes; ISO 15288 as a Systems Engineering standard covering processes and life cycle stages; and ISO 27002 for information security).

7. **Using Free/Libre Open-Source Software (FLOSS) in PFM applications**

Finally, there is a growing interest in using FLOSS solutions in FMIS applications to reduce the cost and complexity of development and improve reusability/interoperability of information systems.

Within the last decade, more than 60 countries and international organizations have developed nearly 275 policy documents related to the use of an open-source approach in the public sector.[6] The rationale behind most of these policy initiatives is the improvement of governance through transparent and effective use of information technology budgets in the public sector, as well as economic/engineering benefits of reusable open source software. A majority of these open-source initiatives (70%) have been accepted, and final actions have been taken by mid-2008.[7] Suitable business models have been developed to implement these policies and successful public sector solutions based on open-source software have emerged. Among various highly visible initiatives, the EU (www.osor.eu) and Latin American (www.softwarepublico.gov.br) open-source portals are worth noting.

Other Suggestions to the World Bank Teams:

■   The World Bank networks/sectors involved in the design and implementation of FMIS projects need to collaborate and coordinate more intensively. Such task teams should possess practical experience in managing complex institutional changes and have an integral view of the public sector results chain as a whole.

■ The FMIS ICT costs (total and per user, also available in FMIS database) presented in this study may provide useful feedback for the verification of FMIS design point calculations and assist in the reduction of risks for corruption or extreme variations in FMIS ICT cost per user.

■ Possible options (COTS/LDSW) for FMIS application software development need to be clarified based on a detailed system design and realistic cost/benefit analysis (considering the total cost of ownership) during project preparation.

■ The excessive use of external consultants to perform the tasks of government officials should be avoided (especially in low-capacity environments), and key PFM organizations should have a capacity building plan starting from the preparation phase of the projects, to be able to assume the responsibility of running all daily operations through FMIS.

■ The involvement of the Bank teams in reviewing the consultant reports, FMIS design and cost estimates, competitiveness analysis, bidding documents (ICB), evaluation reports, contracts and proposed amendments, and the provision of comments to improve the quality and compliance of these key documents contribute substantially to the successful implementation of projects.

■ The task teams should follow all procurement stages closely to avoid delays, especially in large ICB packages. Prompt publication of procurement notices and allocation of adequate time for the preparation of bids or proposals are very important to improve competition and timely completion of planned activities.

■ It is always advisable to perform an ICT assessment (or IT audits) before and after the FMIS implementation to improve IT governance structure and identify possible improvements in infrastructure, database integrity, and information security, based on some industry standards (e.g., COBIT, ITIL).

Concluding Remarks

The first step in designing FMIS projects is to identify the problems to be solved, and mutually agree with key counterparts on priorities and possible solutions. An assessment of the political economy risks and clear understanding of the country context and infrastructure are also important in developing realistic solutions. Successful implementation of proposed solutions will largely depend on building confidence and strengthening institutional capacity starting at project preparation. The development of problem-solving skills in financial management and procurement are also essential for proper management of project activities. Finally, ensuring the availability and sustainability of necessary technical capacity—while also improving IT literacy to implement and maintain large scale PFM information systems—are crucial aspects of FMIS project design and implementation. As with the design and implementation of any complex system, leadership, collaboration, and innovation play important roles in the process.

This study presents the World Bank's experience in the implementation of FMIS solutions from 1984 to 2010, with a focus on the design, implementation, and evaluation of such projects. The preliminary draft FMIS report (prepared by Dorotinsky and Cho in 2003) focused on 32 projects completed by 2002 and looked into the duration, cost, and performance ratings of these projects to identify a number of success and failure factors.

The report documented the mixed results of FMIS projects. The current study attempts to review all completed FMIS projects (T/F) since 1984 with a broader PFM lens, benefiting from improved access to key project-level data available in the World Bank databases and archives.

In addition to the duration, cost and performance ratings, the current study identifies the project characteristics, scope, and cost of T/F systems; ICT solutions; project preparation approach; regional differences in the design and implementation of FMIS solutions; and (importantly) the operational status of the T/F systems. Based on the findings of the current report, 80% of the completed FMIS projects were extended. However, 82% of the FMIS projects were completed within budget and eventually resulted in a sustainable and useful solution as a basis for further PFM reforms. Among 55 completed projects, 49 T/F systems (89%) are fully or partially operational, which suggests that from the perspective of obtaining results and sustainability, many of these projects achieved their technical and operational targets.

Based on the lessons learned, a methodology is suggested for the design and implementation of FMIS projects, following a systematic approach to problem solving in PFM domain. The suggested approach is expected to be useful in clarifying key design parameters through a simple questionnaire to consistently identify *what solution fits which problem in what situation* during project design. Although FMIS solutions constantly evolve and expand in parallel to changes in PFM conditions, as well as the advances in technology, suggested methodology is expected to improve the quality and reliability of next-generation FMIS solutions.

The current focus of FMIS ICT solution providers and client countries are directed towards the development of new open source software and other innovative solutions to meet core FMIS needs with reasonable cost and complexity, as well as common Web publishing standards and formats (e.g., open data initiative) to improve the accountability and transparency in PFM domain. Also, the improvement of knowledge sharing and learning among the client countries (through communities of practice and peer learning platforms) and within the World Bank is very important to develop a common understanding of current challenges and priorities for PFM reforms and promote debates around emerging practices, innovative solutions and sequencing in PFM reforms. Finally, comparisons to similar applications in the private sector are provided to highlight corresponding patterns of success and failure.

It should be noted that the successful completion of FMIS projects depends on many other external factors as well. The adverse effects of country specific political economy issues, global financial events, or changing political environment due to election cycles may have a substantial impact on any properly prepared project during its implementation and result in unexpected delays or failures.

While this study begins to fill a gap in the literature by offering an in-depth focus on particular aspects of the implementation of World Bank projects, much work still remains to be done. In particular, future studies might look into the:

- Impact of FMIS introduction on public financial outcomes (e.g., timely reporting, better decision making) in different countries;
- Significantly higher failure rate for projects in Africa;
- Costs of FMIS project implementation relative to total national annual budgets;
- Variation in procurement patterns among projects;

- Lessons from the implementation of such projects in developed countries;
- Correlation between notable changes in World Bank policies and/or technological advances and the outcomes of FMIS projects; and
- Data and assessments from the operations of other development partners in this arena.

FMIS solutions are tools that may, if well designed and implemented and supplemented by related reforms of PFM, help governments in controlling spending and deficits and achieving greater efficiencies in the budgeting process. However, if FMIS solutions are not combined with a commensurate strengthening of internal controls, they can increase the opportunity for fraud and the misappropriation of funds.

Notes

1. A *complex system* is a network of heterogeneous components that interact nonlinearly, to give rise to emergent behavior. *Emergence* is the way complex systems and patterns arise out of a multiplicity of relatively simple interactions (Wikipedia).
2. Science Magazine, Vol. 284. No. 5411 (1999), "Complexity and the Economy," W. Brian Arthur, 2 April 1999: 107–109.
3. COBIT: Control Objectives for Information and Related Technology.
4. ITIL: Information Technology Infrastructure Library
5. "Quality Assessment of Lending Portfolio," The World Bank Quality Assurance Group (QAG), April 2009.
6. Open Source is an approach to the design, development, and distribution of software freely, offering practical accessibility to source code (Wikipedia).
7. "Government Open Source Policies," CSIS Report, July 2008.

Appendixes

Appendix A. References

Abdul Khan and Mario Pessoa, "Conceptual Design: A Critical Element of a Successful Government Financial Management Information System Project," IMF FAD Technical Note 2010/07, April 30, 2010.

Abdul Khan and Stephen Mayes, "Transition to Accrual Accounting," IMF FAD Technical Note 2009/02, 2009.

Africa Region Working Paper Series No. 25, "Design and Implementation of Financial Management Systems: An African Perspective," January 2002.

Ali Hashim and Allister J. Moon, "Treasury Diagnostic Toolkit," World Bank Working Paper No. 19, 2004.

Anand Rajaram, Tuan Minh Le, Nataliya Biletska and James A. Brumby, "A Diagnostic Framework for Assessing Public Investment Management," August 2010.

Cem Dener, Presentation on "Implementation Methodology of the Integrated Public Financial Management Systems in Europe and Central Asia," World Bank, May 2007.

Davina Jacobs, Jean-Luc Hélis, and Dominique Bouley, "Budget Classification," IMF FAD Technical Note 2009/06, 2009.

Davina Jacobs, "Capital Expenditures and the Budget," IMF FAD Technical Guidance Note 8, April 2009.

DFID, "Review of PFM Reform Literature," January 2009.

Dimitar Radev and Pokar Khemani, "Commitment Controls," IMF FAD Technical Note 2009/04, 2009.

Ian Leinert, "Modernizing Cash Management," IMF FAD Technical Note 2009/03, 2009.

Jack Diamond and Pokar Khemani, "Introducing Financial Management Information Systems in Developing Countries," IMF Working Paper, October 2005.

Leszek Kasek and David Webber, "Performance-Based Budgeting and Medium-Term Expenditure Frameworks in Emerging Europe," The World Bank Report, 2009.

Marc Robinson and Duncan Last, "A Basic Model of Performance Based Budgeting," IMF FAD Technical Note 2009/01, 2009.

PEFA, Public Expenditure and Financial Accountability (PEFA) Program.

Richard Allen and Daniel Tommasi, "Managing Public Expenditure — A Reference Book for Transition Economies," OECD-SIGMA Report, 2001.

Sailendra Pattanayak and Israel Fainboim, "Treasury Single Account: Concept, Design and Implementation Issues," IMF WP/10/143, May 2010.

Salvatore Schiavo-Campo and Daniel Tommasi, "Managing Government Expenditure," Asia Development Bank Report, April 1999.

Science Magazine Vol. 284. No. 5411 (1999) "Complexity and the Economy," W. Brian Arthur, 2 April 1999: 107–109.

The World Bank FMIS Database (1984–2010), updated in August 2010. (Currently available to World Bank users only. An external version is expected to be available in 2011.)

The World Bank, "Payment Systems Worldwide – Outcomes of the Global Payment Systems Survey 2008," FPD Payment Systems Development Group, 2009.

The World Bank, "Public Sector Reform: What Works and Why?" IEG Evaluation Report, 2008.

The World Bank, "Quality Assessment of Lending Portfolio," Quality Assurance Group (QAG), April 2009.

William L. Dorotinsky, Junghun Cho, "World Bank's Experience with Financial Management Information (FMIS) Projects," Draft Report, 2003.

William L. Dorotinsky, Presentation on "Implementing Financial Management Information System Projects: The World Bank Experience- Preliminary Results," Reinventing Government with ICT, World Bank, Nov 19, 2003. (Available to World Bank users only.)

Appendix B. Checklist for the Teams Involved in FMIS Project Design

Designing and implementing a comprehensive FMIS project (Type 1) is a difficult process, as the PFM reform needs and priorities are different for each country. Despite these country-specific conditions, it is possible to follow a consistent approach (as described in chapter 4) to identify key institutional reform and capacity building needs and design appropriate functional and technical solutions accordingly. The FMIS project design stages mapped to the T/F Maturity Framework developed for PEM-PAL Treasury Community of Practice[1] are shown on Figure B.1.

The same methodology can be applied to other types of FMIS projects (expansion of existing systems, emergency TA solutions, and expansion of the systems implemented by the government with other development partners) by checking all steps as in comprehensive FMIS projects and skipping the steps already completed, to ensure consistency during the expansion stage as well.

The lessons learned from the design and implementation of T/F systems are presented below as a checklist to remind a number of important aspects for future projects.

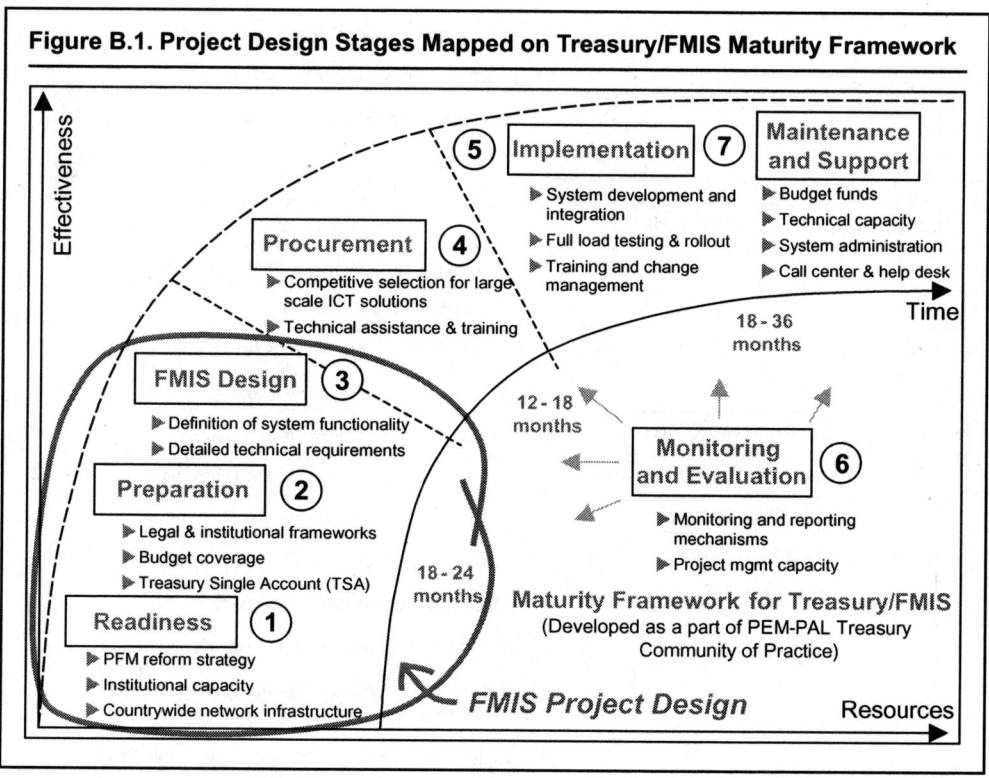

Figure B.1. Project Design Stages Mapped on Treasury/FMIS Maturity Framework

FMIS Project Design Checklist

#	FMIS Project Design Checklist	Key Aspects of Project Preparation
	**Identify the PFM Reform Needs of the Government (What? Why?)**	
1	Assessment of existing PFM practices and institutional capacity	☐ Check availability of PEFA assessment(s) ☐ Other PFM related assessments/projects
2	Identify key counterparts for PFM reforms	☐ Initiate dialogue with key PFM counterparts
3	Develop PFM reform strategy	☐ PFM strategy developed by key counterparts ☐ PFM Action Plan aligned with strategy
4	Identify priorities and sequencing of PFM reform actions	☐ PFM priorities and sequencing clarified together with key counterparts
5	Clarify legal basis/authority for PFM reforms	☐ Legal basis/authority to implement reforms
6	Political economy assessment	☐ Assess political economy & risks to dev outcome
7	Develop Treasury/FMIS Concept Document	☐ Functional review of PFM organizations ☐ Perform gap analysis (current vs. target states) ☐ Identify improvements in business processes ☐ Identify capacity building needs ☐ Identify procedural/legislative changes ☐ Identify organizational/behavioral changes ☐ Define implementation plan and identify risks ☐ Define required FMIS functional capabilities ☐ Cost/benefit analysis
8	Identify advisory support needs during project preparation to address urgent needs	☐ Identify Technical Assistance (TA) and training needs for before and during FMIS implementation ☐ Develop the ToRs for urgent TA/training needs
	**Develop Customized Solutions (How? Where? When?)**	
9	Assessment of existing technical ICT capacity	☐ Availability of ICT assessments (e.g. COBIT/ITIL) ☐ Surveys on IT literacy and workload
10	Identify key counterparts for ICT modernization	☐ Initiate dialogue with key technical people
11	Develop ICT Modernization or e-Gov Strategy	☐ ICT Modern Strategy prepared by counterparts
12	Develop Treasury/FMIS System Design based on the Concept Document	☐ Identify necessary FMIS modules ☐ Develop functional req for FMIS ASW modules ☐ Define FMIS technology architecture ☐ Design FMIS communication network (VPN) + nodes ☐ Define FMIS application software and related central server+data storage requirements ☐ Define FMIS field hardware, network equipment and engineering systems specifications ☐ Main System Center + Disaster Recovery Center

(Continued)

FMIS Project Design Checklist (*Continued*)

#	FMIS Project Design Checklist	Key Aspects of Project Preparation
		☐ Design FMIS Web Portal platform/capabilities
		☐ Cost estimates and competitiveness analysis
		☐ Develop FMIS implementation & training plans
		☐ Develop FMIS support and maintenance plans
		☐ Identify records mgmt and workflow mgmt needs
		☐ Improve system mgmt & info security capacity
13	Prepare realistic implementation plan for key project activities	☐ Duration of proc and impl stages for each activity (one procurement package per activity)
14	Prepare realistic cost estimates for all activities	☐ Define req input & cost estimate for each activity
15	Prepare procurement plan & disbursement estimates for all activities (one to one)	☐ Develop procurement plan & quarterly disbursement estimates aligned with impl plan
16	Identify the FMIS prerequisites To be completed before signing ICT contracts	☐ Development of FMIS Concept Document and System Design in line with the PFM reform goals
		☐ Improve budget classification/chart of accounts
		☐ Improve/establish TSA
		☐ Establish countrywide network
		☐ Improve/establish IT capacity within MoF/Gov
		☐ Prepare MSC + DRC for installations
		☐ Ensure that MoF project team drives all key activities
17	Develop FMIS Technical Requirements and bidding (ICB) documents	☐ Imlement all ICT solutions with one or two ICB packages (two-stage for ASW; single stage for HW)
18	Coordinate with ongoing e-Gov activities (if any)	☐ Ensure interoperability and effective data exchange with related PFM systems/e-Gov solutions/services
Strengthen Capacity and Implement Project (Who?)		
19	Establish a PMG	☐ Ensure that key counterparts are in PMG
20	Establish a PIU within the implementing agency structure	☐ Ensure that a PIU composed of a coordinator, a FM spec, a procurement spec and a translator in place
21	Try using country systems for project mgmt, financial mgmt and procurement, if possible	☐ Check capabilities for coordination & administration of large projects, as well as FM and procurement
22	Establish monitoring and evaluation mechanisms	☐ Develop M&E skills and use proper monitoring and reporting mechanisms throughout project impl
23	Prepare draft bidding documents before the Board approval, if possible	☐ Ensure that key bidding documents are ready to initiate procurement phase after effectiveness
24	Prepare realistic capacity building and change mgmt plans for PFM reforms	☐ Design key capacity building and change mgmt activities to be initiated after project approval
25	Ensure availability of sufficient resources for the sustainability of T/F system	☐ Gov/MoF commitment on necessary resources and funds to sustain T/F system in the future

The task teams involved in the design and implementation of FMIS solutions may wish to benefit from a simplified and slightly expanded form of the "Treasury Questionnaire"[2] during project inception phase. The simplified FMIS Questionnaire is presented below, covering six categories: (i) legal and organization framework; (ii) scope of FMIS operations; (iii) system functionality; (iv) ICT capabilities and infrastructure; (v) technical assistance needs; and (vi) related projects/activities.

FMIS Questionnaire

Country: _____

Prepared by (name + title): _____

Date: yyyy / mm / dd

#	FMIS Questionnaire	Responses
	Part I—Legal and Organizational Framework	
1	Legal basis: Is there a Treasury Law? - if Yes, please **attach** the law or indicate **Web link**: _____	☐ Yes ☐ No
2	- if Yes, the dates of approval + last revision of the Law: Law #: _____	Approved on: yyyy / mm / dd Last revision: yyyy / mm / dd
3	- if No, any other Treasury related legislation? Related legislation: _____	☐ Yes ☐ No Approved on: yyyy / mm / dd
4	When was the Central Treasury organization established? Please **attach** the MoF/Treasury organizational chart.	Established on: yyyy / mm / dd
5	Is the Treasury responsible for: (a) public expenditure mgmt? (b) revenue collection? (c) cash management? (d) issuing securities/bonds? (e) debt/aid management? (f) accounting/financial stmt?	☐ Yes ☐ No ☐ Yes ☐ No ☐ Yes ☐ No ☐ Yes ☐ No ☐ Yes ☐ No ☐ Yes ☐ No
6	Total number of MoF/Treasury offices: Comments: _____	Central: _____ Regional: _____ Districts: _____
7	Total number of MoF/Treasury staff: Comments: _____	Central: _____ Regional: _____ Districts: _____
8	Total number of MoF/Treasury technical specialists (as staff members): Comments: _____	Central: _____ Regional: _____ Districts: _____

#	FMIS Questionnaire	Responses
	Part II—Scope of FMIS Operations	
9	Is there **TSA**? - if Yes, What is the TSA operation mode?[3] - When was the TSA system established? Comments: _____	☐ Yes ☐ No ☐ Client ☐ Correspondent Established on: yyyy / mm / dd

(Continued)

FMIS Questionnaire (*Continued*)

#	FMIS Questionnaire	Responses
10	Are there extra-budgetary funds?[4] - if Yes, EBFs as a % of total expenditures and revenues: Comments: _____	☐ Yes ☐ No EBFs _____ % of total exp EBFs _____ % of total rev
11	Components of Annual Budget serviced by Treasury: Comments: _____	☐ Central ☐ Regional/Local ☐ Extra-Budgetary Funds (EBFs)
12	Annual Budget components included in the TSA: Comments: _____	☐ Central ☐ Regional/Local ☐ Extra-Budgetary Funds (EBFs)
13	Is there a medium-term budgeting/expenditure framework? - If Yes, since when?	☐ MTBF ☐ MTEF Since (year): yyyy
14	Is there a unified **CoA**? Comments: _____	☐ Yes ☐ No
15	Is **BC** aligned with CoA? Please **attach** BC and CoA data structures (all segments + data lengths)	☐ Yes ☐ No
16	Method of accounting used by the Treasury Comments: _____	☐ Cash ☐ Modified-cash ☐ Mod-accr ☐ Accrual
17	Method of accounting used by the Budget Institutions Comments: _____	☐ Cash ☐ Modified-cash ☐ Mod-accr ☐ Accrual
18	Is there a fully operational Treasury System/FMIS[5]? - If Yes, since when?/If No, expected to go live in? Comments: _____	☐ Treasury ☐ FMIS Since: yyyy / mm / dd
19	FMIS supports management of Commitments? - If Yes, since when?/If No, expected to support in? Comments: _____	☐ Annual ☐ Multi-year Since: yyyy / mm / dd

#	FMIS Questionnaire	Responses
Part III—System Functionality		
20	Functional capabilities of existing PFM information systems. • For automated functions, please list related ICT solutions as LDSW or COTS software.	Please indicate the followings: • Responsible dept/unit • Mode of operation (manual/auto)

PFM Functions	Responsible Dept/Unit	Manual/Automated
a) Macroeconomic forecasting		
b) Public Investment Planning		
c) Budget Preparation		
d) Core Treasury System		
• Management of Revenues		
• Purchasing/Commitment		
• Management of Expenditures		
• Cash/Fund Management		
• General Ledger		

(*Continued*)

FMIS Questionnaire (*Continued*)

#	FMIS Questionnaire		Responses
	PFM Functions	**Responsible Dept/Unit**	**Manual/Automated**
	• Financial reports		
	• Asset/Inventory Management		
e)	Internal debt management		
f)	External debt and aid mgmt		
g)	Personnel database (HRMIS)		
h)	Payroll calculations		
i)	Support for Auditing		
j)	Support for Spending Units (portal)		
k)	FMIS: Data Warehouse		
l)	Other (please specify): _____ _____ _____		

#	FMIS Questionnaire	Responses
	Part IV—Information and Communication Technology Capabilities and Infrastructure	

The development of ICT infrastructure for FMIS solutions usually involves four main activities:

► Establishment of countrywide network connections (central + district/local offices).

► Development of web-based Application Software (ASW) for Treasury/FMIS solutions.

► Installation of central servers, data storage units and field hardware for web based applications.

► Installation of network equipment, safety/security systems and system management components.

Establishment of countrywide network (usually a Government contribution) is the first step in implementation of ICT solutions. Other ICT components are implemented through International Competitive Bidding (ICB) process in World Bank funded projects.

#	Question	Responses
21	Is there a countrywide network already established?	☐ Yes ☐ No
22	List network service providers (state owned or private telecom companies)	☐ Yes ☐ No
23	Is there a technical report on possible countrywide network connectivity options? (Dedicated lines, dial up, ADSL, satellite, fiber optic, etc.) - If Yes, please **attach** to this questionnaire.	☐ Yes ☐ No
24	Is there a list of all central and local office locations (nodes) to be connected through a secure countrywide network? - If Yes, please **attach** to this questionnaire.	☐ Yes ☐ No
25	Is there a list of estimated number of system users for each node? - If Yes, please **attach** to this questionnaire.	☐ Yes ☐ No
26	Is there a list of estimated workload of each node (# of reports; number of revenue & expenditure transactions per year; daily maximums)? - If Yes, please **attach** to this questionnaire.	☐ Yes ☐ No
27	Is there an ICT Department within the MoF/Treasury organization? - If Yes, please **attach** the list of specialists in central/local units	☐ Yes ☐ No
28	Is there in-house software development capability within the MoF/Treasury organization? - If Yes, how many programmers and which skills are available?	☐ Yes ☐ No

(Continued)

FMIS Questionnaire (*Continued*)

#	FMIS Questionnaire	Responses
29	Are there local ICT firms specialized in Web-based application software development? - If Yes, how many qualified local firms?	☐ Yes ☐ No

#	FMIS Questionnaire	Responses
Part V—Technical Assistance Needs		
During the preparation and implementation of FMIS projects, a number of Technical Assistance (TA) services can be provided by individual consultants/firms for institutional capacity building and development of solutions for various PFM reform needs.		Please indicate the type of TA needed during the design and implementation of FMIS project.
30	Develop PFM reform strategy	☐ Yes ☐ No
31	Advisory support in budget reforms	☐ Yes ☐ No
32	Advisory support in public expenditure management reforms	☐ Yes ☐ No
33	Advisory support in public sector accounting reforms	☐ Yes ☐ No
34	Functional review of PFM organizations	☐ Yes ☐ No
35	Support on PFM reorganization and new business processes	☐ Yes ☐ No
36	Develop legal, regulatory and/or operational framework (guidelines, procedures, regulations, operating manuals)	☐ Yes ☐ No
37	Improve budget classification/design unified chart of accounts	☐ Yes ☐ No
38	Improve treasury single account (TSA) operations	☐ Yes ☐ No
39	FMIS functional specifications and technology architecture	☐ Yes ☐ No
40	Preparation of the FMIS bidding (ICB) documents	☐ Yes ☐ No
41	Advisory support during the execution of FMIS ICT contracts for checking the compliance with FMIS requirements	☐ Yes ☐ No
42	Review of e-Gov initiatives & coordination with other ICT projects	☐ Yes ☐ No
43	Develop training programs and change management activities	☐ Yes ☐ No
44	Project management	☐ Yes ☐ No
45	Strengthen FM and procurement capacity	☐ Yes ☐ No
46	Other TA needs: _____ _____ _____	☐ Yes ☐ No

#	FMIS Questionnaire	Responses
Part VI—Related Projects/Activities		
47	Is there a completed/ongoing project related with T/F system? If Yes, please list all related activities (funded by the Gov/donors) indicating their objective, scope, duration, budget and main outputs (please **attach** related documents): _____ _____ _____ _____	☐ Yes ☐ No

(*Continued*)

FMIS Questionnaire (*Continued*)

#	FMIS Questionnaire	Responses
	Part VI—Related Projects/Activities	
48	Is there a donor coordination mechanism for PFM related activities? If Yes, please summarize:	☐ Yes ☐ No
	Attachments	
A1	Documents on legal and organizational framework attached?	☐ Yes ☐ No
A2	Organizational diagram of the MoF/Treasury (indicating the number of staff at central/local units) attached?	☐ Yes ☐ No
A3	BC and CoA data structures (all segments+lengths) attached?	☐ Yes ☐ No
A4	Technical report on countrywide network connectivity options attached?	☐ Yes ☐ No
A5	List of all central and local office locations (nodes) to be connected through a secure countrywide network attached?	☐ Yes ☐ No
A6	List of estimated # of system users for each node?	☐ Yes ☐ No
A7	List of estimated workload of each node (# of reports; number of revenue and expenditure transactions per year; daily maximums) attached?	☐ Yes ☐ No
A8	Organizational diagram of the MoF/Treasury IT Department (indicating the number of specialists at central/local units) attached?	☐ Yes ☐ No
A9	Documents on related projects attached?	☐ Yes ☐ No

Notes

1. Public Expenditure Management-Peer Assisted Learning (PEM-PAL) Group (estimated in 2005).
2. Ali Hashim and Allister J. Moon, "Treasury Diagnostic Toolkit," World Bank Working Paper No. 19, 2004.
3. **Client mode:** Treasury sends daily payment requests to the Central Bank, which executes all payments through EPS and returns detailed daily statements from RTGS/ACH. **Correspondent mode:** Treasury is a participant in the EPS to execute all payments directly through a secure link and can get the detailed TSA statements online.
4. **EBFs:** Extra-budgetary funds (e.g., health/social insurance), for which transactions are not directly passed through the Treasury system. EBFs usually operate under separate budget preparation and execution procedures, with their own chart of accounts, and may undermine accuracy and transparency of the financial accounts.
5. **FMIS:** Financial Management Information System (F) usually includes Budget Preparation (B) and Execution (T) capabilities as core modules, sharing an integrated PFM database. Even if B and T exist as separate systems, please consider them as two main components of FMIS. In this questionnaire, Treasury System means the Budget Execution system (T) only.

Appendix C. Use of Electronic Payment Systems and Digital Signature in FMIS Projects

Due to growing interest in using EPS and Digital Signature (DS) applications effectively in daily Treasury/FMIS operations, a workshop was organized as a part of the PEM-PAL Treasury Community of Practice (TCoP) activities in Chisinau in May 2010.

Two survey forms prepared for the TCoP workshop are presented below to highlight some of the key aspects of EPS and DS in the Treasury/FMIS operations of 14 participating ECA countries (AL, AM, AZ, GE, KG, KV, KZ, MD, ME, RU, SI, TJ, TR, and UZ). Workshop presentations and survey results can be found at the PEM-PAL Web site. Some background information to clarify the terminology used in the EPS and DS survey forms is presented later in this section.

Electronic Payment Systems

#	Electronic Payment System (EPS)	Responses	
1	MoU signed with the Central Bank for TSA and EPS operations?	☐ Yes	☐ No
2	A Treasury unit responsible for managing electronic payments?	☐ Yes	☐ No
3	Is there a secure office space suitable for EPS operations?	☐ Yes	☐ No
4	Number of authorized and trained MoF/Treasury personnel working at EPS:	Manager: _____ Staff: _____	
5	A secure network (VPN) connection for TSA/EPS operations? VPN software: _____	☐ Yes	☐ No
6	Dedicated servers with full redundancy and backup solutions?	☐ Yes	☐ No
7	Payments to beneficiaries: Directly or Indirectly (through the Bank accounts of related public entities or spending units)?	☐ Directly	☐ Indirectly
8	Average number of payments/day for central/local budgets:	Central: _____ Regional/Local: _____ Other: _____	
9	Coverage of daily payments for central/local budget via EPS (%):	Central: _____ % Regional/Local: _____ % Other: _____ %	
	**Questions below are expected to be answered together with the TSA operator (e.g., Central Bank)**		
10	How many commercial banks are using the EPS?	# of banks: _____	
11	How many commercial banks are involved in TSA operations? Total number of bank branches participating in TSA?	# of banks: _____ # of branches: _____	
12	How many commercial banks provide on-line (Internet) banking?	# of banks: _____	
13	Is there a high-value payment system (**RTGS**[a])?	☐ Yes	☐ No
14	- If Yes, RTGS system established on?	RTGS estd on: yyyy / mm / dd	
15	- Total number of RTGS transactions per year?	RTGS trans/yr: _____	
16	- Total number of RTGS TSA transactions per year?	RTGS TSA tr/yr: _____	
17	- Maximum number of RTGS TSA transactions per day?	RTGS TSA max/day: _____	
18	Is there a low-value payment system (**ACH**[b])?	☐ Yes	☐ No

(Continued)

Electronic Payment Systems (*Continued*)

#	Electronic Payment System (EPS)	Responses	
19	- If yes, ACH system established on?	ACH estd on: yyyy / mm / dd	
20	- Total number of ACH transactions per year?	ACH trans/yr: _____	
21	- Total number of ACH TSA transactions per year?	ACH TSA tr/yr: _____	
22	- Maximum number of ACH TSA transactions per day?	ACH TSA max/day: _____	
23	EPS communicate/compatible with TARGET2?[c]	☐ Yes	☐ No
24	EPS communicate/compatible with EBA[d] clearing systems?	☐ Yes	☐ No
25	Electronic file exchange based on XML[e] format? If No, Format: _____	☐ Yes	☐ No
26	Exchange of financial information based on SWIFT[f] platform? If No, Platform: _____	☐ Yes	☐ No
27	Using IBAN[g] for domestic/international bank account numbers?	☐ Yes	☐ No

	Digital Signature		
#	Digital Signature	Responses	
1	Law on DS?	☐ Yes	☐ No
2	- If Yes, the dates of approval + last revision of the DS Law #: _____	Approved on: yyyy / mm / dd Last revision: yyyy / mm / dd	
3	Is there a public entity responsible from DS implementation? - If Yes, DS Entity: _____	☐ Yes	☐ No
4	Is DS mandatory in some of the Treasury operations? - If Yes, which services: _____	☐ Yes	☐ No
5	Total number of MoF/Treasury staff using DS in operations?	Staff using DS: _____	
6	Total number of financial transactions signed by using DS/year?	DS usage/yr : _____	
Please skip the questions below if the DS and PKI are not currently used in public or private sector			
7	Is there a PKI[h] infrastructure to support DS applications? - If Yes, PKI software: _____	☐ Yes	☐ No
8	Is there wireless PKI support in the system?	☐ Yes	☐ No
9	Is there a root CA?[i] - If Yes, URL of root CA: _____	☐ Yes	☐ No
10	Are there licensed CAs? - If Yes, number of licensed CAs: _____	☐ Yes	☐ No
11	Are there private CAs? - If Yes, number of private CAs: _____	☐ Yes	☐ No
12	Number of certificates issued by the root CA to date:	Public Sector: _____ Private Sector: _____	
13	Number of certificates issued by the licensed CAs to date:	Public Sector: _____ Private Sector: _____	
14	If CA is not used, other solutions to provide "trust" in PKI?	☐ Web of Trust ☐ Simple PKI ☐ Other (specify): _____	

(Continued)

Electronic Payment Systems (*Continued*)

#	Digital Signature	Responses		
15	Hash function used for DS?	Hash function: _____		
16	Preferred symmetric key techniques (3DES, AES, RC5, etc)?	Symmetric: _____		
17	Preferred asymmetric key techniques (RSA, ECC, DSS, etc)?	Asymmetric: _____		
18	Validity period (years) of public key certificates used in DS:	Root CA: _____ yrs Licensed CA: _____ yrs User: _____ yrs		
19	Key length (bit) of public key certificates used in DS:	Root CA: _____ bit Licensed CA: _____ bit User: _____ bit		

a. **RTGS:** Real Time Gross Settlement system
b. **ACH:** Automated Clearinghouse system
c. **TARGET2:** Trans-European Automated Real-Time Gross Settlement Express Transfer system of the EU Central Banks
d. **EBA:** Euro Banking Assoc (Euro-1 clearing system; Step-1 cross border retail payment; Step-2 pan-European ACH)
e. **XML:** eXtended Markup Language
f. **SWIFT:** The Society for Worldwide Interbank Financial Telecommunications
g. **IBAN:** International Bank Account Number
h. **PKI:** Public Key Infrastructure
i. **CA:** Certificate Authority

Electronic Payment Systems

EPS or EFT operates on the basis of two systems (Figure C.1):

■ The *clearing house system* is where transactions between members of a clearing channel are recorded.

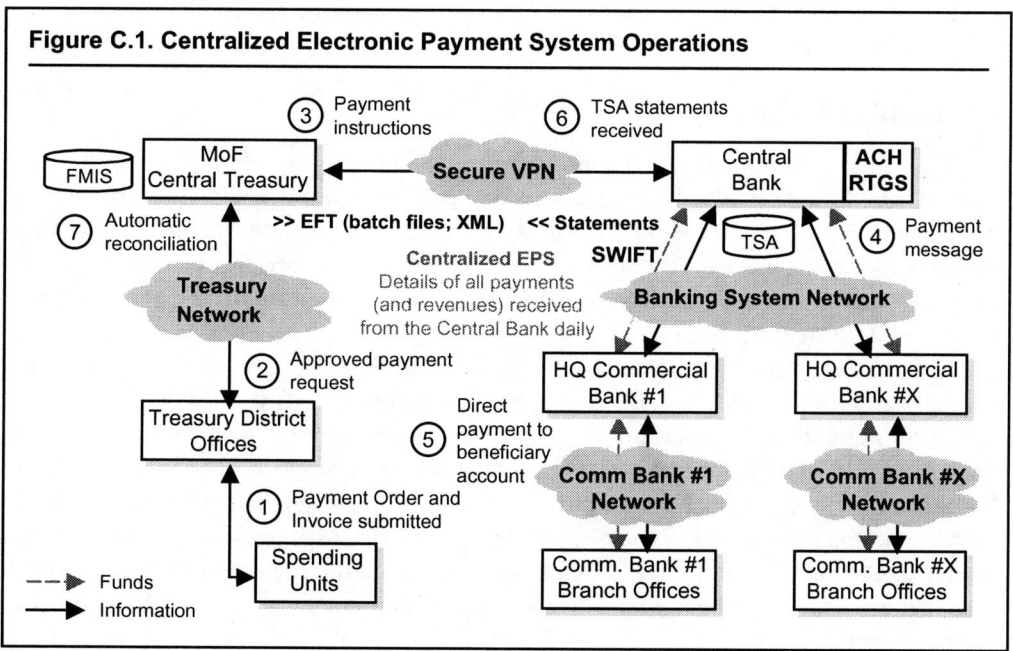

Figure C.1. Centralized Electronic Payment System Operations

■ *Settlement* is the transferring of funds from a payer's account to a payee's account. This can only occur between banks. The Central Bank of each country usually acts as the primary settlement agent. Settlement can occur immediately on a gross basis or be delayed on a net basis.

Real-Time Gross Settlement (RTGS) systems are funds transfer systems where transfer of money takes place from one bank to another on a "real-time" and "gross" basis. Settlement in real time means payment transaction is not subjected to any waiting period. The transactions are settled as soon as they are processed. "Gross settlement" means the transaction is settled on one to one basis without bunching or netting with any other transaction. Once processed, payments are final and irrevocable. In terms of liquidity and systemic risks, high-value payment systems (RTGS) are the most important due to the large value and time sensitive nature of the payments. RTGS solutions are mostly implemented by the central banks. The private sector clearing houses use an RTGS model similar to the Clearing House Interbank Payment System (CHIPS).

The Automated Clearing House (ACH) system has been developed as a low-value payment system. It processes large volumes of credit and debit transactions in batches and at low cost. ACH credit transactions include payroll, pension, and annuity payments. ACH debit transactions include consumer bill payments, such as utility bills, phone bills, and insurance premiums. It is mainly operated by the central banks. In some countries, the ACH systems are privately owned and operated but authorized and regulated by the central banks.

The Society for Worldwide Interbank Financial Telecommunications (SWIFT) is a global telecommunications network. It provides a strict message format for the exchange of financial information between financial institutions. Messages automatically pass through electronic links built between SWIFT and the local electronic clearing systems in different countries. More recently, SWIFT has been applied to the transferring of the entire letter of credit process onto the Internet and providing Web-based functionality for business-to-business (B2B) transactions with SWIFTNet.

What is Digital Signature?

A DS[1] (digital signature scheme) is a mathematical scheme for demonstrating the authenticity and integrity of a digital message or document. A valid digital signature gives a recipient reason to believe that the message was created by a known sender, and that it was not altered in transit. Digital signatures are commonly used for software distribution, financial transactions, and in other cases where it is important to detect forgery and tampering (Figure C.2).

The message to be signed is first *hashed* to produce a short digest that is then signed. Digital signatures employ a type of *asymmetric cryptography* (Rivest, Shamir Adleman (RSA), Elliptic Curve Cryptography (ECC), Digital Signature Standard (DSS), etc.), where the key used to encrypt a message is not the same as the key used to decrypt it. Each user has a pair of cryptographic keys—a public key and a private key. The private key is kept secret, whereas the public key may be widely distributed. Messages are encrypted with the recipient's public key and can only be decrypted with the corresponding private key. The keys are related mathematically, but the private key cannot be feasibly derived from the public key.

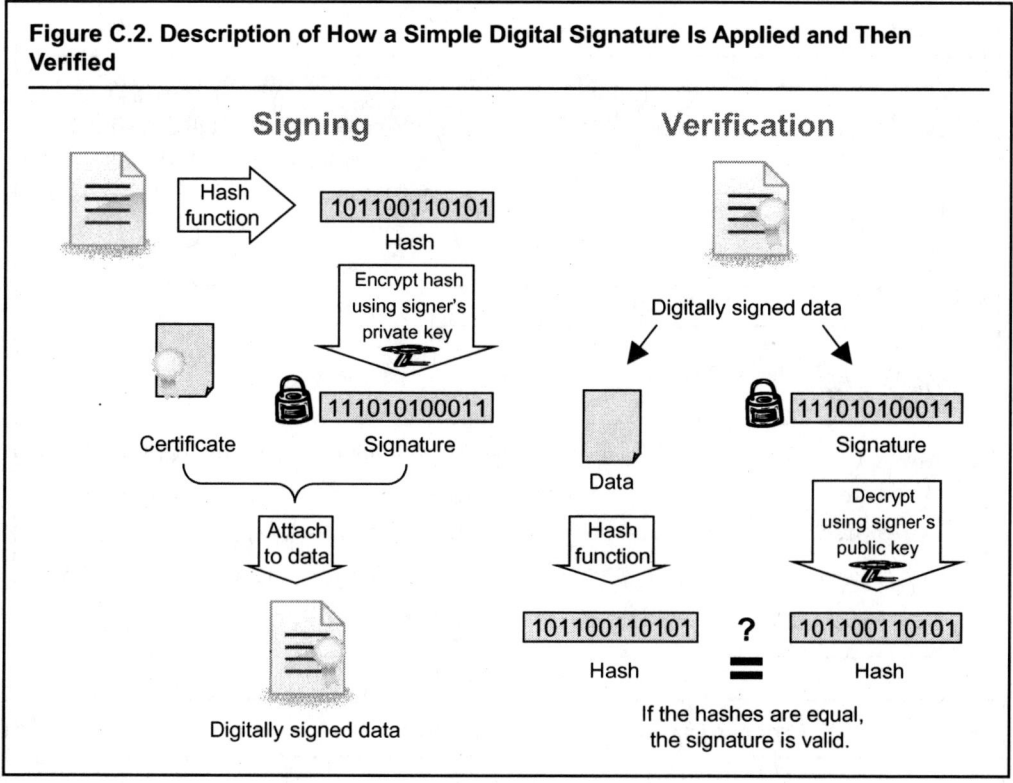

Figure C.2. Description of How a Simple Digital Signature Is Applied and Then Verified

What is Electronic Signature?

An Electronic Signature (ES) is any legally recognized electronic means that indicates that a person adopts the contents of an electronic message. In most ES applications, there is no cryptographic assurance of the sender's identity, and no integrity check on the text received. Popular ES standards include the OpenPGP supported by Pretty Good Privacy (PGP) and Gnu Privacy Guard (GnuPG), and some of the Secure/Multipurpose Internet Mail Extension (S/MIME) Internet Engineering Task Force (IETF) standards.

Digital signatures are often used to implement ES, but not all ES use DS (see Figure C.3). In some countries, including the United States and members of the European Union,[2] ES have legal significance. However, laws concerning ES do not always make clear whether they are digital cryptographic signatures.

What is Public Key Infrastructure?

Public Key Infrastructure (PKI)[3] is a suite of hardware, software, people, policies and procedures needed to create, manage, distribute, use, store, and revoke public key certificates in order to provide "trust" for secure electronic communications and transactions in open environments (Figure C.4). For each user, the user identity, the public key, their binding, validity conditions and other attributes are made unforgeable in digital certificates issued by the CA. Main PKI components are as follows:

- **Certification Authority** (CA): Generates digital certificates (i.e., signing people's public key and identity information with its own private key). The user identity must be unique within each CA domain.

Figure C.3. Electronic vs. Digital Signature

ES vs. DS	Electronic Signature	Digital Signature
Concept	Electronic data as an identifier	Digital signature using asymmetric encryption/decryption method 1359829394897765839 1929393923939239239 4929495993593953 9994304938455490594 4939523489843485755 8
Problem	Reusable	Impossible to reuse

No forgery	Can't make a signed document without a private key
No modification	Can't modify the signed document without the private key
Entity authentication	The private key holder is the maker of the document
No reuse	Can't substitute the digital signature of "A" document to "B"
Nonrepudiation	Can't repudiate signing of the private key holder

(Encryption/decryption type: RSA, DSS (Digital Signature Standard), ESIGN, Schnorr, KCDSA)

Source: Electronic Payment System in Korea

Figure C.4. PKI Process to Issue Digital Certificates

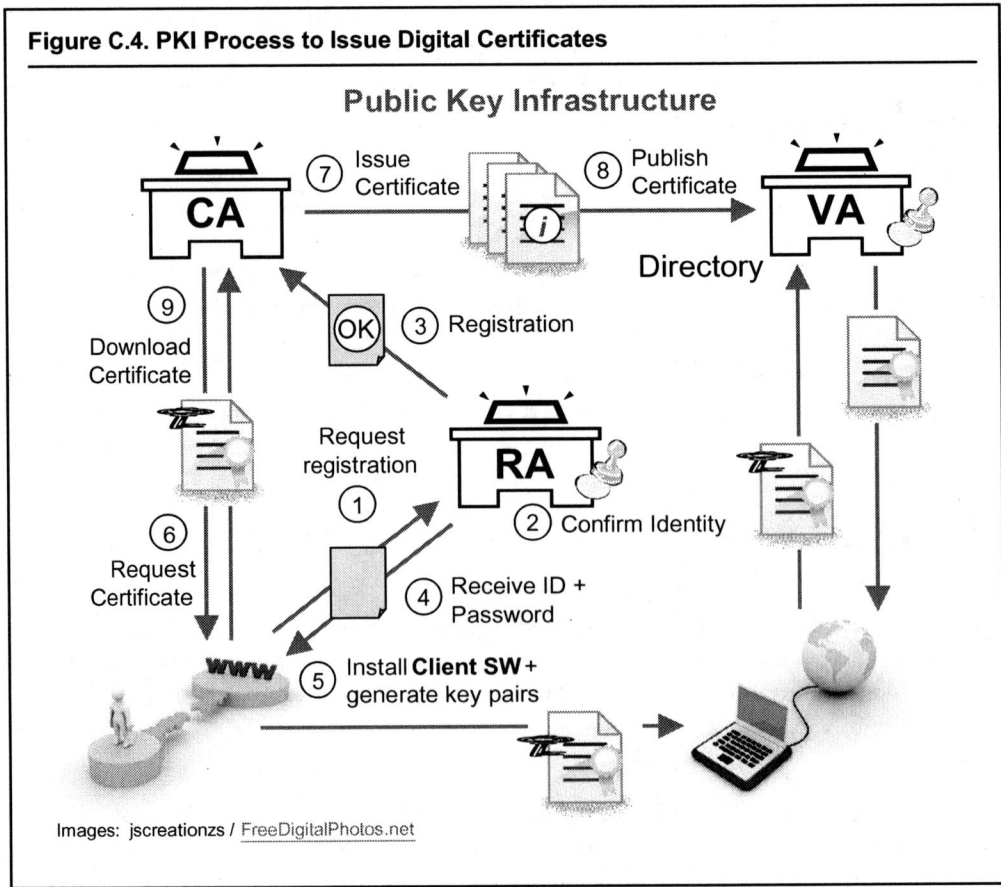

Images: jscreationzs / FreeDigitalPhotos.net

- **Registration Authority** (RA): Verifies identity and associates that identity with their public key.
- **Validation Authority** (VA) or **Directory**: Confirms whether a specific certificate produced by this CA is still valid or not (e.g., lost or compromised private keys, or change of information contained).
- **Client Software:** Generates public and private key pairs.

PKI provides:

- Strong *authentication* through use of *digital certificates*
- Privacy and data integrity through use of *encryption*
- *Non-repudiation* through the use of digital signatures

When deploying a PKI, organizations can choose between purchasing standalone PKI systems for in-house deployment (build) and outsourcing an integrated PKI platform (buy).

PKI solutions provide public keys and bindings to user identities which are used for encryption and/or sender authentication of e-mail messages, documents, users' access to applications, secure communication, and mobile signatures (mobile signatures are electronic signatures that are created using a mobile device and rely on signature or certification services in a location-independent telecom environment).

Notes

1. Wikipedia: Digital Signature
2. EU: Community Framework for Electronic Signatures
3. Wikipedia: Public Key Infrastructure

Appendix D. Procurement Options for the Implementation of FMIS Solutions

In World Bank–funded FMIS projects, International Competitive Bidding (ICB) procedure is followed for the procurement of required Information and Communication Technology (ICT) solutions.

The technical implementation of (T/F) systems includes the following ICT components:

[0] Establishment of countrywide network connections (physical communication lines, usually as a government contribution),

[1] Development of Web-based ASW, mostly as a combination of customized COTS + LDSW to cover all FMIS needs,

[2] Installation of central servers (database & application servers) and data storage units required for the ASW (at the main system center and business continuity center),

[3] Installation of standard field hardware (servers, user workstations, and peripherals) in central and field offices, and

[4] Installation of active/passive network equipment, system and user management tools, and engineering support solutions.

In most of the projects, three variants are visible for the design of procurement (ICB) packages related to the FMIS ICT solutions:

Option 1: **A single responsibility contract (two-stage ICB)**
One ICB package covering the implementation of all ICT components [1]+[2]+[3]+[4].

Option 2: **Two contracts LINKED with each other:**
ICB-1: Two-stage ICB for the development of application software [1], including the demonstration of proposed ASW.
ICB-2: One-stage ICB for the installation of all hardware and network equipment [2]+[3]+[4].
In this case, implementation of [2] depends on the inputs to be provided by ASW developer [1] to ensure compatible central server solutions, and there is a delay in the initiation of ICB-2 due to this linkage.

Option 3: **Two separate INDEPENDENT contracts:**
ICB-1: Two-stage ICB for the development of ASW and installation of central hardware [1]+[2] with demonstration of proposed ASW + servers during the first stage.

ICB-2: One-stage ICB for the installation of standard field hardware, engineering support systems and network equipment [3]+[4].

The preferences of ECA countries in completed/active FMIS projects are shown below:

Option 1: Georgia (F), Moldova (F), Tajikistan (F) [planned]
Option 2: Albania (T), Azerbaijan (T), Russian Federation (T)
Option 3: Kyrgyz Republic (T/F), Ukraine (F)

Figure D.1 presents the key steps and linkages of these procurement options.

Suggestions to improve the design of FMIS procurement packages:

■ It is advisable to have two separate independent ICB packages (Option 3) to reduce the time and complexity of ICT implementation. Another possibility is to use Option 1 for a well-defined and relatively small scale implementation of the Treasury/FMIS solutions.

■ All "mandatory" requirements should to be met for the selection of a supplier. Technical evaluation/merit points should be considered only when there is a need to define and evaluate "desirable" requirements to add value to existing mandatory requirements.

■ In FMIS projects where the technical requirements are well defined, the weight of price should be kept as high as possible (80% or more) to benefit from the competition in reducing the bid price while ensuring the delivery of good-quality ICT solutions based on mandatory requirements. The weight of technical evaluation for desirable features can be up to 20%, if there is a need to consider some optional high value technical requirements in addition to mandatory conditions.

■ Warranty period is usually three years for all ICT components starting from the final operational acceptance of the while T/F system. Post-warranty period is usually two years, starting from the end of the warranty period. The Supply and Installation (S&I) cost usually covers the full cost of warranty period for all ICT components including parts included maintenance, as well as free support and upgrades of all software solutions. Such details can be included in the cost table "Table 2.5: Supply and Installation Table" within the bidding document to clarify the unit price of various components.

■ The definition of RC needs to be clarified in the bidding documents. Items that can be considered "recurrent," such as additional annual technical support, software upgrade needs, and relevant hardware expansions, should be identified clearly. Services that may be required to implement additional capabilities, expansion of hardware capacity to cover additional scope are not recurrent in nature. Also, telecommunication service charges cannot be included, as these are usually paid from the state budget under a network service contract.

It should be remembered that, in case RC are listed in the bidding document, all relevant items included in "Table 2.6: Recurrent Cost Table" in the bidding document need to be evaluated together with the Supply and Installation cost and will be a part of the contractual commitment of the Supplier. The Bank funds can be used to cover S&I + Warranty costs only, whereas the RC should be funded from the Purchaser's budget. In such cases, a clear commitment of the Purchaser is needed for necessary RC funding.

Alternatively, the Recurrent Costs can be excluded from the bid, by stating this clearly in Section VI, Clause 7.3. In this case, there is no need to specify any item in Table 2.6 and recurrent costs are not considered during bid evaluation.

■ FMIS licensing requirements can be simplified under the special conditions of contract as follows:

The Purchaser will have the right to define unlimited number of FMIS users with specific roles and responsibilities. However, only X system users will have the right for simultaneous (concurrent) access to any Application Software module at any time, using

Figure D.1. Procurement Options for the Implementation of FMIS ICT Solutions

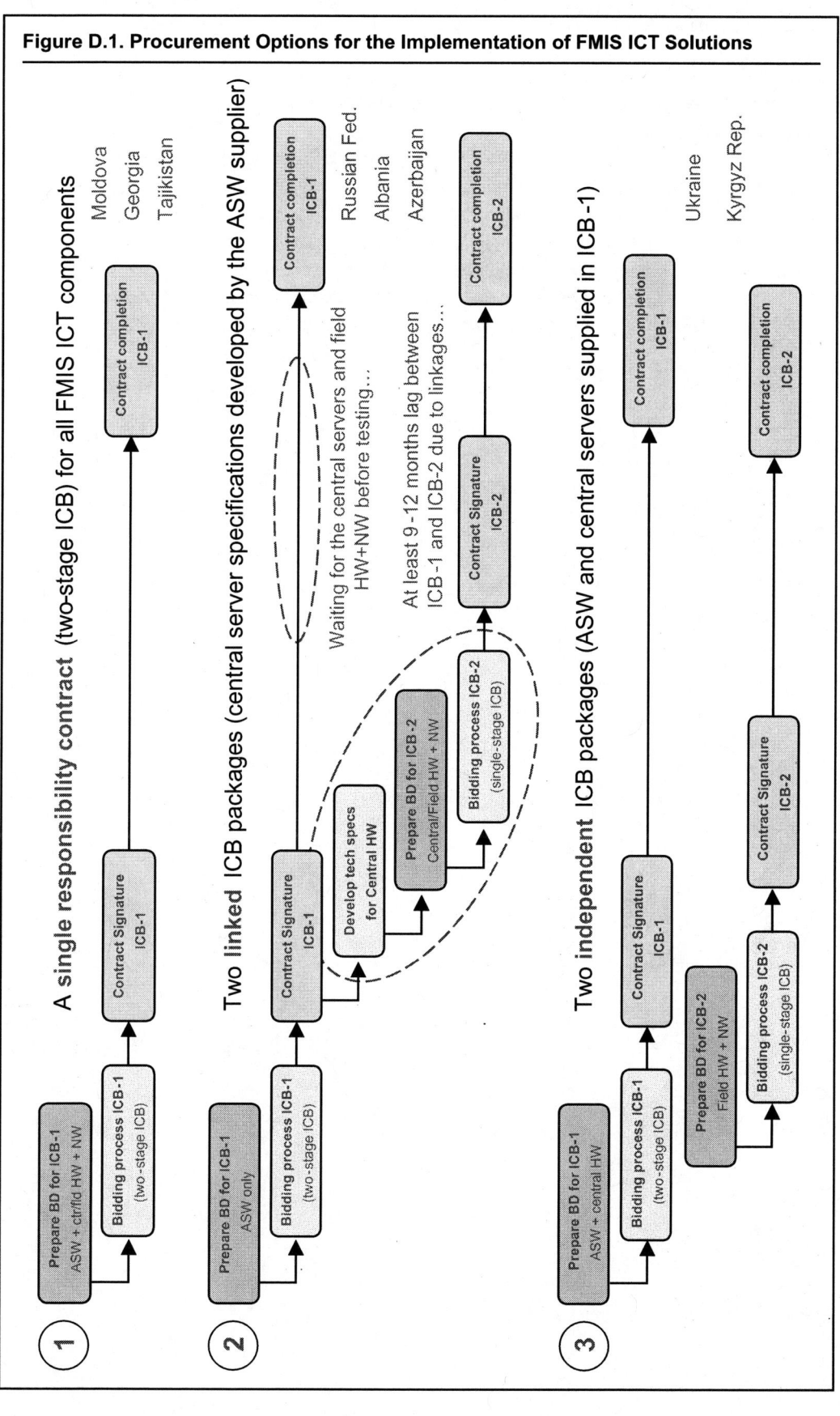

the licenses provided by the Supplier according to the contract. The FMIS concurrent user licenses shall be perpetual.

The Purchaser may request additional concurrent user licenses (up to Y additional licenses), if necessary. For additional concurrent user licensing needs, the rates (unit prices) as specified in the Supplier's Bid (Table 2.5, Supply and Installation Cost Table) will be used and a separate contract will be signed for such optional items.

There won't be any user license fee for Web Portal, web publishing, custom/LDSW modules or for external users accessing the FMIS modules through a web portal. The Web portal should provide secure authorized access to unlimited number of users for PFM needs.

Appendix E. Progressive Development of FMIS in Guatemala and Nicaragua

The development of FMIS solutions in more than 10 Latin American countries has been achieved in consecutive steps, starting with the implementation of core Treasury/FMIS solution at the MoF central organization and then gradually expanding the core system to other line ministries, and finally to their district/local offices through 3 or 4 projects. Two country cases are summarized below to explain such progressive FMIS development efforts in Guatemala and Nicaragua.

Development of SIAF in Guatemala

Guatemala SIAF Development	SIAF I—Integrated Fin Mgmt Prj P007213 1995–99	SIAF II—Integrated Fin Mgmt Prj II P048657 1997–2002	SIAF III—Integrated Fin Mgmt Prj III P066175 2002–08	SIAF III—Additional Financing P106993 2009–11
PFM Functionality	**SICOIN** (Integrated Accounting Module) for Central Gov: budget authorizations + treasury + accounting	**SICOIN** for Central Gov: budgeting + accounting + treasury Integration of **decentralized entities** and **state enterprises**. **SICOIN** rollout to all Central Gov entities **SICOIN** integrated w/ banking system Project management system (**SIGEPRO**) Development and roll out of the **budget formulation** module	Transition to Web-based platforms **SIGES** Mgmt Module for committed + actual expenditures **SIAFMUNI** for local gov **Wage Bill** module and personnel registry for the Central Gov **GUATECOMPRAS** for public procurement **SIGES** registers purchases orders and links purchased goods with inventory module **SIAFMUNI** for PEM needs of municipal gov Transparency portal based on **SICOIN**	Consolidation of the web-based **SICOIN** Consolidation of the **Wage Bill** module **GUATECOMPRAS** for electronic tenders submission (paperless) **SIGES** infra contracts module aligned to GUATECOMPRAS Web platform for local governments (**SICOINGL**) to support the PFM of municipal governments (income from cadastre fees, water, electricity, disputes, taxpayers current account)
Interfaces with other systems	None	**SIGADE** (the debt management system DMFAS, developed by UNCTAD) for external debt mgmt. The internal debt is managed by the Central Bank through an in-house developed SW TIN (tax payer identification number) validation managed by the SAT which is	**SIGADE** (External Debt System) version 5.3 SAT TIN validation SIGES—SICOIN Wage Bill linked with SIGES, SICOIN & SAT GUATECOMPRAS—BANCASAT RETENIVA (withholding VAT system) SICOINWEB linked w/ Min of Health & public	SICIONGL—SIAFMUNI SEGEPLAN (**SNIP**) Public Investment Mgmt Banking system for taxes and municipal fees Wage Bill—Social Security systems SIGES—SAT Central Bank: online cash monitoring

(Continued)

Development of SIAF in Guatemala (*Continued*)

Guatemala SIAF Development	SIAF I—Integrated Fin Mgmt Prj P007213 1995–99	SIAF II—Integrated Fin Mgmt Prj II P048657 1997–2002	SIAF III—Integrated Fin Mgmt Prj III P066175 2002–08	SIAF III—Additional Financing P106993 2009–11
		the integrated Tax and Customs administration	enterp-decentr mgmt systems SIAFMUNI—Comptroller's Office	Online monitoring of the account balances and electronic statements for all public accounts
Scope	Central Government entities comprising the overall ministries and secretaries	Central Gov entities Incorporation of decentralized and autonomous entities, and state enterprises	Central Gov entities Incorporation of local governments. Wage Bill management module	Consolidation of the previous phases + municipal enterprises & the financial system
Single Treasury Account (STA)	In 1997 the Treasury office cleaned up and closed the Central Gov entities' commercial banks accounts in order to consolidate a Common Fund through the creation of a STA at the Central Bank in accordance with the national Constitution	STA for the Central Gov at the Central Bank to manage the revenue collection of both taxes and non-taxes sources Payments are done by electronic transfers from the STA to the beneficiaries' accounts at the banking system	Consolidation of the STA (registry of all current designated accounts and the commercial banks submit all transactions electronically) Using digital signature to proceed with payments Entities can authorize electronic transfers to the vendors' bank accounts.	Incorporation into the STA of loans, credits, and grants balances Direct payment orders from the STA to vendors with contracts financed by loans and grants
Unified Chart of accounts	Unified charts of accounts for Central Gov (conceptualization, definition, and implementation)	Unified charts of accounts for Central Gov plus decentralized institutions (maintenance and update)	Unified charts of accounts for Central Gov, decentralized institutions and local governments (maintenance and update)	Unified charts of accounts for Central Gov, decentralized inst and local gov (new concept and design for Central Gov)
Improved budget classification	The Organic Budged Law (decree 101–97): Budget classification should be based on programmatic basis New Manual of Budget Classification: Institutional, geographic, object and functions, type of expenditure, financing source, economic classification for revenues and expenditures and by object as well.	Incorporation of the physical monitoring module to monitor institutional goals Implementation of the metrics classification module Introduction of the Budget Manual for formulating, modifying, and executing to the overall Central Gov and decentralized entities Strengthening of the budget quarterly financial programming	Budget classification manual is updated online Incorporating the budget goals and indicators module Inst budget classific updated in accordance to the IMF 2001 guidelines Redefine Central Gov and decentr entities with data mining (since 1998) Flagship of the prioritized government programs Multi-year budget formulation methodology	Revised institutional, functional, and object classifications were incorporated in accordance to the IMF 2001 guidelines New function class and adaptation of the expenditure matrix Implement dynamic classification to monitor programs, entities and expenditure vehicles such as the trust funds Implementation of the public investment module

(*Continued*)

Development of SIAF in Guatemala (Continued)

Guatemala SIAF Development	SIAF I—Integrated Fin Mgmt Prj P007213 1995–99	SIAF II—Integrated Fin Mgmt Prj II P048657 1997–2002	SIAF III—Integrated Fin Mgmt Prj III P066175 2002–08	SIAF III—Additional Financing P106993 2009–11
Coverage of budget expenditures	Central Gov exp registry for budget, accounting and treasury transactions Spending Unit registry using SIAFITO Payments by checks to state vendors and public employees	100% Central Gov + 15 auton+decentr entities 70% of payments via electronic transfers to vendors/ public empl 100% of the Central Gov transactions, incl transfers, are registered	SICOINWEB enable the entities operate online in a deconcentrated manner Loans and grants for municipal governments are incorporated to the functionalities of SIAFMUNI and SICOINGL	Incorporation of the financial investments contracts registration and management for municipal governments
Coverage of revenue collection	The SAT was created in 1998. The Treasury office collects all taxes and duties payments through designated accounts in the banking system where taxpayers present their declarations.	Commercial banks submit to SICOIN daily rev collection (text files) The BANCASAT system is used by the SAT for tax payments (70% of tax payments are through web-based BANCASA)	Commercial banks submit all the information in XML format to the SICOIN system (tax + non-tax rev). The STA cash flow planning improved significantly	Real-time cons bw Central Bank & SICOIN All accounts are monitored online through SICOIN The Treasury office can forecast the STA balances daily
Technology architecture	Client-server with decentralized databases in Central Gov Batch consolidation of data using BD ORACLE SIAFITO is based on SYSBASE database (client-server)	Client-server with decentralized databases distributed among the Central Gov entities Central data consolidation in batch by the MoF	Fully Web-based architecture for Central Gov Distributed databases for local governments Web-based systems for wage bill + personnel reg	Fully Web-based architecture for Central Gov Web-based system with a central database for local governments Web-based wage bill + personnel registry
Application Software (ASW)	Locally developed software (SW) based on Oracle Developer Suite (ORACLE forms, ORACLE report, Designer) POWER BUILDER and SYSBASE for the local application	Locally developed SW based on Developer Suite (ORACLE forms, ORACLE report, Designer) BD manager: ORACLE DB 7.3.4 for the central application and decentralized entities	Locally developed SW based on .NET Developer Suite. MYSQL for local governments. DB manager: ORACLE standard for Central Gov and decentralized entities CRYSTAL reports	Locally developed SW based on .NET, Visual Basic, ORACLE standard data base manager. AJAX technology. CRYSTAL reports
ASW Developer	In-house SW dev by the SICSYM; local indiv cons for system admin	In-house SW dev by indiv consultants and few international ones	In-house SW development by indiv local consultants	In-house SW development by local individual consultants
Warranty	NA	NA	NA	NA
Number of Offices Connected	5 pilot entities for SICOIN	45 Central Gov entities for SICION	396 Central Gov (CG) exec units, auton+decentr entities (DE), and SoEs.	Goal: 500 Centr Gov exec units, auton+dec ent, and SoEs.

(Continued)

Development of SIAF in Guatemala (*Continued*)

Guatemala SIAF Development	SIAF I—Integrated Fin Mgmt Prj P007213 1995–99	SIAF II—Integrated Fin Mgmt Prj II P048657 1997–2002	SIAF III—Integrated Fin Mgmt Prj III P066175 2002–08	SIAF III—Additional Financing P106993 2009–11
	40 Central Gov entities for SIAFITO		326 municipal gov connected to SIAFMUNI 7 municipal gov (the major ones) connected to the SICOINWEB	284 municipal gov connected to SICOINGL 7 municipal gov (the major ones) connected to the SICOINWEB
Number of system users	300 approx	2,000 approx	SICOINWEB: 3,636 CG SICOINWEB: 3,874 DE SIGES: 4,093 SICOINGL:1,549 GUATENOMINAS (Wage Bill): 1,000 GUATECOMPRAS (Procurement): 4,000 SIAFMUNI: 2,000 SICOINGL: 70	SICOINWEB: 3,800 CG SICOINWEB: 3,900 DE SIGES: 5,000 SICOINGL:1,800 GUATENOMINAS (Wage Bill): 1,600 GUATECOMPRAS (Procurement):4,500 SICOINGL: 2,500
Number of Concurrent users	100 approximately	900 approximately	SICOINWEB: 2,200 CG SICOINWEB: 2,100 DE SIGES: 1,300 GUATENOMINAS (Wage Bill): 504 GUATECOMPRAS (Procurement): 800 SICOINGL: 50	SICOINWEB: 2,601 CG SICOINWEB: 2,371 DE SIGES: 1,336 GUATENOMINAS (Wage Bill): 600 GUATECOMPRAS (Procurement): 1,000 SICOINGL:1,800
ITC Capacity	Analyst/Progr: 8 NW/Telco mgr: 1 Technical support 2: DB administrator: 2 National Director: 1 Int'l consultants: 11	Analyst/Progr: 20 NW/Telco mgr: 1 Technical support 2: DB administrator: 2 National Director: 1 Int'l consultants: 2	Analyst/Progr: 30 NW/Telco mgr: 1 Technical support 2: DB administrator: 2 National Director: 1 Int'l consultants: 1	Analyst/Progr: 35 NW/Telco mgr:1 Technical support 2: DB administrator: 3 National Director: 1
Any IT Assessment/ Audit	Operational audit to the systems performed by specialized firms hired by the project	Operational audit to the systems performed by specialized firms hired by the project	Operational audit to the systems performed by specialized firms hired by the project	Operational audit to the systems performed by specialized firms hired by the project
Completion level	Central implementation at the Central Gov	Implementation of the budget formulation, execution and accounting modules in the overall Central Gov entities	Implementation of the Treasury, Accounting, Budget formulation and execution modules in the overall Central	Integrated administrative and financial system operating in a deconcentrated

(*Continued*)

Development of SIAF in Guatemala (*Continued*)

Guatemala SIAF Development	SIAF I—Integrated Fin Mgmt Prj P007213 1995–99	SIAF II—Integrated Fin Mgmt Prj II P048657 1997–2002	SIAF III—Integrated Fin Mgmt Prj III P066175 2002–08	SIAF III—Additional Financing P106993 2009–11
			Gov entities, decentralized and local governments	manner at the Central Gov & Decentr Entities
Business continuity solutions	Backup on tapes containing the database and applications saved at the Central Bank	Backup on tapes containing the database and applications saved at the Central Bank	Continuity alternative site (10 minutes to replicate)	Continuity alternative site (10 minutes to replicate)
Project prep period (month)	13	6	24	12
Donor funds	None	None	None	None
Total cost of project ($M)	10.3	17.5	33.2	20.5
WB funds ($M)	9.4	15.7	29.7	20 (14.0 SIAF + 6.0 SAG)
Cost of SIAF IT component	5.6	7.6	NA	NA
Government funding ($M)	0.6	0.3	0.49	0.54
Avg time for procurement	NA	NA	NA	NA
Duration of SIAF IT impl	12 months	6 months	18 months (01.01.2003–06.30.2004)	12 months

Development of FMIS in Nicaragua

Nicaragua FMIS Development	IDC—Institutional Dev Credit P035080 1996–99	EMTAC—Economic Mgmt TA P049296 1999–2004	PSTAC—Public Sector TA Credit P078891 2004–09	Proposed Project P111795 2010–14
PFM Functionality	Central Budget, Accounting and Treasury management based on an application provided by the Argentinean government, free of charge. Ad-hoc Budget Formulation capability.	Intranet application for Central Budget, Accounting and Treasury management including the use of revolving funds plus specific module for Budget Formulation at spending unit (SU) level. Wage bill management for treasury funds.	Central government Budget (incl budget formulation and execution at SU level, MTBF, physical execution for infrastructure projects, and municipal transfer application TRANSMUNI) Accounting (incl the Investment-Saving Account consolidation)	New FMIS covering all core PFM functions for central government and decentralized agencies.

(*Continued*)

Development of FMIS in Nicaragua (*Continued*)

Nicaragua FMIS Development	IDC—Institutional Dev Credit P035080 1996–99	EMTAC—Economic Mgmt TA P049296 1999–2004	PSTAC—Public Sector TA Credit P078891 2004–09	Proposed Project P111795 2010–14
		Ad-hoc Budget Formulation capability.	and Treasury management (incl improvements for revolving funds, payment planning, monthly cash plan, and electronic transfers). Separate application for decentralized entities.	
Interfaces with other systems	None	None	Public Debt at conceptual level. Public Investment SNIP fully operational. HR Mgmt System and Public Procurement (both partially impl, manually integrated). Internal Revenue fully operational. Asset Mgmt System for Public Real Estate Properties (fully implemented at Central Government).	System capable to fully interoperate with other public sector information systems.
Scope	Ministry of Finance Directorates	Central Government agencies	Central Government agencies operating on line, and decentralized agencies registering post transactions.	Central Government at all Spending Unit levels.
Single Treasury Account functionality	Partially implemented (initial effort to concentrate over revenues)	Limited development and implementation for earmarked incomes to finance expenditures of Central Gov agencies.	Partial implementation of STA and EFT for Central Gov Expenditures (20% of Spending Units)	STA for all financial sources of Central Government agencies.
Unified Chart of Accounts	Implementation of a single Chart of Accounts for Central Government agencies.	Consolidation of the single Chart of Accounts for Central Government agencies.	Consolidation of the single Chart of Accounts for Central Government agencies.	Unified Chart of Accounts for the whole public sector.
Budget Classification	Budget classification, manuals and tables for budget consolidation purposes.	The budget classification remains with minor changes.	The budget classification remains including new manuals for the annual budget consolidation under the MTBF approach.	Standard budget classification for budget consolidation of the overall public sector according to IMF standards.

(Continued)

Development of FMIS in Nicaragua (*Continued*)

Nicaragua FMIS Development	IDC—Institutional Dev Credit P035080 1996–99	EMTAC—Economic Mgmt TA P049296 1999–2004	PSTAC—Public Sector TA Credit P078891 2004–09	Proposed Project P111795 2010–14
Coverage of budget expenditures	Post recording of expenditures by Central Government agencies included in the annual budget.	Online recording of treasury executed funds by Central Government agencies included in the annual budget. Post recording of some external executed funds.	Full recording of treasury as well as external funds by the Central Government agencies included in the annual budget.	Online recording of budgeted expenditures for Central Government agencies.
Coverage of revenue collection	Full coverage for current revenues.	Full coverage for current revenues and earmarked incomes.	Full coverage for current revenues, earmarked incomes, and external grants and credits.	Full coverage for current revenues, earmarked incomes, decentralized collections, and external grants and credits.
Technology Architecture	Client-server platform	Upgraded technological platform (Web-simulated)	Upgraded technological platform (Web-simulated, soon to be discontinued)	Three-tier Web-based platform.
Application Software (ASW)	Adaptation of SIDIFF from Argentina ▨ LDSW on Oracle RDBMS.	Locally developed SW (based on SIAF solution from Guatemala) using Internet developer suite, Oracle forms, Oracle report, Designer. (SW application server Oracle 8.1, database Oracle DB 8.1)	Locally developed SW (Internet Developer suite, Oracle forms, Jdeveloper, Oracle report Designer). Also, Eclipse, CVS (SW application server Oracle 10G, database Oracle DB 10G)	TBD.
ASW developer	International consultant firm and local in-house consultants	International individual consultants and local in-house consultants	Mostly local in-house consultants and fewer international individual consultants	TBD.
Number of offices connected	3 General MoF Directorates	45 Central Government executing units	76 Central Government and Decentralized executing units (38 through Intranet and 38 through VPN)	150 Central Government spending units.
Number of system users	150	1,007	2,832 (SIGFA 1,204; SIGFA-A 295; SISEC 168; SNF 126; SIBE 435; TRANSMUNI 208; SIGFAPRO 324;)	3,000

(Continued)

Development of FMIS in Nicaragua (*Continued*)

Nicaragua FMIS Development	IDC—Institutional Dev Credit P035080 1996–99	EMTAC—Economic Mgmt TA P049296 1999–2004	PSTAC—Public Sector TA Credit P078891 2004–09	Proposed Project P111795 2010–14
Number of concurrent users	60	300	700	1,500
IT Assessment or IT Audit	None	System's audit by specialized firms.	System's audit by specialized firms.	System's audit by specialized firms and certification by the CGR.
Business Continuity Solution	Tape backup of the databases and applications. The backup system consisted of recorded tapes protected in a safe.	Tape backup of the databases and applications. The backup system consisted of recorded tapes protected in safes (Treasury + Central Bank). Weekly information updates and recording of tapes. The tapes for the CB are updated monthly.	Tape backup of the databases and applications. The backup system consisted of recorded tapes protected in safes (Treasury + Central Bank). Weekly information updates and recording of tapes. The tapes for the CB are updated monthly.	Fully redundant facility functioning as a mirror of the main data center.
Project preparation period (months)	12	4	11	10
Total Cost of Project (US$ million)	28.470	22.100	36.200	10.0 (estimated)
Total Cost of FMIS solution (US$ million)	4.613	6.357	1.835	NA

Appendix F. Projects in IDA Countries

International Development Association (IDA) funding has contributed to the design and implementation of Financial Management Information Systems (FMIS) in 27 countries so far. Based on the data available from the FMIS database updated in 2010, there are 46 projects funded through IDA for the development of Treasury System or FMIS (T/F) solutions since 1984 (Table F.1). Twenty-three out of 55 completed projects were in IDA countries (12 completed in Africa). Similarly, 23 out of 32 projects are being implemented in IDA countries (12 active in Africa). Almost 66% of the IDA funding ($747M out of $1,133M) has been allocated to Africa in completed/active FMIS projects so far (Table F.2).

These PFM projects have contributed to the strengthening of capacity in the central government institutions responsible for budget preparation, execution and reporting. The FMIS projects have funded the design and development of information systems to support implementation of PFM reforms, improve transparency, and strengthen the institutional capacity for improving the efficiency of public expenditure management.

Improvements in PFM practices and efficiency gains observed in Burkina Faso, Sierra Leone, Uganda and Zambia are examples of these contributions. Despite these, Africa has the highest rate of failure in FMIS projects (4 out of 12 completed projects did not result in any operational PFM system), mainly due to initial attempts to implement ambitious FMIS solutions without adequate consideration of the limitations in capacity and infrastructure.

Table F.1. Regional Distribution of FMIS Projects in IDA Countries

Region	# of IDA Countries	# of T/F Projects	Completed Projects	Active Projects	Summary of T/F Status* in IDA Countries
AFR	13	24	12	12	4 FO + 4 PO + 5 IP
EAP	5	7	1	6	1 FO + 4 IP
ECA	3	3	-	3	3 IP
LCR	3	6	5	1	2 FO + 1 IP
MNA	1	1	1	-	1 PO
SAR	2	5	4	1	2 FO
Totals	**27**	**46**	**23**	**23**	9 FO + 5 PO + 13 IP in 27 countries

(*) Status: Fully (FO, Partially Operational (PO), or In Progress (IP)

Table F.2. Total Funding for FMIS Projects in IDA Countries

IDA Funding in 46 FMIS Projects (1984–2010)	Completed Projects (23)	Active Projects (23)	Total Funds (US$ Million)	% of Total
Total cost of FMIS projects (US$ million)	620	1,149	1,769	
WB IDA funding	509	624	1,133	64%
WB funds for ICT components	227	347	574	33%
WB funds for FMIS ICT investment	116	230	346	20%

Appendix G. Project Disbursement Profiles by Region

The disbursement profiles of each completed FMIS project are presented in this Appendix (total disbursement in US$ versus the World Bank fiscal year in quarters), together with the restructuring date(s) and/or extension periods, if any (see the legend below for an explanation of the symbols used).

Additional notes included under each chart summarize the main reason(s) for delay, restructuring, or extension due to the Borrower (Brw) or the World Bank (WB). The operational status of the T/F system is also indicated to clarify the outcome.

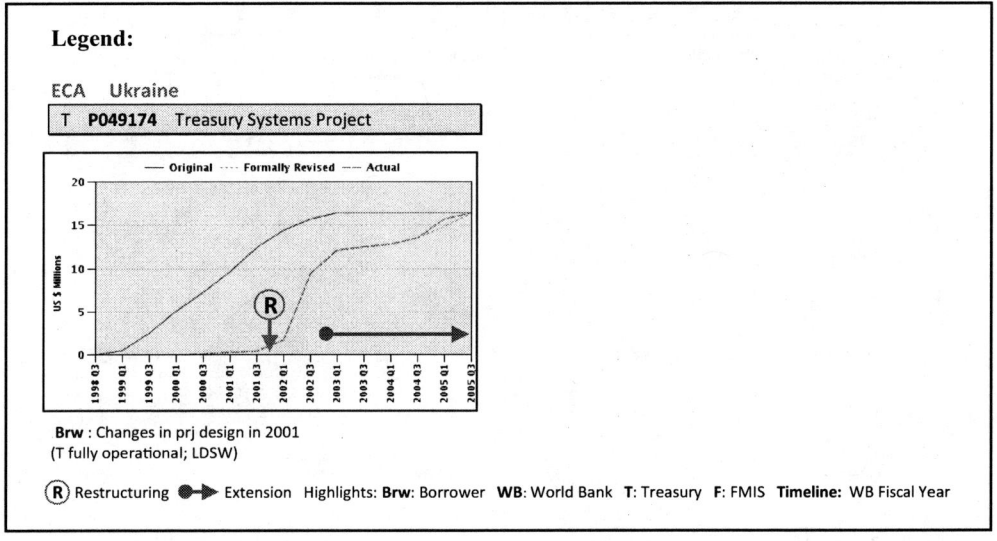

Africa

AFR   Burkina Faso

| T   P000301   Public Institutional Development Prj |

Brw : Poor project management until 1997
(F operational C+L)

AFR   Cape Verde

| F   P057998   Public Sector Ref & Cap Bldg Prj - II |

Brw : Extended due to changes in project activities
(F not implemented)

AFR   Gambia, The

| F   P057995   Capacity Bldg for Economic Mgmt Prj |

Brw : Delay in activ; resist + WB : Ambitious design
(F operational at center)

AFR   Ghana

| F   P045588   Public Financial Management TA Prj |

WB : Weak project design; Cost overrun
(F not implemented; T pilot only)

AFR   Kenya

| F   P066490   Public Sector Mgmt TA Project |

Brw : Changes in legislation
(F not fully operational; 3 pilot sites)

AFR   Madagascar

| F   P074448   Governance & Institutional Dev Prj |

Brw : Change in scope; LA amnd; Political instability
(F operational at center)

Ⓡ Restructuring   ●▶ Extension Highlights: **Brw**: Borrower **WB**: World Bank **T**: Treasury **F**: FMIS **Timeline:** WB Fiscal Year

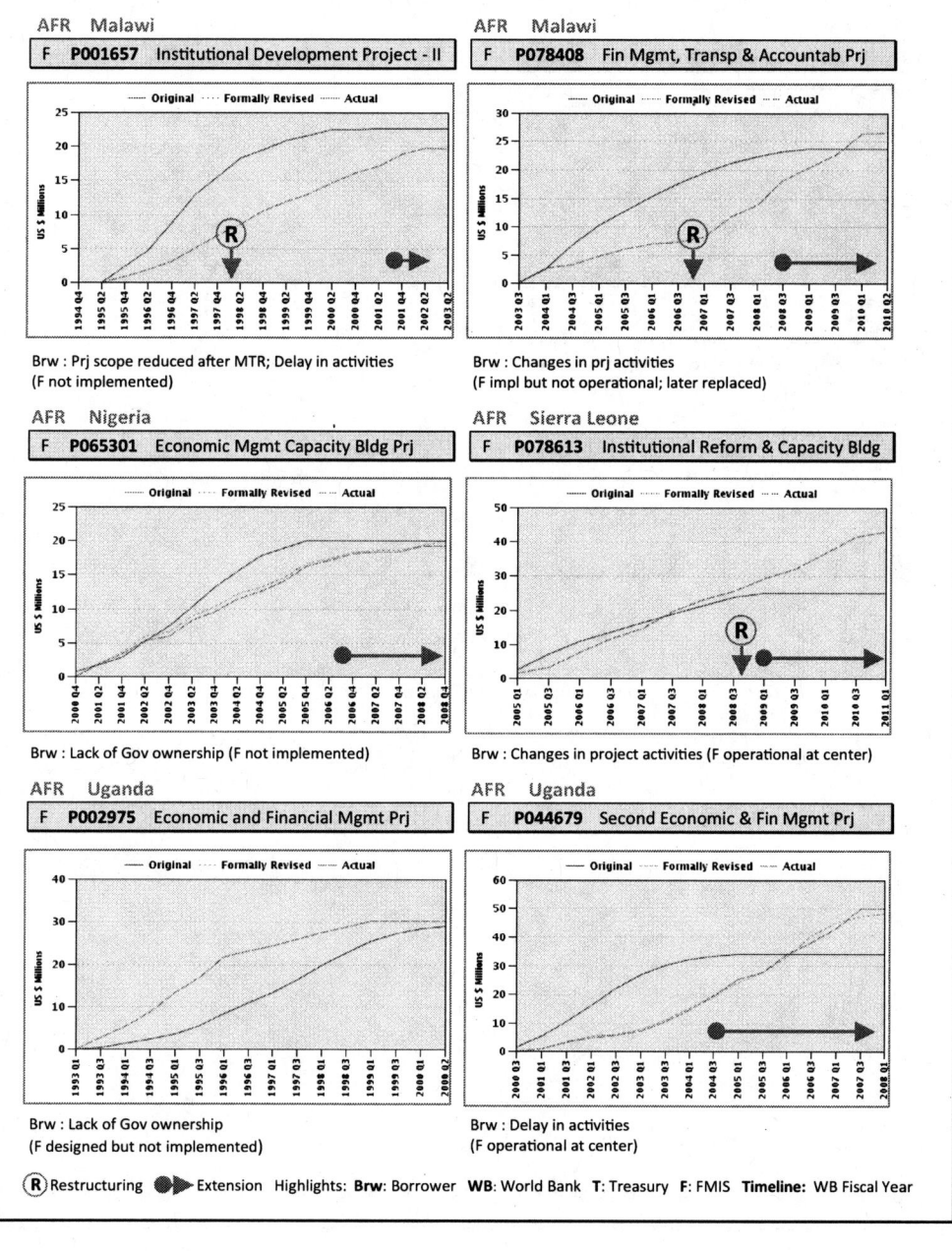

AFR Malawi
F P001657 Institutional Development Project - II

Brw : Prj scope reduced after MTR; Delay in activities
(F not implemented)

AFR Malawi
F P078408 Fin Mgmt, Transp & Accountab Prj

Brw : Changes in prj activities
(F impl but not operational; later replaced)

AFR Nigeria
F P065301 Economic Mgmt Capacity Bldg Prj

Brw : Lack of Gov ownership (F not implemented)

AFR Sierra Leone
F P078613 Institutional Reform & Capacity Bldg

Brw : Changes in project activities (F operational at center)

AFR Uganda
F P002975 Economic and Financial Mgmt Prj

Brw : Lack of Gov ownership
(F designed but not implemented)

AFR Uganda
F P044679 Second Economic & Fin Mgmt Prj

Brw : Delay in activities
(F operational at center)

(R) Restructuring ●▶ Extension Highlights: **Brw**: Borrower **WB**: World Bank **T**: Treasury **F**: FMIS **Timeline:** WB Fiscal Year

AFR   Zambia

F   **P050400**   Public Service Capacity Building Prj

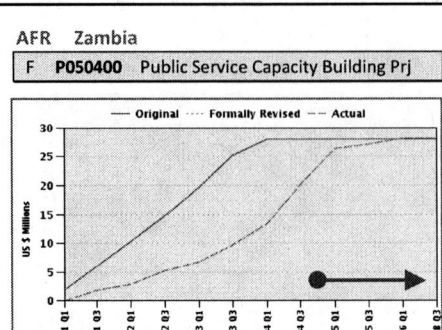

Brw : Delay in activ + WB : Lack of Donor (GTZ) support
(F not implemented)

(R) Restructuring ●▶ Extension Highlights: **Brw**: Borrower **WB**: World Bank **T**: Treasury **F**: FMIS **Timeline:** WB Fiscal Year

East Asia and Pacific

EAP   China

F	**P036041**	Fiscal Technical Assistance Project

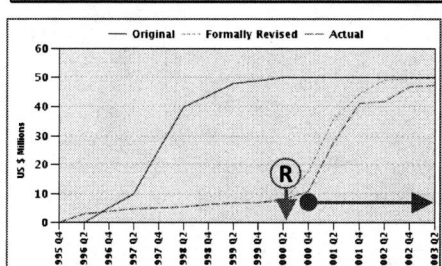

Brw : Changes in Gov priorities
(F operational at center)

EAP   Indonesia

T	**P004019**	Accountancy Development Prj - II

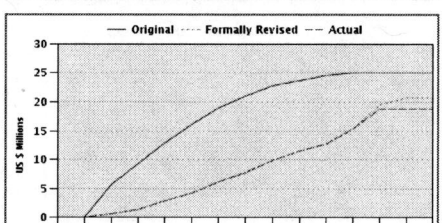

WB : Weak prj design; T impl with extensive delay
(T operational)

EAP   Mongolia

T	**P051855**	Fiscal Accounting Technical Assist.

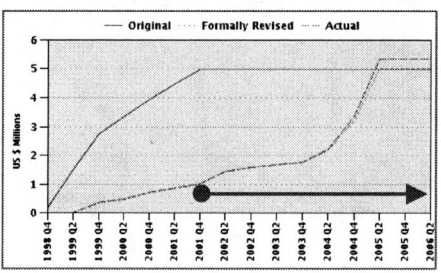

Brw : Poor prj mgmt; Two failed ICB for T
(T operational)

(R) Restructuring ●▶ Extension Highlights: **Brw**: Borrower **WB**: World Bank **T**: Treasury **F**: FMIS **Timeline:** WB Fiscal Year

Europe and Central Asia

ECA   Albania

T P069939   Public Administration Reform Project

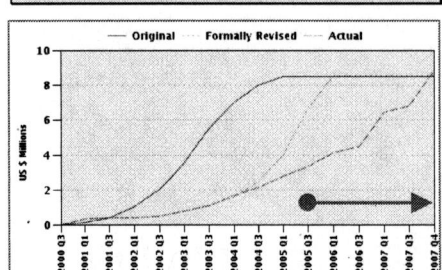

Brw : Lack of Gov ownership + B : Weak prj design
(T not fully oper)

ECA   Azerbaijan

T P066100   Institution Building TA - II

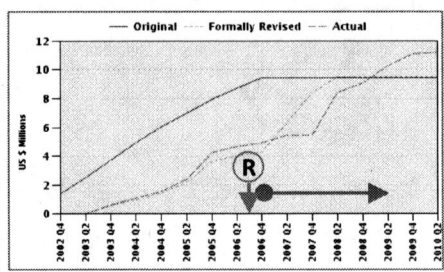

Brw : Lack of Gov own; Poor prj mgmt
(T pilot impl; not oper)

ECA   Hungary

F P043446   Public Finance Management Project

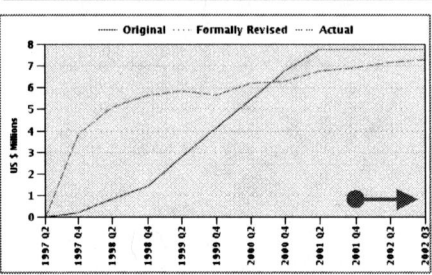

Brw : Extended to benefit from savings/unused funds
(F operational)

ECA   Kazakhstan

T P037960   Treasury Modernization Project

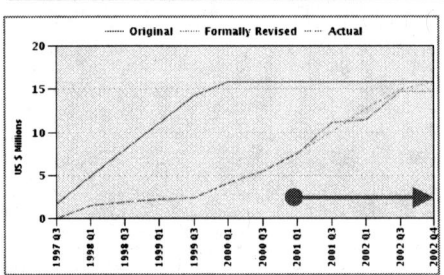

Brw : Change of Capital in 1997; Ext due to lengthy ICB
(T operational)

ECA   Slovak Republic

F P069864   Public Finance Management Project

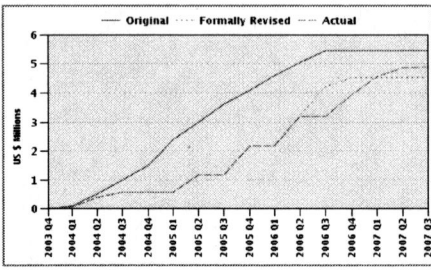

Brw : Minor delay due to changes in activities
(F operational)

ECA   Türkiye

T P035759   Public Finance Management Project

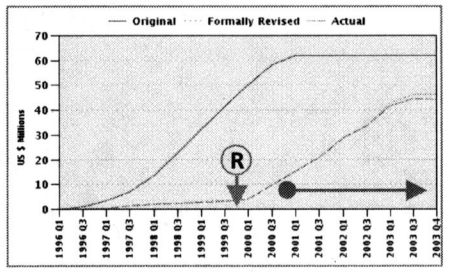

WB : Complex prj design; scope reduced
(T fully operational w Gov funding)

(R) Restructuring ●▶ Extension Highlights: **Brw**: Borrower **WB**: World Bank **T**: Treasury **F**: FMIS **Timeline:** WB Fiscal Year

ECA   Ukraine

| T | P049174 | Treasury Systems Project |

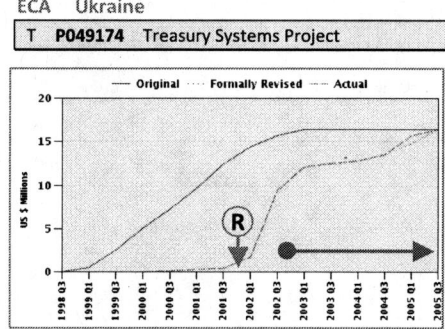

Brw : Changes in prj design in 2001
(T fully operational; LDSW)

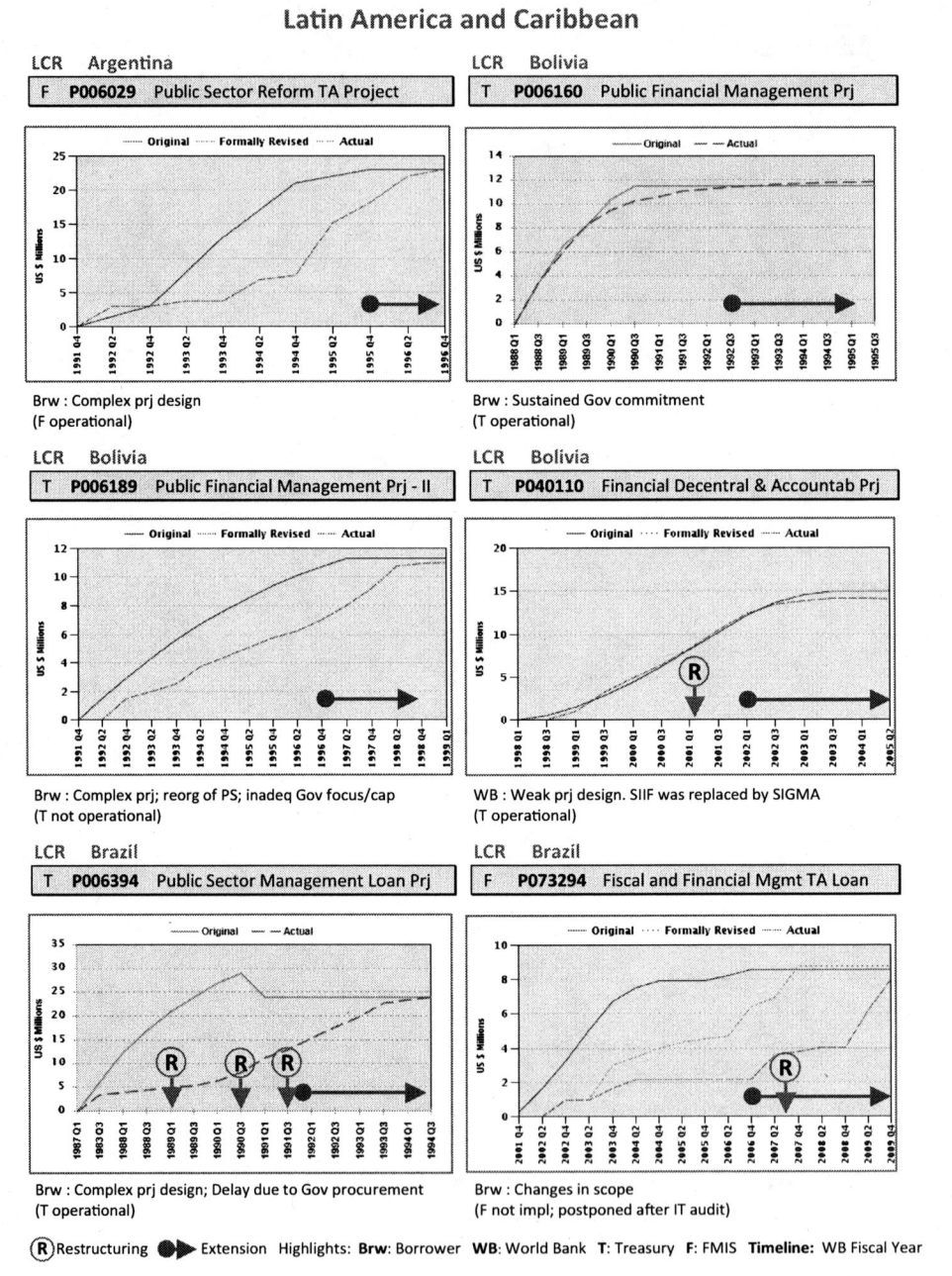

Latin America and Caribbean

LCR   Argentina

| F **P006029**   Public Sector Reform TA Project |

Brw : Complex prj design
(F operational)

LCR   Bolivia

| T **P006189**   Public Financial Management Prj - II |

Brw : Complex prj; reorg of PS; inadeq Gov focus/cap
(T not operational)

LCR   Brazil

| T **P006394**   Public Sector Management Loan Prj |

Brw : Complex prj design; Delay due to Gov procurement
(T operational)

LCR   Bolivia

| T **P006160**   Public Financial Management Prj |

Brw : Sustained Gov commitment
(T operational)

LCR   Bolivia

| T **P040110**   Financial Decentral & Accountab Prj |

WB : Weak prj design. SIIF was replaced by SIGMA
(T operational)

LCR   Brazil

| F **P073294**   Fiscal and Financial Mgmt TA Loan |

Brw : Changes in scope
(F not impl; postponed after IT audit)

(R) Restructuring ●► Extension Highlights: **Brw**: Borrower **WB**: World Bank **T**: Treasury **F**: FMIS **Timeline:** WB Fiscal Year

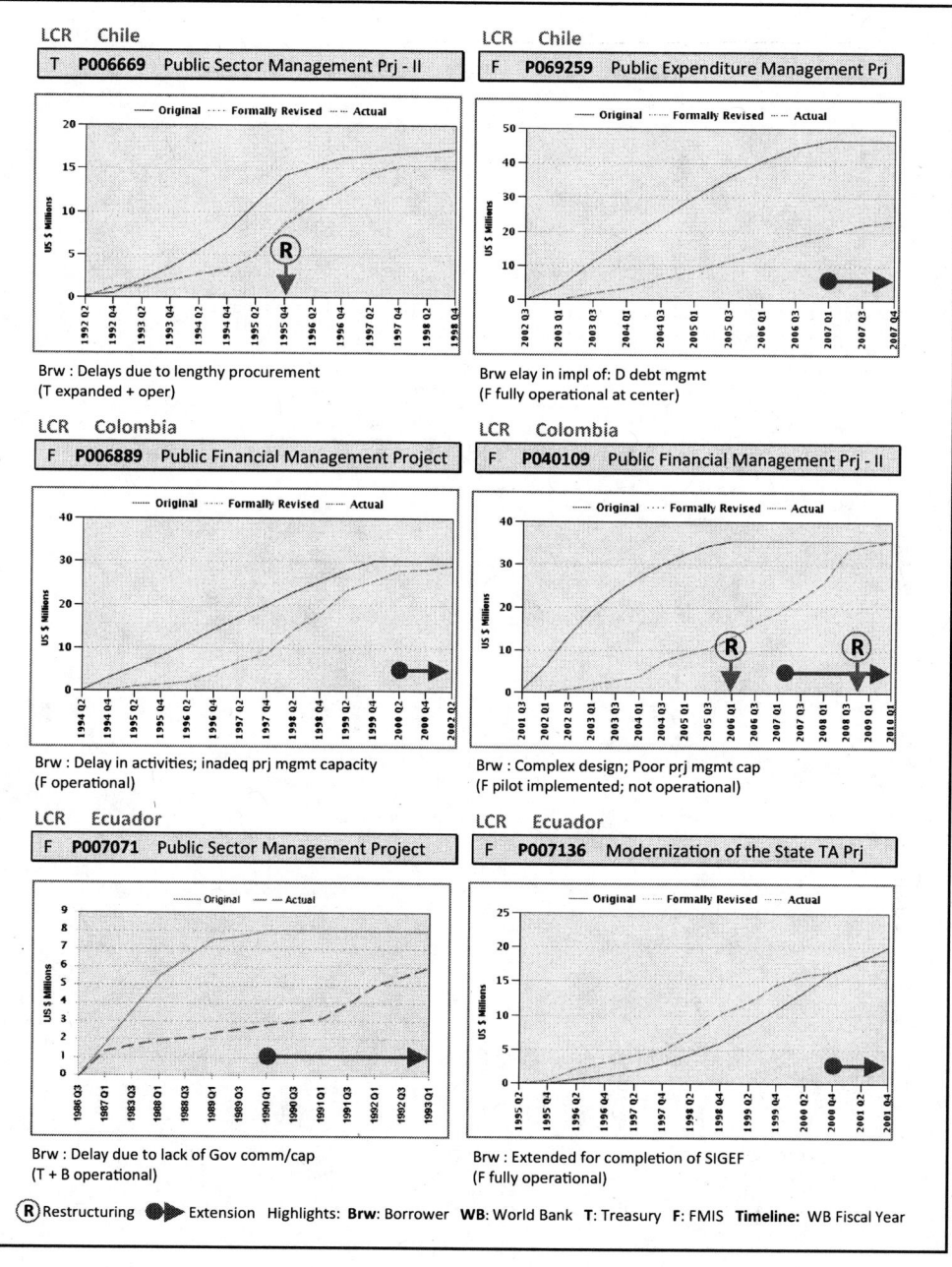

LCR   Chile

| T | **P006669** | Public Sector Management Prj - II |

Brw : Delays due to lengthy procurement
(T expanded + oper)

LCR   Chile

| F | **P069259** | Public Expenditure Management Prj |

Brw elay in impl of: D debt mgmt
(F fully operational at center)

LCR   Colombia

| F | **P006889** | Public Financial Management Project |

Brw : Delay in activities; inadeq prj mgmt capacity
(F operational)

LCR   Colombia

| F | **P040109** | Public Financial Management Prj - II |

Brw : Complex design; Poor prj mgmt cap
(F pilot implemented; not operational)

LCR   Ecuador

| F | **P007071** | Public Sector Management Project |

Brw : Delay due to lack of Gov comm/cap
(T + B operational)

LCR   Ecuador

| F | **P007136** | Modernization of the State TA Prj |

Brw : Extended for completion of SIGEF
(F fully operational)

(R) Restructuring ●▶ Extension Highlights: **Brw:** Borrower **WB:** World Bank **T:** Treasury **F:** FMIS **Timeline:** WB Fiscal Year

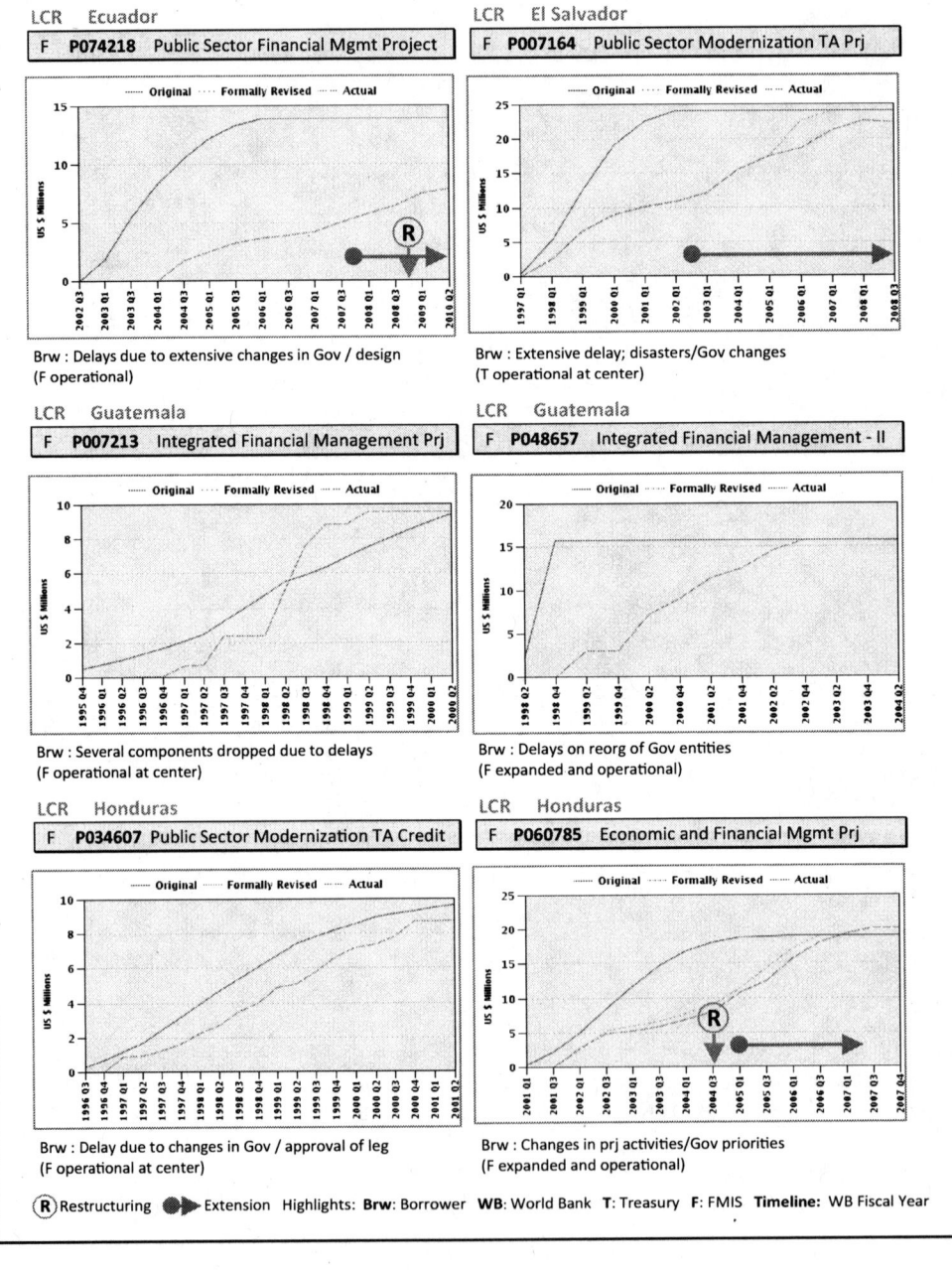

LCR   Ecuador

F **P074218**   Public Sector Financial Mgmt Project

Brw : Delays due to extensive changes in Gov / design
(F operational)

LCR   El Salvador

F **P007164**   Public Sector Modernization TA Prj

Brw : Extensive delay; disasters/Gov changes
(T operational at center)

LCR   Guatemala

F **P007213**   Integrated Financial Management Prj

Brw : Several components dropped due to delays
(F operational at center)

LCR   Guatemala

F **P048657**   Integrated Financial Management - II

Brw : Delays on reorg of Gov entities
(F expanded and operational)

LCR   Honduras

F **P034607** Public Sector Modernization TA Credit

Brw : Delay due to changes in Gov / approval of leg
(F operational at center)

LCR   Honduras

F **P060785**   Economic and Financial Mgmt Prj

Brw : Changes in prj activities/Gov priorities
(F expanded and operational)

(R) Restructuring Extension Highlights: **Brw**: Borrower **WB**: World Bank **T**: Treasury **F**: FMIS **Timeline:** WB Fiscal Year

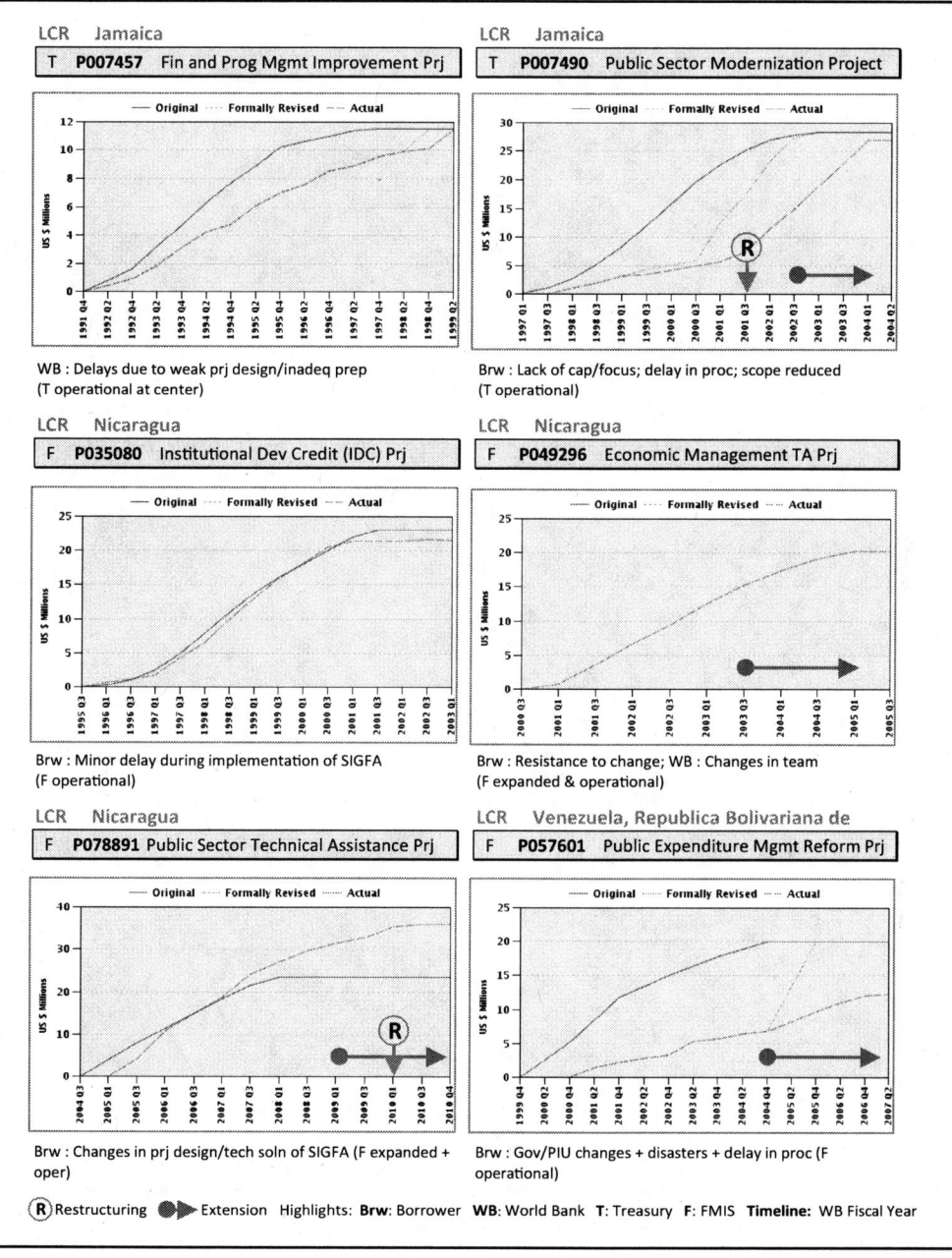

LCR   Argentina

| T   P037049 Public Investm Strengthening TA Prj |

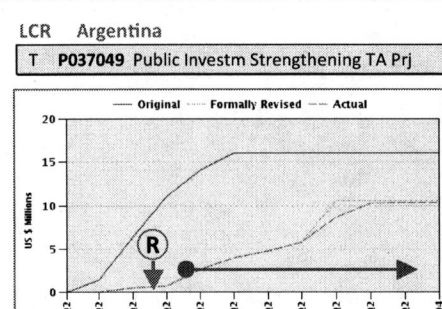

Brw : Changes in Gov & prio; WB : Weak prj design
(expansion of SIDIF)

Ⓡ Restructuring ⬤▶ Extension Highlights: **Brw**: Borrower **WB**: World Bank **T**: Treasury **F**: FMIS **Timeline:** WB Fiscal Year

Middle East and North Africa

MNA Algeria

| F | **P064921** | Budget System Modernization |

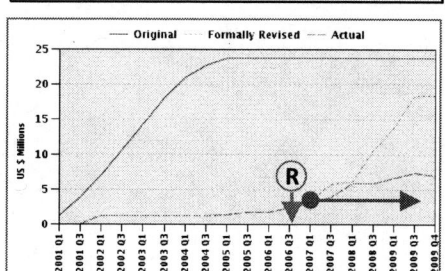

Brw : Weak impl capacity; WB : complex design
(F not implemented)

MNA Yemen

| F | **P050706** | Civil Service Modernization Project |

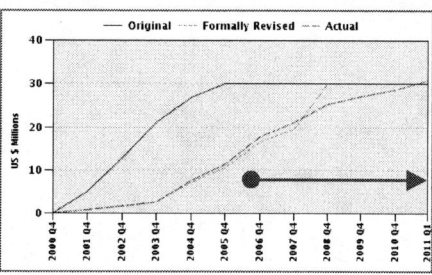

Brw : Political unrest; Delay in AFMIS; WB : Team chg
(F not operational)

Ⓡ Restructuring ◖▶ Extension Highlights: **Brw**: Borrower **WB**: World Bank **T**: Treasury **F**: FMIS **Timeline:** WB Fiscal Year

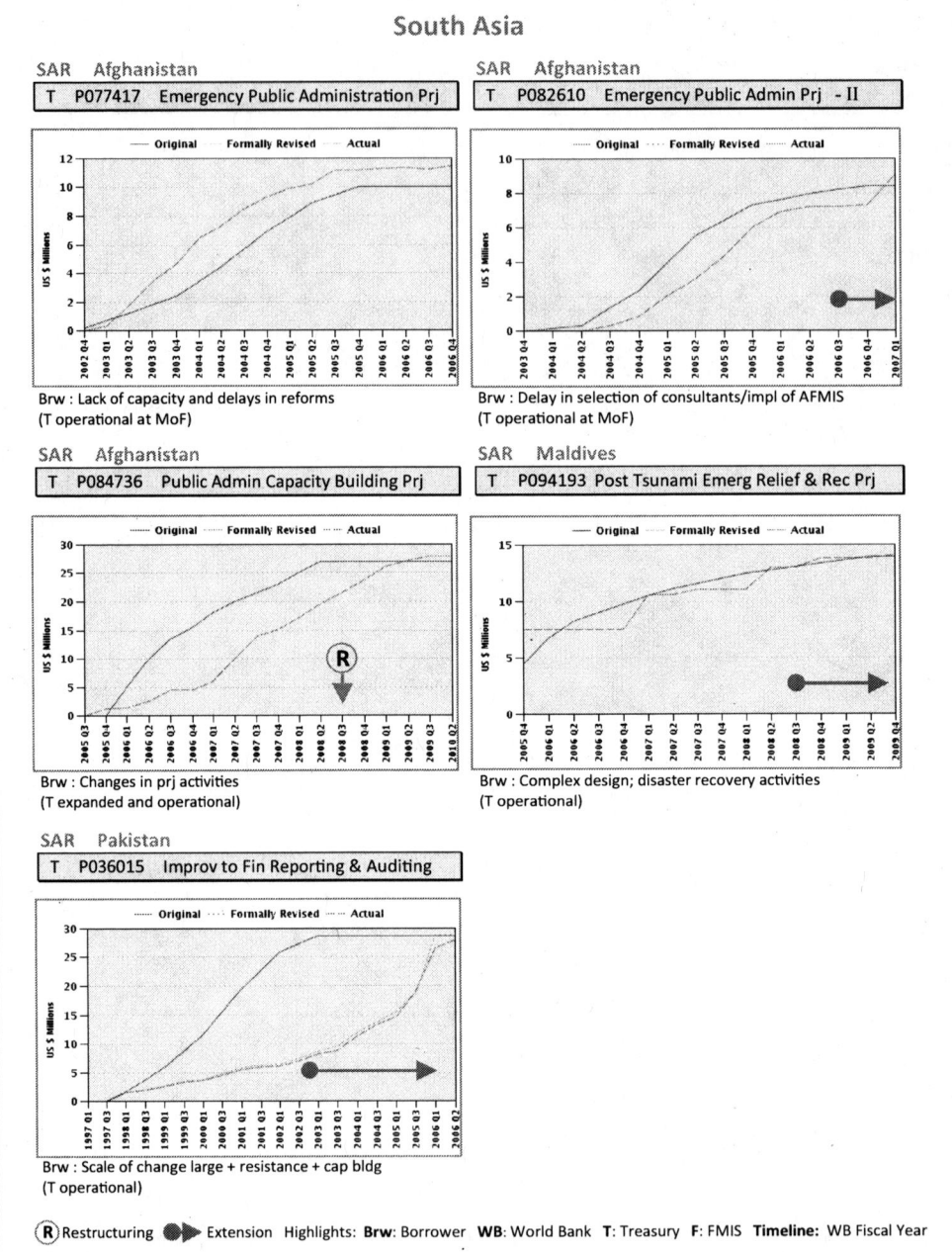

South Asia

SAR   Afghanistan

| T   P077417   Emergency Public Administration Prj |

Brw : Lack of capacity and delays in reforms
(T operational at MoF)

SAR   Afghanistan

| T   P082610   Emergency Public Admin Prj - II |

Brw : Delay in selection of consultants/impl of AFMIS
(T operational at MoF)

SAR   Afghanistan

| T   P084736   Public Admin Capacity Building Prj |

Brw : Changes in prj activities
(T expanded and operational)

SAR   Maldives

| T   P094193 Post Tsunami Emerg Relief & Rec Prj |

Brw : Complex design; disaster recovery activities
(T operational)

SAR   Pakistan

| T   P036015   Improv to Fin Reporting & Auditing |

Brw : Scale of change large + resistance + cap bldg
(T operational)

(R) Restructuring ●➤ Extension   Highlights: **Brw**: Borrower   **WB**: World Bank   **T**: Treasury   **F**: FMIS   **Timeline:** WB Fiscal Year

Appendix H. Good Practice FMIS Indicators for Project Teams

Since the introduction of the PEFA Performance Measurement Framework in 2006, a positive development has emerged in which the PEFA framework is used during the preparation and implementation of FMIS projects for initial assessment and monitoring of progress in PFM functions and performance. Some of the PEFA performance indicators used in active FMIS projects (e.g., Burkina Faso, Nigeria, Albania, Tajikistan, Ukraine, Mongolia, and Colombia) is shown in Table H.1.

Table H.1. PEFA Performance Indicators Used in Active FMIS Projects

		Public Financial Management High-Level Performance Indicators	Scoring Method	Dimension Score				Score
				1	2	3	4	
	A	**Public Financial Management Out-Turns: Credibility of the Budget**						
→	PI-1	Aggregate expenditure out-turn compared to original approved budget	M1					
	PI-2	Composition of expenditure out-turn compared to original approved budget	M1					
→	PI-3	Aggregate revenue out-turn compared to original approved budget	M1					
	PI-4	Stock and monitoring of expenditure payment arrears	M1					
	B	**Key Cross-Cutting Issues: Comprehensiveness and Transparency**						
→	PI-5	Classification of the budget	M1					
→	PI-6	Comprehensiveness of information included in budget documentation	M1					
→	PI-7	Extent of unreported government operations	M1					
→	PI-8	Transparency of intergovernmental fiscal relations	M2					
	PI-9	Oversight of aggregate fiscal risk from other public sector entities.	M1					
→	PI-10	Public access to key fiscal information	M1					
	C	**Budget Cycle**						
	C (i)	Policy-Based Budgeting						
	PI-11	Orderliness and participation in the annual budget process	M2					
→	PI-12	Multiyear perspective in fiscal planning, expenditure policy and budgeting	M2					
	C (ii)	Predictability and Control in Budget Execution						
	PI-13	Transparency of taxpayer obligations and liabilities	M2					
	PI-14	Effectiveness of measures for taxpayer registration and tax assessment	M2					
	PI-15	Effectiveness in collection of tax payments	M1					
→	PI-16	Predictability in the availability of funds for commitment of expenditures	M1					
→	PI-17	Recording and management of cash balances, debt and guarantees	M2					

(Continued)

Table H.1. PEFA Performance Indicators Used in Active FMIS Projects (*Continued*)

		C	Budget Cycle (*continued*)							
→		PI-18	Effectiveness of payroll controls	M1						
→		PI-19	Competition, value for money and controls in procurement	M2						
		PI-20	Effectiveness of internal controls for non-salary expenditure	M1						
		PI-21	Effectiveness of internal audit	M1						
		C (iii)	Accounting, Recording, and Reporting							
→		PI-22	Timeliness and regularity of accounts reconciliation	M2						
		PI-23	Availability of information on resources received by service delivery units	M1						
→		PI-24	Quality and timeliness of in-year budget reports	M1						
		PI-25	Quality and timeliness of annual financial statements	M1						
		C (iv)	External Scrutiny and Audit							
→		PI-26	Scope, nature and follow-up of external audit	M1						
		PI-27	Legislative scrutiny of the annual budget law	M1						
		PI-28	Legislative scrutiny of external audit reports	M1						
		D	Donor Practices							
→		D-1	Predictability of Direct Budget Support	M1						
→		D-2	Financial info provided by donors for budgeting & reporting on prj & prog aid	M1						
		D-3	Proportion of aid that is managed by use of national procedures	M1						

Table H.2. Sample FMIS Project Outcome and Results Indicators

PDO	Outcome Indicators	Use of Results Information
Strengthen public financial management by improving operational efficiency and transparency.	• Fiscal and budgetary projections are analyzed under a multi-annual perspective and are linked to budget and expenditure policies through MTBF. • Internal and external users' satisfaction over the quality of services and information provided by FMIS has improved. • Required time for the preparation and issuance of financial statements is reduced by 50%. • Budget execution results and performance of all contracts are published in the MoF Web portal monthly.	• Monitor improvements in budget and expenditure policies associated with the introduction of MTBF. • Monitor improvements in perception of quality of services and information provided by FMIS. • Monitor improvements in financial management efficiency and transparency. • Monitor efficiency of budget execution and public procurement.

Intermediate Results	Results Indicators	Use of Results Monitoring
Component 1: Improvement of PFM Functions		
Budget Preparation: The MTBF and the methodology of results-based budgeting have been introduced in all central government agencies and their district offices.	By YYYY all central government agencies and their district offices are preparing the budget plans using a multi-year and results-based budgeting methodology.	Monitor and evaluate public expenditure effectiveness and performance orientation.

(*Continued*)

Table H.2. Sample FMIS Project Outcome and Results Indicators (*Continued*)

Intermediate Results	Results Indicators	Use of Results Monitoring
Public Investment: Public Investment Planning and Management capabilities have been implemented through FMIS.	XXX% of Central Government public investment projects are planned and monitored through FMIS.	Monitor the improvements in the public investments monitoring and evaluation system.
Commitments: Commitment control and monitoring function has been improved to provide daily monitoring of all obligations.	At least XXX% of Central Government commitments are controlled and monitored through FMIS.	Monitor improvements in commitment management.
Accounting: Financial statements for central government agencies are produced according to international classification standards and are published within the applicable legal time frame.	Central government budget and financial statements are delivered by YYYY in accordance with: i) IPSAS, ii) 2001 IMF Manual for Government Financial Statistics, and iii) the applicable legal framework.	Monitor the improvements in complying with international accounting standards and IMF Manual for Government Financial Statistics for public expenditure transparency.
Cash Management: Treasury cash management has been optimized through the operation of a fully automated Treasury Single Account with electronic payment capabilities.	At least XXX% of Central Government payments are processed electronically using the TSA procedures.	Monitor improvements in cash management.
Public Debt: Foreign and domestic public debt is updated and recorded automatically in the FMIS.	XXX% of foreign public debt and XXX% of domestic public debt is recorded automatically through FMIS-DMFAS interface, generating automatic multi-currency accounting records.	Monitor the improvements in public debt management.
Asset Management: All Central Government assets are recorded centrally and reported to related users.	XXX% of Central Government assets are recorded and reported through FMIS interface (Web portal) for central agencies and spending units.	Monitor the improvements in asset management.
Procurement: Central Government procurement operations (after contract signature) are managed through FMIS.	XXX% of Central Government contracts are recorded through FMIS.	Monitor the execution of contracts and report efficiency and transparency of public procurement.
Civil Service: Human resource and payroll management are supported in FMIS.	XXX% of Central Government agencies have adopted the new HR management processes, including personnel records and electronic payroll.	Monitor the improvements in the quality of HR management and the development of a meritocratic civil service.
Component 2: Design and development of Financial Management Information System		
Necessary technology infrastructure (network connections and system centers) was prepared in all Central Government agencies and district offices for FMIS implementation.	Network physical connections established and main system center + disaster recovery center premises prepared by the Government.	Monitor the establishment of technical infrastructure before FMIS implementation.

(Continued)

Table H.2. Sample FMIS Project Outcome and Results Indicators (*Continued*)

Intermediate Results	Results Indicators	Use of Results Monitoring
FMIS application software is fully operational to support countrywide PFM operations on a daily basis at central agencies and districts.	Customization/development of the new FMIS application software has been completed, tested and rolled-out; the system is 100% operational and supporting all Central Gov financial operations.	Monitor the development and effective use of FMIS.
Component 3:Capacity Building		
A permanent training, capacity building and knowledge management model on public financial management and public sector administration units is in place and a critical mass of users have received specialized training.	XXX% of the relevant MoF unit staff trained to operate and maintain the new FMIS and to provide functional support to users. XXXX public servants trained on Web-based FMIS applications.	Monitor implementation of training and capacity building programs.
A dedicated technical team is in place within the MoF to manage FMIS and provide technical support to users.	At least XX dedicated technical specialists recruited and trained (XX at central level, XX at district offices) to manage FMIS system centers, databases, information security, and user access and provide technical support to all system users.	Monitor the establishment of necessary technical capacity to sustain FMIS ICT solutions.

Note: The above PDO and IR sample indicators were derived from various project appraisal documents (including several active and a pipeline project in Nicaragua (P111795)) and presented in generic forms.

Appendix I. FMIS Project Timelines (1984–2010)

Cat	Project ID	Project Name	Region	Country	Prj Stat	Tot Yrs	T/F Stat
T	P000301	Public Institutional Development Project	AFR	Burkina Faso	C	9.6	1
T	P078596	Administration Capacity Building Project	AFR	Burkina Faso	A	8.1	3
F	P057998	Public Sector Reform And Capacity Building Project (02)	AFR	Cape Verde	C	3.8	0
T	P104041	Enhancing Governance Capacity	AFR	Congo, Democratic Republic of	A	5.7	3
F	P057995	Capacity Building for Economic Management Prj	AFR	Gambia, The	C	9.8	2
F	P117275	Integrated Financial Management Information System Project	AFR	Gambia, The	A	3.4	3
F	P045458	Public Financial Management Technical Assistance Project	AFR	Ghana	C	7.7	2
F	P120942	e-Ghana (Additional Financing)	AFR	Ghana	A	2.9	3
F	P066490	Public Sector Management Technical Assistance Project	AFR	Kenya	C	5.1	2
F	P090567	Institutional Reform and Capacity Building Technical Assistance Project	AFR	Kenya	A	6.0	3
F	P109775	Public Financial Management - IFMIS	AFR	Liberia	A	4.1	3
F	P074448	Governance and Institutional Development Project	AFR	Madagascar	C	7.8	2
F	P103950	Governance and Institutional Development Project II	AFR	Madagascar	A	5.6	3
F	P001657	Institutional Development Project (2)	AFR	Malawi	C	13.4	2
F	P078408	Financial Mgmt, Transparency and Accountability Prj (FIMTAP)	AFR	Malawi	C	7.4	2
F	P065301	Economic Management Capacity Building Prj	AFR	Nigeria	C	9.2	0
F	P088150	Federal Government Economic Reform and Governance Project	AFR	Nigeria	A	8.6	3
F	P078613	Institutional Reform & Capacity Building	AFR	Sierra Leone	C	5.6	2
F	P108069	Public Financial Management	AFR	Sierra Leone	A	5.6	3
F	P070544	Accountability, Transparency & Integrity Program	AFR	Tanzania	A	6.1	3
F	P002975	Economic and Financial Management Project	AFR	Uganda	C	9.0	0
F	P044679	Second Economic and Financial Management Project	AFR	Uganda	C	8.7	2
F	P090867	Local Government Management and Services Delivery Project	AFR	Uganda	A	5.7	3
F	P050400	Public Service Capacity Building Project	AFR	Zambia	C	6.5	0
F	P082452	Public Sector Management Program Support Project	AFR	Zambia	A	5.7	3
F	P087945	Public Financial Management and Accountability	EAP	Cambodia	A	6.9	3
F	P113309	Public Financial Management II	EAP	Cambodia	P		4
T	P036041	Fiscal Technical Assistance Project	EAP	China	C	8.6	2
T	P004019	Accountancy Development Project (2)	EAP	Indonesia	C	7.3	1
F	P085133	Government Financial Management and Revenue Administration Project	EAP	Indonesia	A	10.1	3
F	P077620	Financial Management Capacity Building Credit	EAP	Lao People's Democratic Republic	A	9.1	3
T	P107757	Treasury Modernization	EAP	Lao People's Democratic Republic	P		4
T	P051855	Fiscal Accounting Technical Assistance (c-3081)	EAP	Mongolia	C	8.1	1
T	P077778	Economic Capacity Building TA (ECTAP)	EAP	Mongolia	A	8.6	3
F	P098426	Governance Assistance Project	EAP	Mongolia	A	6.3	3
F	P092484	Planning and Financial Management Capacity Building Program	EAP	Timor-Leste	A	6.4	1
F	P075399	Public Financial Management Reform Project	EAP	Viet Nam	A	9.1	3

FMIS project timelines (Continued)

Cat	Project ID	Project Name	Region	Country	Prj Stat	Tot Yrs	T/F Stat
T	P069939	Public Administration Reform Project	ECA	Albania	C	7.5	1
F	P105143	MDTF for Capacity Building & Support to Implement the Integrated Planning System	ECA	Albania	A	4.6	3
T	P066100	(former IBTA-II) Highly Pathogenic Avian Influenza Preparedness Project	ECA	Azerbaijan	C	9.9	1
F	P063081	Public Sector Financial Management Reform Support	ECA	Georgia	A	6.4	3
F	P043446	Public Finance Management Project	ECA	Hungary	C	6.7	1
T	P037960	Treasury Modernization Project	ECA	Kazakhstan	C	8.5	1
F	P071063	Governance Technical Assistance Project	ECA	Kyrgyz Republic	A	8.7	3
F	P082916	Public Financial Management Technical Assistance Project	ECA	Moldova	A	7.8	3
F	P064508	Treasury Development Project	ECA	Russian Federation	A	13.1	1
F	P069864	Public Finance Management Project	ECA	Slovak Republic	C	5.6	1
F	P099840	Public Finance Management Modernization	ECA	Tajikistan	A	8.0	3
F	P035759	Public Finance Management Project	ECA	Türkiye	C	8.5	1
T	P049174	Treasury Systems Project	ECA	Ukraine	C	7.9	1
F	P090389	Public Finance Modernization Project	ECA	Ukraine	A	7.5	3
F	P006029	Public Sector Reform Technical Assistance Project	LCR	Argentina	C	6.7	1
F	P037049	Public Investment Strengthening Technical Assistance Project	LCR	Argentina	C	12.4	1
T	P006160	Public Financial Management Project	LCR	Bolivia	C	8.4	2
F	P006189	Public Financial Management (2) Project	LCR	Bolivia	C	7.6	2
F	P040110	Financial Decentralization & Accountability Prj	LCR	Bolivia	C	6.9	2
T	P006394	Public Sector Management Loan Project	LCR	Brazil	C	9.6	1
F	P073294	Fiscal and Financial Management Technical Assistance Loan	LCR	Brazil	C	7.8	0
T	P066669	Public Sector Management Project (2)	LCR	Chile	C	8.1	1
F	P069259	Public Expenditure Management Project	LCR	Chile	A	6.5	1
F	P103441	Second Public Expenditure Management	LCR	Colombia	C	8.3	1
F	P006889	Public Financial Management Project	LCR	Colombia	C	10.0	2
F	P040109	Public Financial Management Project (02)	LCR	Colombia	A	3.3	1
F	P106628	Improving Public Management Project	LCR	Ecuador	C	8.5	2
F	P007071	Public Sector Management Project	LCR	Ecuador	C	7.2	1
F	P007136	Modernization of the State Technical Assistance Project	LCR	Ecuador	C	7.4	1
F	P074218	Public Sector Financial Management Project	LCR	El Salvador	C	12.8	2
F	P007164	Public Sector Modernization Technical Assistance Project	LCR	El Salvador	P	5.3	4
F	P095314	Second Public Sector Modernization Project	LCR	El Salvador			

FMIS project timelines (Continued)

Cat	Project ID	Project Name	Region	Country	Prj Stat	Tot Yrs	T/F Stat
F	P007213	Integrated Financial Management Project	LCR	Guatemala	C	4.7	2
F	P048657	Integrated Financial Management II	LCR	Guatemala	C	5.2	1
F	P066175	Integrated Financial Management III - TA Prj	LCR	Guatemala	A	9.8	3
F	P034607	Public Sector Modernization Technical Assistance Credit	LCR	Honduras	C	7.8	2
F	P060785	Economic and Financial Management Project	LCR	Honduras	C	6.6	1
F	P110050	State Modernization	LCR	Honduras	P		4
T	P007457	Financial and Program Management Improvement Project	LCR	Jamaica	C	11.4	2
T	P007490	Public Sector Modernization Project	LCR	Jamaica	C	9.9	1
F	P035080	Institutional Development Credit (IDC) Project	LCR	Nicaragua	C	7.8	2
F	P049296	Economic Management Technical Assistance	LCR	Nicaragua	C	4.7	1
F	P078891	Public Sector Technical Assistance Project	LCR	Nicaragua	C	6.7	1
F	P111795	Public Financial Management Modernization Project	LCR	Nicaragua	P		4
F	P100635	OECS E-Government for Regional Integration Program (APL)	LCR	OECS Countries	A	5.2	3
F	P057601	Public Expenditure Management Reform Project	LCR	Venezuela, Republica Bolivariana de	C	7.6	1
F	P064921	Budget System Modernization	MNA	Algeria	C	9.3	0
F	P050706	Civil Service Modernization Project	MNA	Yemen, Republic of	C	12.4	2
F	P117363	Public Finance Modernization Project	MNA	Yemen, Republic of	P		4
T	P077417	Emergency Public Administration Project	SAR	Afghanistan	C	3.6	2
T	P082610	Emergency Public Administration Project II	SAR	Afghanistan	C	5.4	2
T	P084736	Public Admin Capcity Building Project	SAR	Afghanistan	C	4.9	1
T	P099980	Public Financial Management Reform Project	SAR	Afghanistan	A	4.1	1
T	P120289	Public Financial Management Reform II	SAR	Afghanistan	P		4
T	P094193	Post Tsunami Emegency Relief and Reconstruction Project	SAR	Maldives	C	5.0	1
T	P036015	Improvement to Financial Reporting and Auditing Project	SAR	Pakistan	C	12.2	1
T	P076872	Second Improvement to Financial Reporting and Auditing Project	SAR	Pakistan	A	8.5	1

28 Treasury
66 FMIS (T+B)
94

AFR	25	Closed	55
EAP	12	Active	32
ECA	14	Pipeline	7
LCR	32		94
MNA	3		
SAR	8		
94			

31	T/F Operational
22	T/F Operational (pilot)
28	T/F in Progress
7	Pipeline
6	T/F not Implemented
94	Treasury/FMIS total

Legend: Concept Note — Approval — Effectiveness — Prep — Eff — Impl (disbursement) — Orig Closing Date — Actual Closing Date — Extension

Appendix J. Treasury/FMIS Projects in ECA Region

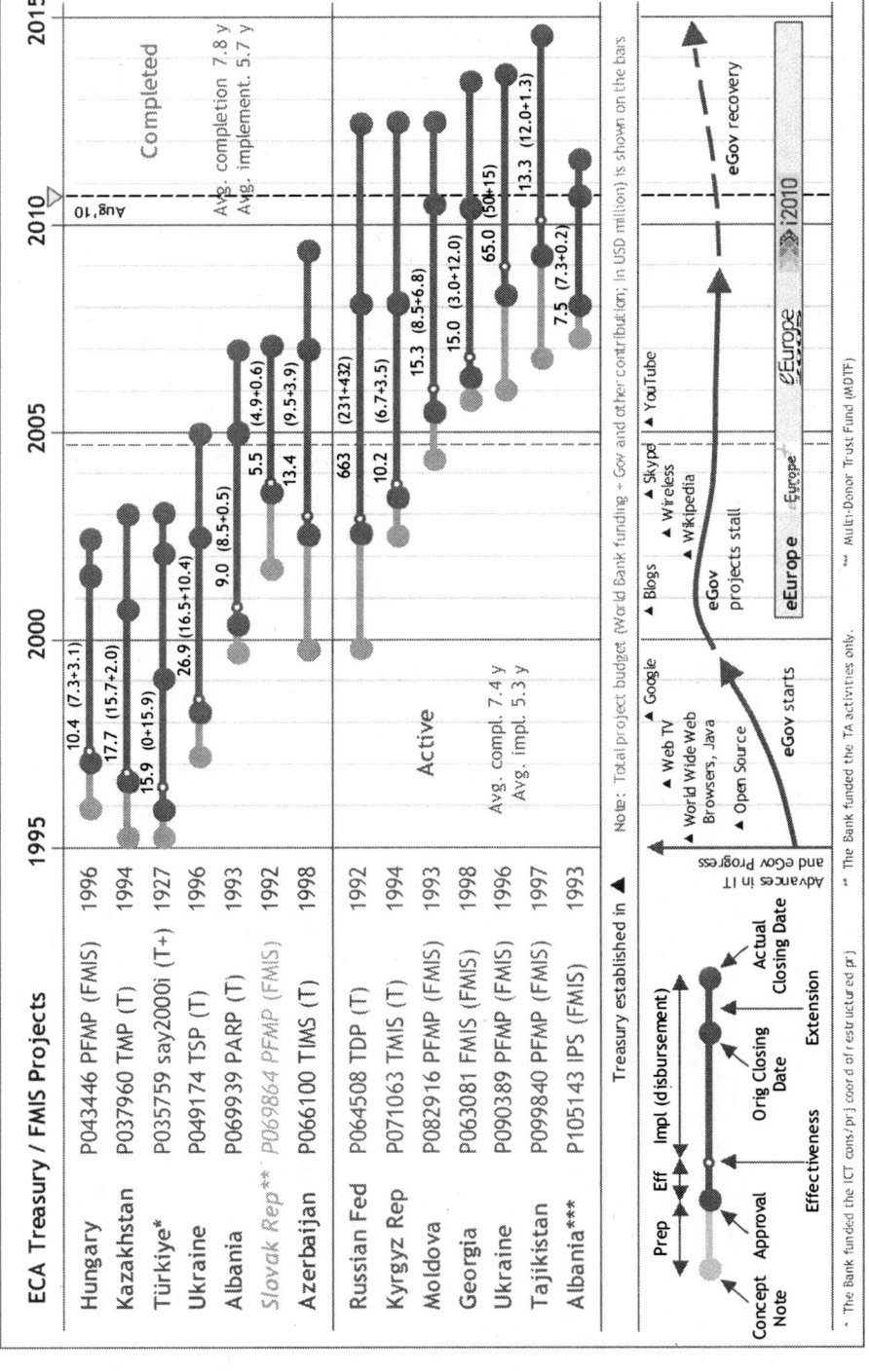

#	Cat	Region	Country	Prj Stat	T/F Type
1	T	AFR	Burkina Faso	A	1
2	F	AFR	Cape Verde	C	0
3	T	AFR	Congo, Democratic Republic of	A	1
4	F	AFR	Gambia, The	P	1
5	F	AFR	Ghana	C	1
6	F	AFR	Kenya	A	5
7	F	AFR	Liberia	A	3
8	F	AFR	Madagascar	A	1
9	F	AFR	Malawi	C	1
10	F	AFR	Nigeria	P	2
11	F	AFR	Sierra Leone	A	1
12	F	AFR	Tanzania	A	2
13	F	AFR	Uganda	A	1
14	F	AFR	Zambia	A	2
15	F	EAP	Cambodia	A	1
16	F	EAP	China	C	1
17	T	EAP	Indonesia	A	1
18	T	EAP	Lao People's Democratic Republic	A	1
19	F	EAP	Mongolia	A	1
20	F	EAP	Timor-Leste	A	1
21	F	EAP	Viet Nam	A	1
22	T	ECA	Albania	A	1
23	T	ECA	Azerbaijan	C	1
24	F	ECA	Georgia	A	1
25	T	ECA	Hungary	C	1
26	T	ECA	Kazakhstan	C	1
27	F	ECA	Kyrgyz Republic	A	1
28	F	ECA	Moldova	A	1
29	T	ECA	Russian Federation	A	1
30	F	ECA	Slovak Republic	C	1
31	F	ECA	Tajikistan	A	1

Operational status of FMIS projects in 51 countries (Continued)

#	Cat	Region	Country	Prj Stat	T/F Type
32	T	ECA	Türkiye	C	1
33	F	ECA	Ukraine	A	1
34	F	LCR	Argentina	C	1
35	T	LCR	Bolivia	C	1
36	T	LCR	Brazil	C	1
37	F	LCR	Chile	A	1
38	F	LCR	Colombia	A	1
39	F	LCR	Ecuador	C	1
40	F	LCR	El Salvador	P	1
41	F	LCR	Guatemala	A	1
42	F	LCR	Honduras	P	1
43	T	LCR	Jamaica	C	1
44	F	LCR	Nicaragua	P	1
45	F	LCR	OECS Countries	A	1
46	F	LCR	Venezuela, Republica Bolivariana de	C	1
47	F	MNA	Algeria	C	0
48	F	MNA	Yemen, Republic of	A	1
49	T	SAR	Afghanistan	A	3
50	T	SAR	Maldives	C	3
51	T	SAR	Pakistan	A	1

Year axis: 1984 – 2016

Summary counts:

T	16
F	35
	51

Region		Status		
AFR	14	Closed	17	42
EAP	7	Active	29	3
ECA	12	Pipeline	5	-3
LCR	13		51	0
MNA	2			1
SAR	3			2
	51			51

Legend:
- T/F Operational (Completed)
- T/F Partially Operational
- T/F Expected Go-Live (Active)
- T/F Planned (Pipeline)
- T/F Not Implemented

Notes:
- Above timelines denote the operational period of T/F systems developed through Bank funded projects
- In some countries, several consecutive projects were implemented to expand or upgrade existing T/F.
- Dashed lines denote the transition to full scale operations / partially operational systems.

Appendix L. Implementation Status of All Projects Included in the FMIS Database (August 2010)

(Legend is at the end of the table)

Region	Country	Project ID	Project Name	T/F	Approval Date	Closing Date	Prj Status	T/F Status	T/F Type	Summary of Project Implementation
AFR	Burkina Faso	P000301	Public Institutional Development Project	T	Jun-92	Dec-00	C	1	1	TS (T): Budget Exp Mgmt (T) + Public Inv (IS) + HR/payroll calc (IS) + Statistics + Procurement + Debt mgmt (IS) + Judicial reform
AFR	Burkina Faso	P078596	Administration Capacity Building Project	T	Mar-05	Feb-11	A	3	2	TS (T): Expansion of Computerized Integrated Circuit (CIC) + Design of budget planning + MTEF
AFR	Cape Verde	P057998	Public Sector Reform And Capacity Building Project (02)	F	Nov-99	Dec-02	C	0	0	SIGOF (F): Designed but not implemented (lack of legal framework and inadequate funding) + Judicial IS + Statistics
AFR	Congo, DR	P104041	Enhancing Governance Capacity	T	Apr-08	Feb-13	A	3	1	TS(T): Treasury + HRMIS + Payroll + PFM IS at provincial levels as well
AFR	Gambia, The	P057995	Capacity Building for Economic Management Prj	F	Jul-01	Dec-08	C	2	1	IFMIS (F): Implemented (4 yr delay due to resist) + Tax + Customs (Asycuda) + IFMIS scope reduced during restructuring
AFR	Gambia, The	P117275	Integrated Financial Mgmt Information System Project	F	Jul-10	Dec-12	A	4	2	IFMIS (F): Rolling out IFMIS to the 38 remaining Gov ministries and Central Bank
AFR	Ghana	P045588	Public Financial Management Technical Assistance Project	F	Nov-96	Jul-03	C	2	1	FMIS (F): Not fully oper (T pilot impl; no MTBF; ICT infr not ready) + Cash + Debt Mgmt + Procurement + Auditing + Tax + HRMIS
AFR	Ghana	P120942	e-Ghana (Additional Financing)	F	Jun-10	Dec-12	A	3	1	FMIS (F): Expansion and upgrade of existing FMIS
AFR	Kenya	P066490	Public Sector Management Technical Assistance Project	F	Jul-01	Jun-05	C	2	2	FMIS (F): Partially implemented (3 pilot; MTEF not functional) + HRMIS + Payroll (only pilot)
AFR	Kenya	P090567	Institutional Reform and Capacity Building Technical Assistance Project	F	Jan-06	Nov-10	A	3	5	FMIS (F): Activate FMIS + Procurement + HR and Payroll (IPPD) + centrally first (6 Min) + rollout out to 40 Min later + MDTF
AFR	Liberia	P109775	Public Financial Management - IFMIS	F	May-08	Feb-12	A	3	3	FMIS (F): Budget Prep + Execution w/ GL) + HRMIS through an Emergency Recovery Loan

(Continued)

Appendix L. Implementation Status of All Projects Included in the FMIS Database (August 2010) (*Continued*)

Region	Country	Project ID	Project Name	T/F	Approval Date	Closing Date	Prj Status	T/F Status	T/F Type	Summary of Project Implementation
AFR	Madagascar	P074448	Governance and Institutional Development Project	F	Nov-03	Jun-09	C	2	1	SIGFP (F): Not fully operational due to political instabilities since 2009
AFR	Madagascar	P103950	Governance and Institutional Development Project II	F	Jun-08	Aug-12	A	3	2	SIGFP (F): Rollout of SIGFP + major components on Revenue Admin and Procurement reforms
AFR	Malawi	P001657	Institutional Development Project (2)	F	Jun-94	Jun-01	C	2	1	FMIS (F): Piloted at center (MTEF + T + HR & Payroll)
AFR	Malawi	P078408	Financial Mgmt, Transparency and Accountability Prj (FIMTAP)	F	Mar-03	Sep-09	C	2	2	IFMIS (F): Expansion not completed (5 pilot Min only; old budget prep SW Epicor for budgeting)
AFR	Nigeria	P065301	Economic Management Capacity Building Prj	F	May-00	Dec-07	C	0	0	IFEMIS (F): Not implemented. Network established but SW not developed; lack of ownership. PHRD and EU funds not utilized. .
AFR	Nigeria	P088150	Federal Government Economic Reform and Governance Project	F	Dec-04	Feb-13	A	3	2	FMIS (B+T) + HRMIS + Payroll + Procurement for Federal Gov: (ICB in progress)
AFR	Sierra Leone	P078613	Institutional Reform & Capacity Building	F	May-04	Mar-09	C	2	1	IFMIS (F): MTBF + T developed in MoF and 9 Min (replacing FMAS); MDTF components to be completed in 2011
AFR	Sierra Leone	P108069	Public Financial Management	F	Jun-09	Jul-13	A	3	2	IFMIS (F): Support for IFMIS rollout at central level; Expansion of FMIS capabilities (HR).
AFR	Tanzania	P070544	Accountability, Transparency & Integrity Program	F	May-06	Dec-11	A	3	2	IFMS (F): Expansion of IFMS (piloted in 10 Min in 1998); In 2004, IFMS rolled-out to reg adm + Disaster Recovery Sys impl in 2006
AFR	Uganda	P002975	Economic and Financial Management Project	F	Aug-92	Jun-99	C	0	0	FMIS (F): Designed but not implemented.
AFR	Uganda	P044679	Second Economic and Financial Management Project	F	Nov-99	Dec-06	C	2	2	IFMIS (F): Expansion at central level (14/22 Min); B and T not well integrated; expanded to C+L w/ cost overrun + Statistics + GDLC

(Continued)

Appendix L. Implementation Status of All Projects Included in the FMIS Database (August 2010) (Continued)

Region	Country	Project ID	Project Name	F/T			A/P			Description
AFR	Uganda	P090867	Local Government Management and Services Delivery Project	F	Dec-07	Dec-11	A	3	2	IFMIS (F): Active prj expanded to districts + Support FINMAP (existing system)
AFR	Zambia	P050400	Public Service Capacity Building Project	F	Mar-00	Jun-05	C	0	0	IFMIS (F): Not implemented; Donors (GTZ) couldn't support; MoF upgraded existing Financial Management System (FMS)
AFR	Zambia	P082452	Public Sector Management Program Support Project	F	Jan-06	Dec-10	A	3	2	IFMIS (F): Piloted in 5 Min and 2 Prov + HR + Payroll + Activity Based Budg (ABB) + Debt Mgmt
EAP	Cambodia	P087945	Public Financial Management and Accountability	F	Jun-06	Jan-12	A	3	1	FMIS (F): T + IBIS (B); integrated with Procurement + Debt Mgmt + Tax
EAP	Cambodia	P113309	Public Financial Management II	F	Aug-12		P	4	2	Project details not available yet
EAP	China	P036041	Fiscal Technical Assistance Project	F	Apr-95	Dec-02	C	2	1	GFMIS (F): Pilot only + Tax Admin reform (CTAIS) + links with e-Gov prog
EAP	Indonesia	P004019	Accountancy Development Project (2)	T	Sep-94	Dec-00	C	1	1	GAS (T): Exp/Rev processing + Accounting. Weak design and delay in implementation.
EAP	Indonesia	P085133	Government Financial Management and Revenue Administration Project	F	Dec-04	Dec-13	A	3	1	SPAN (F): FMIS scaled down; not incl HRMIS & Payroll + Second phase (dropped). Tax + Customs + Procurement impl separately.
EAP	Lao People's DR	P077620	Financial Management Capacity Building Credit	T	Jun-02	Apr-11	A	3	2	GFIS (T): Expand GFIS to all ministries + provinces
EAP	Lao People's DR	P107757	Treasury Modernization	T	Nov-11		P	4	1	TIMS (T): Development of a new Treasury Info Mgmt System (TIMS)
EAP	Mongolia	P051855	Fiscal Accounting Technical Assistance (c 3081)	T	Jun-98	Sep-05	C	1	1	GFMIS (T): Operational in Jan 2005, after 2 failed ICBs + Debt Mgmt System
EAP	Mongolia	P077778	Economic Capacity Building TA (ECTAP)	F	Jun-03	Sep-11	A	3	2	Expansion of GFMIS (T to F) w/ Budget Prep (MTBF), Procurement & HRMIS + linked w/ Debt Mgmt (DMFAS)
EAP	Mongolia	P099426	Governance Assistance Project	F	May-06	Jan-12	A	3	2	GFMIS (F): Expansion of GFMIS + Debt Mgmt + substantial Tax Adm component

(Continued)

Appendix L. Implementation Status of All Projects Included in the FMIS Database (August 2010) (Continued)

Region	Country	Project ID	Project Name	T/F	Approval Date	Closing Date	Prj Status	T/F Status	T/F Type	Summary of Project Implementation
EAP	Timor-Leste	P092484	Planning and Financial Management Capacity Building Program	F	Mar-06	Jul-11	A	1	1	FMIS (F): Rev Mgmt (Tax+Customs) + HR & Payroll + MacroEco Forecasting (large prj scope and counterparts)
EAP	Viet Nam	P075399	Public Financial Management Reform Project	T	May-03	Feb-11	A	3	1	TABMIS (F): T rollout in progress since 2009 + Budget Planning (during extension) + Debt Mgmt (DFMAS)
ECA	Albania	P069939	Public Administration Reform Project	T	Mar-00	Dec-06	C	1	1	AMoFTS (T): Completed but TSA not fully operational yet; oper in 2010 + HR & payroll completed but not used (lack of comm)
ECA	Albania	P105143	MDTF for Capacity Bldg & Support to Implement Integrated Planning Sys	F	Jan-08	Sep-11	A	3	1	AFMIS (F): Expansion of AMoFTS to F; IPSIS + EAMIS + HRMIS & Payroll + GovNet expansion
ECA	Azerbaijan	P066100	(former IBTA-II) Highly Pathogenic Avian Influenza Preparedness Prj	T	Jun-02	Sep-09	C	1	1	TIMS (T): Dev in 2006; delay in rollout due to lack of commitment Sys integ by USAID (Carana); WB funded IT infrastructure only.
ECA	Georgia	P063081	Public Sector Financial Management Reform Support	F	Feb-06	Mar-12	A	3	1	PFMIS (F): New FMIS + HRMIS & Payroll for the MoF + integrated with DMFAS + CS reform + Chamber of Control
ECA	Hungary	P043446	Public Finance Management Project	F	Dec-96	Jun-02	C	1	1	FMIS (F): Operational with B + T + Debt Mgmt
ECA	Kazakhstan	P037960	Treasury Modernization Project	T	Jul-96	Dec-02	C	1	1	TS (T): Core Treasury became fully functional in 2008
ECA	Kyrgyz Republic	P071063	Governance Technical Assistance Project	F	May-03	Feb-11	A	3	1	FMIS (F): TMIS (T) + HRMIS & Payroll + integration w Debt Mgmt + Budget Prep (B) added later
ECA	Moldova	P082916	Public Financial Management Technical Assistance Project	F	Jun-05	Dec-11	A	3	1	FMIS (F): Core FMIS + HR & Payroll for the MoF + integration w/ Debt Mgmt (DMFAS) + Internal Audit Reform & IS
ECA	Russian Federation	P064508	Treasury Development Project	T	Jun-02	Jun-12	A	1	1	FTAS (T): FTAS developed in 2009. Roll out initiated in Jan 2010. Completion expected in Dec 2011.

(Continued)

Appendix L. Implementation Status of All Projects Included in the FMIS Database (August 2010) (*Continued*)

ECA	P069864	Public Finance Management Project	F	Jun-03	Jan-07	C	1	1	FMIS (F): Operational with MTBF and program budgeting + T; Bank provided only TA; System impl by the MoF.
ECA	P099840	Public Financial Management Modernization	F	May-09	Aug-14	A	3	1	FMIS (F): Capacity building + IT infrastructure in progress during APL-1. FMIS is expected during APL-2 (2015–16).
ECA	P035759	Public Finance Management Project	T	Sep-95	Dec-02	C	1	1	say2000i (T + HR + Payroll): Operational since Jan 2002 + Integrated w/ B + Tax + Customs + Debt
ECA	P049174	Treasury Systems Project	T	Feb-98	Dec-04	C	1	1	AS Kazna (T): LDSW as a distributed web-based solution (installed in oblast centers). Change in scope 1997–2002.
ECA	P090389	Public Finance Modernization Project	F	Jan-08	Jun-13	A	3	1	PFMS (F): FMIS designed, procurement in progress + core FMIS + interfaces w/ Debt Mgmt + Tax + Customs
LCR	P006029	Public Sector Reform Technical Assistance Project	F	Jun-91	Jun-97	C	1	1	SIDIF (F): Core FMIS operational + Debt Mgmt (DMFAS) + Customs + HR and Asset Reg not implemented.
LCR	P037049	Public Investment Strengthening Technical Assistance Project	F	Nov-95	Dec-06	C	1	2	SIDIF (F): Expansion + Public Inv Sys (SNIP) + Inventory of inv prjs (BAPIN) + Local Unified SIDIF (SLU) + Design of the web-SIDIF
LCR	P006160	Public Financial Management Project	T	May-87	Jun-94	C	2	1	SAFCO (T): Developed + Cash Mgmt + Tax + Customs + Banking system improved
LCR	P006189	Public Financial Management (2) Project	T	Jun-91	Dec-97	C	2	1	SIIF (T): Pilot impl 6/20 Min (no expansion due to high cost of telco + change in gov + lack of IT unit to sustain).
LCR	P040110	Financial Decentralization & Accountability Prj	T	Aug-97	Mar-03	C	2	1	SIGMA (T): Central level (instead of SIIF expansion). Expansion of SIGMA to local level was funded by IDB + Debt mgmt + Audit
LCR	P006394	Public Sector Management Loan Project	T	Jun-86	Dec-93	C	1	1	SIAFI (T): Only budget execution implemented properly; B not implemented; ambitious design, complex procurement

(Continued)

Appendix L. Implementation Status of All Projects Included in the FMIS Database (August 2010) *(Continued)*

Region	Country	Project ID	Project Name	T/F	Approval Date	Closing Date	Prj Status	T/F Status	T/F Type	Summary of Project Implementation
LCR	Brazil	P073294	Fiscal and Financial Management Technical Assistance Loan	F	May-01	Dec-08	C	0	0	SIAFI-21 (T): Extension of SIAFI to a web-based solution; not impl (postponed by Gov decision) + Debt Mgmt (SID) + SIGPLAN (PPA)
LCR	Chile	P006669	Public Sector Management Project (2)	T	Oct-91	Jun-98	C	1	2	SIGFE (T): Expansion; Mainly Tax + Customs impl + SSI + Treasury is resp fm rev collection
LCR	Chile	P069259	Public Expenditure Management Project	F	Feb-02	Jun-07	C	1	1	SIGFE (T) + SIAP (B) implemented largely + Perf Indicators defined for each inst + HRMIS developed by SONDA as pilot
LCR	Chile	P103441	Second Public Expenditure Management	F	Aug-07	Jun-13	A	3	2	SIGFE-II (T) + SIAP (B) expanded + introduce FM system for municipalities + SIAPER (HRMIS) will be fully implemented
LCR	Colombia	P006889	Public Financial Management Project	F	Dec-93	Mar-01	C	1	1	SIIF (F): Operational + Tax + Customs + Debt Mgmt (DMFAS)
LCR	Colombia	P040109	Public Financial Management Project (02)	F	Mar-01	Dec-09	C	2	2	SIIF-II (F): New web-based SIIF to be oper in 2011; not ready due to tech+oper issues. SIIF is operational + Tax & Customs
LCR	Colombia	P106628	Improving Public Management Project	F	Feb-10	Dec-12	A	3	2	SIIF (F): Integration of SIIF, SUIFP and Customs + Tax (MUISCA)
LCR	Ecuador	P007071	Public Sector Management Project	F	Apr-85	Mar-93	C	2	2	TS (B+T): Fin Info System (T) + SIGMA for macroeconomic mgmt + DEUDEX public debt monitoring sys + Prog Budgeting System
LCR	Ecuador	P007136	Modernization of the State Technical Assistance Project	F	Dec-94	Mar-01	C	1	1	SIGEF (F): Operational (84% PEM) + SIGEF Treasury partially implemented 20 central & 62 prov units + HRMIS + Str Planning
LCR	Ecuador	P074218	Public Sector Financial Management Project	F	Mar-02	Feb-09	C	1	2	SIGEF (F): Web based SIGEF (e-SIGEF) was designed and impl (similar to Guatemala). e-SIGEF is operational since Jan 2008
LCR	El Salvador	P007164	Public Sector Modernization Technical Assistance Project	F	Sep-96	Aug-07	C	2	1	SAFI (F): Developed and used in 89 gov entities + HRMIS + Procurement

(Continued)

LCR	El Salvador	P095314	Second Public Sector Modernization Project	F	Nov-09	Dec-14	P	4	2	SAFI (F): Improvement of SAFI (perf based budg+ TSA and CoA + integrate w/proc, tax collection, HRMIS/payroll + new Stats Sys
LCR	Guatemala	P007213	Integrated Financial Management Project	F	May-95	Jun-99	C	2	1	SIAF (F): Implemented for central gov only + Debt Mgmt and Audit components dropped
LCR	Guatemala	P048657	Integrated Financial Management II	F	Dec-97	Sep-02	C	1	2	SIAF (F): Expansion of SIAF + Debt (DMFAS) and Cash Mgmt + SNIP (Inv Planning) piloted
LCR	Guatemala	P066175	Integrated Financial Management III—TA Prj	F	Mar-02	Jun-11	A	3	2	SIAF (F): Expanded incl cash and debt mgmt + Municipal FM solution + HRMIS + Audit support + e-Government
LCR	Honduras	P034607	Public Sector Modernization Technical Assistance Credit	F	Feb-96	Jun-00	C	2	1	SIAFI (F): Operational in 5 Secs from Jan 1999 + HRMIS + Procurement + Inv Planning
LCR	Honduras	P060785	Economic and Financial Management Project	F	Sep-00	Sep-06	C	1	2	SIAFI (F): Expansion of SIAFI + Dropped HRMIS (SIARH) and Procurement later
LCR	Honduras	P110050	State Modernization	F	Jul-11		P	4	2	SIAFI (F): Expansion of SIAFI to municipalities
LCR	Jamaica	P007457	Financial and Program Management Improvement Project	T	Jun-91	Jun-98	C	2	1	FMIS (T): Implemented at central level in 17 Min (incl cash mgmt, but no commitment control) + HRMIS
LCR	Jamaica	P007490	Public Sector Modernization Project	T	Sep-96	Sep-03	C	1	2	FMIS (T): Only T improved. HRMIS designed but not fully impl + mainly PS modern + FinMan designed (web based) during prj.
LCR	Nicaragua	P035080	Institutional Development Credit (IDC) Project	F	Mar-95	Dec-01	C	2	1	SIGFA (F): Oper at central level since Jan 1998 + substantial institutional reform
LCR	Nicaragua	P049296	Economic Management Technical Assistance	F	Jan-00	Jun-04	C	1	2	SIGFA (F): Extension of SIGFA at central level to all line ministries
LCR	Nicaragua	P078891	Public Sector Technical Assistance Project	F	Mar-04	Dec-09	C	1	2	SIGFA (F): Extension of SIGFA + Improve SNIP (Inv Plan)
LCR	Nicaragua	P111795	Public Financial Management Modernization Project	F	Dec-10	Dec-15	P	4	2	SIGAF (F): New Web-based FMIS for central gov (to replace SIGFA) + new HRMIS+Payroll & contract mgmt + integrate w/Debt + PIM

(Continued)

Appendix L. Implementation Status of All Projects Included in the FMIS Database (August 2010) (*Continued*)

Region	Country	Project ID	Project Name	T/F	Approval Date	Closing Date	Prj Status	T/F Status	T/F Type	Summary of Project Implementation
LCR	OECS Countries	P100635	OECS E-Government for Regional Integration Program (APL)	F	May-08	Jun-12	A	3	2	FMIS (F) : Expansion of SmartStream (T) in 4 OECS cnts (HR, B. Acct) + Tax (SIGTAS) + Customs (ASYCUDA) + eProc + other eGov
LCR	Venezuela	P057601	Public Expenditure Management Reform Project	F	Jun-99	Jun-06	C	1	1	SIGECOF (T): Impl at central + 56% of local level 321/576 units + HRMIS + Debt (DMFAS) integration
MNA	Algeria	P064921	Budget System Modernization	F	Feb-01	Feb-09	C	0	0	IBMS (F): FMIS planned but not implemented. SIG-BUD (B) was developed for perf-based program budgeting only.
MNA	Yemen, Rep	P050706	Civil Service Modernization Project	F	Apr-00	Jun-10	C	2	1	AFMIS (F): Implemented in the MoF and 3 ministries + substantial HRMIS and payroll
MNA	Yemen, Rep	P117363	Public Finance Modernization Project	F	Dec-10		P	4	2	AFMIS (F): Expansion of AFMIS
SAR	Afghanistan	P077417	Emergency Public Administration Project	T	Apr-02	Sep-05	C	2	3	AFMIS (T): Implemented at the MoF
SAR	Afghanistan	P082610	Emergency Public Administration Project II	T	Jun-03	Sep-08	C	2	4	AFMIS (T): Implemented at the MoF (additional funding to complete the work with another consultant)
SAR	Afghanistan	P084736	Public Admin Capacity Building Project	T	Jan-05	Jun-09	C	1	4	AFMIS (T): Expansion of AFMIS; operational in 12 provinces and all line ministries in 2009.
SAR	Afghanistan	P099980	Public Financial Management Reform Project	T	May-07	Dec-10	A	1	4	AFMIS (T): Expansion of AFMIS. all Line Min (34) and 18 prov connected in Nov'09 (Assets + Proc + HRMIS + payroll)
SAR	Afghanistan	P120289	Public Financial Management Reform II	T	Oct-10		P	4	4	AFMIS (T): Expansion of AFMIS
SAR	Maldives	P094193	Post Tsunami Emergency Relief and Reconstruction Project	T	Mar-05	Dec-09	C	1	3	TS (T): Treasury system was developed and operational at pilot and several sites. T roll-out to be completed in 2010.
SAR	Pakistan	P036015	Improvement to Financial Reporting and Auditing Project	T	Sep-96	May-05	C	1	1	PIFRA I (T): Budget Execution + Accounting + HRMIS

(Continued)

Appendix L. Implementation Status of All Projects Included in the FMIS Database (August 2010) (*Continued*)

SAR	Pakistan	P076872	Second Improvement to Financial Reporting and Auditing Project	T	Sep-05	Dec-10	A	1	2	PIFRA II (T): Rolled out initiated in 2009. Completion expected in 2011.

Regional distribution

25	AFR
12	EAP
14	ECA
32	LCR
3	MNA
8	SAR
94	

Category

Treasury (T)	28
FMIS (F)	66
	94

	Prj.St.	Status	Type	
C	55	31	47	1
A	32	22	33	2
P	7	28	3	3
	94	7	4	4
		–	1	5
		6	6	0
		94	**94**	

Nomenclature:

T/F Category of the project: [**F**: FMIS (B+T); **T**: Treasury system; **B**: Budget Preparation]

Prj Status: Project status [**C**: Closed; **A**: Active; **P**: Pipeline]

T/F Status: [**1**: T/F is fully/partially oper;   **2**: T/F pilot/reduced scope impl;   **3**: Implem. in progress;   **4**: Pipeline project   **0**: T/F not impl or not operational]

T/F Type: [**1**: Comprehensive T/F system;   **2**: Expansion of existing T/F;   **3**: T/F emergency solution;   **4**: Exp of existing T/F emerg soln;   **5**: Exp of existing T/F impl by others   **0** : Not operational]

Appendix M. FMIS Data Mapper

The FMIS Data Mapper presents a snapshot of 94 FMIS projects funded by the World Bank in 51 countries on Google Maps.

Related project documents can be displayed or downloaded from the World Bank external web site using the link on the web site in the information box of each project.